intraday tactics on forex - appli

UNDERSTANDING
PRICE ACTION

Practical Analysis
of the
5-Minute Time Frame

Bob Volman

LIGHT TOWER
PUBLISHING

Published by: Light Tower Publishing

ISBN 978-90-822786-0-6

ProRealTime charts used with permission of www.ProRealTime.com

upabook@gmail.com

Excerpts of the book can be downloaded from:

www.upabook.wordpress.com

Table of Contents

Part 1: Practical Analysis

Part 2: Evaluation and Management

Preface

In these modern times of high-tech trading devices, with all the latest gadgets at the push of a button, price action traders may come off as somewhat old-school. With nothing in front of them but the bars in the chart, there is little in their workspace that bears witness of the digital wave. Are they mere relics from a fading past, soon to be extinct, or could it be that there is merit in this seemingly stubborn defiance of trading evolution?

One way to answer this is to point out the actual benefits of every indicator craze that has swept across the trading landscape for the past so many years. Not an easy chore by any means. A simpler solution, perhaps, is to focus attention on the price action trader instead and see if we can come to appreciate his one and only tool, the naked chart.

With the latter idea in mind, *Understanding Price Action* is written not just to establish the virtues of the price action method, but to serve as a practical guide on the matter. The core premise within is that any dedicated student, before long, should be able to trade confidently and profitably from a clean chart without ever feeling lost or otherwise deprived.

For the purpose of illustration, any price chart could basically do, but few are better suited for the job than the 5-minute chart of the eur/usd currency pair. A true creature of habit, this market has long since been the favorite of countless traders around the globe and it's hard to think of a more accessible platform for the technical discussions in the chapters ahead.

When taking up the task of writing this guide, the objective was not just to show a pallet of trading concepts on a number of cherry-picked charts, but to give a fair impression also of their practical implementation on a day-to-day basis. For this purpose, the book has been split into two parts.

Part 1 lays out the principles of price action and discusses entry and exit techniques on a broad range of educational charts. In Part 2 we will examine how these findings hold up on a more continuous basis. Included within is a series of *six months of consecutive 5-minute sessions* of the eur/usd. Besides providing a massive amount of study material, this series should leave little doubt behind as to the amazing continuity and exploitability of price action themes from one session to the next.

One of the most common questions I received in response to my first book, *Forex Price Action Scalping*, was if the principles and setups pointed out on a fast scalping chart (70-tick) could also be applied to the higher intraday frames, like the 2 or 5-minute, or even the hourly for that matter. There can only be one answer to this question: price action principles are transposable to *any* time frame of choice because they bear within them the universal laws of supply and demand. This is not bounded by the time in which it takes place, nor is it a prerogative of any one market. From one instrument or time frame to another, subtle adaptations may be called for, if only to accommodate for the differences in average range or motion; but the trading concepts of the price action method are just as applicable to futures, indices, stocks, commodities, bonds, or what have you, as they are to the Forex markets.

As will be demonstrated also, price action principles are not only free from the boundaries of market and frame, they stand above the nature of the trading environment as well. To illustrate this point, a special section is included on how to tackle a very persistent climate of low volatility by slightly tweaking standard procedure to better suit the conditions at hand. We will examine this adaptation process from the viewpoint of a faster intraday frame on several currency pairs and some popular non-Forex markets.

In regard to the absolute novice, it should be noted that to keep the focus at all times directed towards analysis, it is chosen not to disturb the pace of this book with endless pages of introductory fluff that is readily available either online or in more generic trading books. From a technical perspective, however, *Understanding Price Action* is written for both the novice and the experienced trader, and for all who have taken interest in exploring the benefits and possibilities of the price action method.

Free excerpts of the book can be downloaded from:

www.upabook.wordpress.com

Part 1

Practical Analysis

Chapter 1

A Time to Trade and a Time to Study

While the indicator hype has far from run its course, more and more traders are coming to see the virtues of the "less is more" philosophy. And with reason. There is something strikingly serene about a chart stripped down to the bare essentials. There are no riddles to decipher, no conflicting signals to evade, there is nothing cluttering up the screen. It's all about facts—and they are out in the open. The bars in the chart hold nothing back, nor will their message ever lag behind. With these benefits in mind, the price action trader adheres to a very simple premise: if a high-odds trade cannot be spotted straight off the chart, it is just not there.

Still and all, without a proper understanding of market mechanics, no trader of any kind is likely to escape the notorious lessons of the market and the costly fees that come with it. The journey through the learning stages is never an easy process and there will be pain and hardship along the way. Chances are, quite a few will never surpass this dreaded stage of initiation. On the good side, there is a lot a trader can do to increase his chances of survival, and at little cost to boot: in a nutshell, he needs to educate himself properly.

Bear in mind, this is not to suggest that *all* can be taught from the drawing board; it merely serves to stress the importance of preparation. If the goal is indeed to survive in a field where so many others have perished before their time, how can it not pay to enter well prepared from the outset.

It is up to the student how long to commit to the safety of the sidelines. For some it may take several months of reviewing the same old principles over and over again, for others the light may turn green much sooner than that. But even when all the concepts and techniques are starting to make perfect sense, aspiring traders are well advised not to delve into the markets without a solid plan in place. Lessons need to be learned, but there is little point in allowing one's auditions to be unnecessarily costly or self-defeating.

Next to jumping in headfirst, hurriedly adopting a third party method, just to get going, is another popular practice among many new entrants. But when applied as a mere shortcut to education, this approach, too, is not likely to hold up in the line of duty, particularly when the current market environment proves unfavorable to the chosen method in question. The preferable route, by far, is to always put ample time and effort into constructing a personal methodology, suited for all seasons, and devoid of the vagaries and whims of third party discretion.

Although a fully functional and standalone method *will* be offered in the chapters ahead, and referred to as "our" methodology, please understand that this is done so for practical purposes and not to suggest that the reader should obligingly apply whatever is put forth. The concepts and techniques, of course, can serve as a structural groundwork for any customized method.

It may take some time and experimenting to find out what style of trading suits a trader best. But regardless of personal preference, all techniques should at least harbor the same objective, which is to exploit *repetition*. The first task, therefore, for any student, is to build up a mental database of price action principles in action. In the following two chapters we will have a close look at these essentials, from both a theoretical and practical point of view. From there on, our focus will be on the finer subtleties of trading the 5-minute chart.

Chapter 2

Price Action Principles—Theory

Price action principles form the basic ingredients of all sound trading techniques. While their variations in appearance are practically infinite, as are the ways they can be implemented into a plan of attack, all will find footing in a small set of elementary concepts that repeat over and over again in any technical chart. The core principles relate to:

Double pressure.
Support and resistance.
False breaks, tease breaks and proper breaks.
False highs and lows.
Pullback reversals.
Ceiling test.
Round number effect.

Figure 2.1 provides a schematic impression of the principles in action; if presented in regular bars this may very well have been a typical 5-minute chart of the eur/usd pair meandering in a 50 pip range over the course of a session—or any other chart, for that matter.

Rather than delving into these price charts straightaway, let us establish a solid foundation for all our further studies by exploring each of the seven principles from a theoretical viewpoint first.

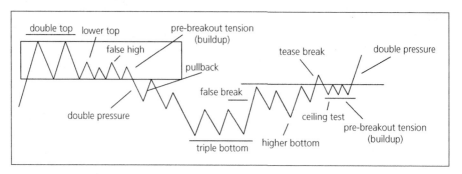

Figure 2.1. Schematic illustration of the core principles of price action.

Double Pressure

Since no trader can take his own trades to target, we are all dependent on the actions and reactions of our fellow traders in the field. Does this mean we are mere puppets hanging from the market's fickle strings? Far from it. But we need to play our game cleverly. Before putting capital at risk on any one trading idea there is an important concept to take into account: for prices to follow through in substantial fashion, we need assistance from *both* sides of the market. Should we aim to take position on, say, the bull side, it may not suffice to only find companions in the bullish camp. Preferably, we would like to see a decent number of bears quickly bail out to protect themselves from the very rising market we are trying to exploit. The more bears forced to buy back their shorts, the better the odds for our trade to reach its destination before the situation sees chance to reverse.

When both bull and bear temporarily join forces on the same side of the market—not with similar enthusiasm, we can imagine—we have what we can refer to as a *double-pressure* situation. Considering the many seesaw motions in any chart, these imbalances between supply and demand are far from unique; but it is fair to suggest also that they sooner tend to self-correct than blossom into anything substantial. In a certain set of conditions, however, double pressure could start to feed on itself, and this could really set the wheels in motion. Should we see prices head out one way much more than the other, this is generally referred to as *follow-through*.

Rather than responding to its presence, arguably a more promising way to take advantage of follow-through is to anticipate its origin so as to take position in its primary stage. This implies that these events do not always appear out of the blue. Indeed, it can safely be stated that in any session of any market sooner or later the price action will build up to a boiling point from where the pressure is likely to escape in double-pressure manner. To detect these "sweetspots" in the chart, the crucial boundaries between attack and defense, is essentially what a breakout method is all about.

While most traders will find merit in the double-pressure concept, many may not sympathize with the idea of trading breaks. Some will even argue that in today's tight markets the failure rate of the average breakout (of whatever kind) is so high that this once much-appreciated strategy is now a poor proposition at best. This critique is not entirely out of place. Many breaks indeed fail to follow through, and not seldom by design. Yet if we learn to make distinctions between the high and low-odds varieties there is no need for pessimism on the part of trading breaks, quite the contrary. In the chapters ahead, we will see hundreds of examples of breakouts that should leave little room for argument as to their tradability with high odds attached.

But in all cases, conditions are king. Even a break in line with the dominant pressure runs a high risk of failure if poorly set within the technical picture. Always more telling than its mere occurrence is the way a break is built up. By and large, the best opportunities stem from a visible fight over the breakout level in question—a number of alternating bars in which bulls and bears battle it out in a relatively tight vertical span. These tug-o-wars can materialize in any number of ways, but not seldom only a handful of bars are needed to recognize the sweetspot in the chart, and with it, the potential for a serious pop. We can refer to these cluster progressions as *buildup* or *pre-breakout tension*.

Figure 2.2 shows a random series of very common buildup situations that often precede a breakout of sorts. In a regular chart, these sideways progressions may be a little less straightforward (not necessarily), but the element of buildup is never hard to detect: prices keep pushing at and bouncing off a level of interest, until either the defenders or the attackers throw in the towel.

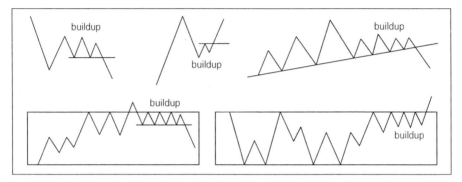

Figure 2.2. Double-pressure pops after buildup.

While each buildup cluster has a bull and a bear side, in the vast majority of tradable cases only one will qualify for trading purposes. It is interesting to note also that this side is generally the most defined, which stands to build up the pre-breakout tension even more. At the "non-break" side, however, the price action can still send out very telling signals and this, too, can play a role in the timing of the break.

When it comes to taking position, the break of a specific bar in a buildup progression *could* trigger an entry in the market, but this is never a standalone event; there are always more parameters to take into account. To judge any situation in its proper light, a solid understanding of price action principles is essential.

Support and Resistance

In mainstream Technical Analysis, the concept of *support and resistance* is by far the granddaddy of all price technical phenomena. The general idea is that the levels in the chart from where prices previously bounced may prove their resilience again at a later stage, but will be broken at some point. It takes little charting experience to find merit within this observation.

An interesting side-effect of support and resistance is that when these "barrier levels" are eventually overcome, their earlier significance is not necessarily lost. Once broken, these levels often reverse their initial roles, meaning that former support may now turn into resistance when touched from below, and resistance, once broken topside, may act as support when touched from above. This, too, is a highly visible technical phenomenon and it is not hard to imagine how countless strategies are solely designed to exploit it.

Despite their prominent role in the price action, however, it is best to entertain a neutral view on all these peaks and troughs and use them mainly as a source of information. The novice in particular is not recommended to adopt the aggressive contrarian approach of shorting former highs and buying former lows in anticipation of these levels to hold up; nor is he advised to blindly long new highs or short new lows in anticipation of these breaks to follow through.

Rather than acting on support and resistance straightaway, whether for a break or a bounce, the conservative practice is to first monitor how the market handles itself in and around these levels, and then take it from there. For example, the perforation of a former high is likely to have more of an impact when the level gets taken out as a result of a tug-o-war progression beneath it (buildup). Much less so when prices come up from lower levels and then go straight on to clear the former high—these type of breaks are known to backfire quite painfully. As to the latter, it is vital to realize that there are numerous parties in the market whose favorite game is not to trade but to *counter* the break, particularly those set poorly.

Support and resistance levels can serve many purposes, but their biggest virtue is that we can derive from their presence an idea on the dominant party in the chart. This is valuable information; not only will it point us in the proper direction for our trades, it will tell us also which side of the market to shun. For we shouldn't trade against dominance.

A very effective way to identify the dominant party is to simply follow the overall slope of the market. When a chart is dominated by the bulls, even modestly, prices will make new highs on the whole and the bearish corrections along the way will have a hard time surpassing former lows.

And even when prices start to falter in the higher region of the chart, bulls are technically still in control as long as they manage to keep the market up in levels higher than or equal to a former significant low.

Inevitably, at some point the ruling party will run out of ammo and as a result they may no longer be able to recoup so well from whatever setbacks they are forced to incur. This could be a sign of a power shift ahead. But the stronger the earlier dominance, the less likely the market will turn on any first reversal attempt.

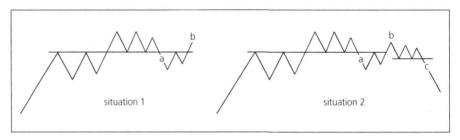

Figure 2.3. It takes time for a market to roll over. All else equal, the break at point *c* provides better odds for bearish follow-through than the one at point *a*.

Compare the two situations in Figure 2.3. Up until point *b*, both charts are identical. The failed bear attack at point *a* serves to illustrate the danger of accepting an otherwise reasonable break that is technically still set against the dominant pressure. Since this break followed a "classic" topping progression (double top plus lower top), eager bears may have been tricked into thinking that a turn was at hand. But they traded in defiance of the bullish dominance, which so far had only shown signs of waning *momentum*.

The bear break at point *c*, in Situation 2, already stands a much better chance of finding follow-through. The premise behind the better odds is found in progression *b-c*, which shows a failure of the bulls to undo the bear break at *a*, which, in terms of probability, is now more likely to inspire bears to play short and bulls to bail out (double pressure). And not unimportant either, contrarians will probably be less keen on defying this break.

Of course, in the bigger scheme of things, and depending on whatever parameters are taken into account, both the break at *a* and *c* could be unfavorable; and even the break at *a* may have been playable, why not: but when compared among themselves, trading the break at point *c* is definitely the better bet, simply because there is now more information available that favors the bearish cause.

Identifying the dominant pressure correctly is paramount in any breakout method. Aspiring traders in particular should either trade in line with this pressure, or take position from a neutral base whose break is likely to promote a new dominant order; but they are well advised not to defy whatever dominance is in place.

This is not to suggest that trading *against* dominance is considered an inferior proposition, most certainly not. But before going this more aggressive, contrarian route, it really is recommended to learn to trade confidently and profitably *in line* with the pressure first.

Contrarian tactics do deserve our utmost attention, though, if only for the fact that the extent of counterpressure will play a crucial role in the failure or success of a breakout. The more we come to understand the favorite game of our opponents, the sooner we will be able to recognize a poisonous break on offer. All this will be taken up as we march along. Some of these counterbreak tactics may even strike a pleasant chord with the reader, and they can always be implemented at some future point.

False Breaks, Tease Breaks and Proper Breaks

Even when set in line with the current dominant pressure, there are basically three ways for the market to go about a break: terribly, poorly or properly. Before we take up the differences, allow me to once again stress that one crucial concept that is so vital to grasp: as much as trading breakouts is a favorite pastime among many participants in the market, equally popular is the contrarian game, which harbors within it the exact opposite line of thought: contrarians take pride in positioning themselves against the event. At first this may seem odd; out of all the possible places to take a counter position, why pick a break and risk getting trampled on by a potential double-pressure stampede? The answer is not hard to guess: the contrarian anticipates the breakout to fail.

Contrarian tactics are certainly not for everyone, for the dangers within them are evident. However, we can rest assured that there are many parties in the market who have mastered the art of the counter-strike to perfection. It is what they do all day long. And it is not just the typical break they tend to bully; with equal pleasure they take their shots at a rising or falling market by shorting or buying whatever comes towards them.

With powerful enemies always on the prowl, we cannot afford to only concentrate on the bright side of our trading ideas—the likelihood of opposition demands equal attention. But let us not forget that the contrarian, too, needs to carefully weigh his prospects before taking his chances on defying a break, for no party can ever have his way with the market unchallenged. As we can see, the breakout trader and the contrarian may entertain opposing views, their task is essentially the same: to determine the *nature* of the break.

If a break is not built up "properly", chances are it will have a hard time convincing the bulk of breakout traders that the event is for real. Not seldom, a lack of participation immediately becomes evident when the same bar that caused the break instantly reverses—a nasty little *oops*-moment for all those who traded it. At other times, we may see prices follow through a bit, only to then peter out and undo the break after all. Regardless of how these things play out in the situation at hand, a poorly set break stands a high chance of failure simply because many breakout traders will not deem the odds good enough to trade the event for *continuation*, while at the same time plenty of contrarians may be tempted to trade the break for *failure*.

Also, when confronted with a faltering break, parties positioned in line with it, from whatever earlier level, may decide to exchange their holdings for the safety of the sidelines, thereby further increasing the pressure against the break—and with it, the odds for its failure. Of course, not always will a poor break resolve itself in favor of the contrarian cause, or we might as well become contrarians ourselves. But any chart will show that the dreaded false break is not a rarity by any means.

Before we go on to examine the favorable scenario, it may help to first look at some situations to avoid. There are two type of breakouts that should at least come across as highly suspect. The most obvious one we will refer to as the *false break trap*; the second type, less malign but still very much to shun, we can look upon as the *tease break trap*. Bear in mind, it is never the outcome that determines these labels, it is the way the breaks are set when they occur. In other words, it is very well possible that an excellent break will find no follow-through whatsoever, whereas a terrible break might take off and never look back. In terms of probability, the outcomes are sooner reversed.

Whether or not to take position on a break is always a function of how well the technical credentials of the chart back up the prospects for follow-through. At least three things demand examination in all situations: (a) is the break set in line with the dominant pressure or against it; (b) is the market ranging or trending; (c) are there obstacles overhead or underfoot that could possibly obstruct an advance or decline.

While these are the core essentials that will determine whether the chart *conditions* speak favorably of the venture (we will discuss their particulars in more detail along the way), they do not warrant participation by themselves. Always a mandatory routine before taking position on any type of break is to assess the way the market behaved just *prior* to the event. If we don't find buildup there, the offer is best declined.

Consider the three situations in Figure 2.4. All else equal and assuming the short entries at *e* were all technically sound in regard to the dominant pressure, these situations perfectly illustrate the principle of the false break trap, the tease break trap and the proper break respectively.

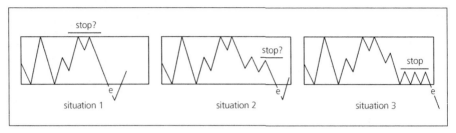

Figure 2.4. Difference in buildup prior to a breakout not only affects the likelihood of follow-through, but the level for protection as well.

Earlier on we stressed the importance of buildup and how it tends to play a determining role in the success or failure of a break. The premise behind this principle is not hard to grasp: the stronger we see a level defended before it yields, the more dominance displayed by the ultimate victors. But there is another good reason why the *absence* of buildup tends to compromise the follow-through potential on a break. It concerns the placement of the protective stop.

On any wager, the level for protection plays a major part in the total concept of a trade. You simply cannot enter the market without a sound idea of when to get out in case prices fail to follow through. In all cases, there is a point of no return beyond which a trade has lost validity and needs to be scratched. Obviously, there are no hard and fast rules on the matter and all will depend on strategy specifics and a trader's personal perception of the situation at hand. But let us try to shed some light on the entry/stop issue by examining a very common technique that should not raise too many eyebrows as to its technical merit; in case of a short position, it is to place the stop somewhere above the last distinctive high prior to entry.

If we apply this tactic to the three situations in Figure 2.4, the differences are evident. All entries were taken at point *e*, but the levels for protection ranged from wide to tight.

Without discarding the benefits of a "wide" stop per se, we can generally state the following: the wider a stop needs to be placed to find *technical* justification, the less attractive the breakout becomes from a continuation perspective, and the more attractive when seen through contrarian eyes. (Situation 1).

For further explanation, let us examine the tease break scenario in Situation 2. Here the bears were offered a somewhat better entry and a better technical level to protect themselves also. Still, the buildup left a lot to be desired since it did not really take place at the bottom barrier of the range progression; the level for protection, too, resided quite some distance away from entry. This type of break is likely to attract more sideline bears than the one on the left, but it still provides decent opportunity from a contrarian point of view.

On balance, breaks of the tease break variety (and we will see many of them) do stand a pretty good chance to follow through, but they may not do so straightaway. Hence the idea of a tease. As seen in Situation 2, a typical response of the market is to first counter the break in an attempt to undo it; but as prices move back inside the range, they may then hit upon the lows of whatever buildup lies higher up. From such an area of resistance (former support), prices may edge down again and even go on to break the bottom barrier successfully second time around.

All of this could play out in any number of ways and in some situations a stop may get hit and in others, it may survive. The point is that the tease breakout, despite being less premature than the very poor break, still poses a big threat to anyone playing the market with a tight stop. Since a tight stop will be a key feature within our operating tactics, to be discussed in Chapter 5, our focus is best directed towards the breakouts of top-notch quality.

An excellent way to play a break is shown in Situation 3. Now we can truly see the virtues of proper buildup. Not only did this break stem from a *barrier fight*, with bears coming out on top, a breakout trader could now place a stop *tightly* above the buildup progression. The breakout may still fail soon after, but technically seen, this is the more favorable scenario.

Pleasant here also is that the principle of support and resistance may help out once again should prices at some point travel back up to challenge the broken barrier from below (common practice). Now representing both the bottom of the broken range *and* the bottom of the latest buildup, the barrier stands a much better chance to fend off the contrarian bulls on impact; furthermore, bulls *in* position could grab the opportunity to quickly sell out, while empty-handed bears could make excellent use of the pullback to hop on the bandwagon in second instance. That implies double pressure on the sell side again.

As we can see, a breakout not only involves a broken level, there are quite a few variables, forces and perceptions at work and all need to be taken into account when assessing the odds. The most important message to take away from the above is to simply avoid all breaks that are not built up solidly.

On the good side, plenty of breaks are set so poorly that they are easy to dodge by anyone with just a basic understanding of break play tactics. A non-buildup break as discussed in Situation 1, for example, is one such event that is best left alone. As to the line between a tease break variant and a proper break, in all fairness, it can be rather thin at times. We best take up these differences in more detail once we start to do our analysis on the 5-minute charts.

False Highs and Lows

When a bar takes out a high or low of a neighboring bar, we can refer to the current bar as a *breakout bar*. If a subsequent bar takes out the breakout bar in the same direction, this new bar is now the breakout bar, and so on. Always more interesting than the mere occurrence of a break, though, is to find out how the market handles the event. For example, a bull break followed by bull break is a sign of follow-through and thus an indication of bullish enthusiasm, for as long as it lasts. Should we see the market respond to a bull break with a bearish bar and this bar then gets broken at the bottom by another, that gives us valuable information also: technically seen, we are dealing with a *false high*. It is considered false because the bull break failed to follow through and was followed by a bear break in turn.

When compared to the failed breakout of a carefully built up pattern, the failed breakout of a single bar is usually of less significance—but it is a false break nonetheless. To minimize confusion, in most cases we will refer to the pattern break failures as false breaks (usually more bars involved) and to the single bar failures, or failures of a broken top or bottom, as either a *false high* or *false low*.

A false high or low in a trending swing may only reflect a minor hiccup in the dominant pressure and as such may have little impact on the current directional consensus. But when situated at a crucial spot, say, in a buildup cluster, a false high or low could be a major tell as to the most likely outcome of the skirmish at hand. Seeing the break at their end fail, the parties affected adversely may no longer feel so confident remaining in position. Should more counterpressure come forth, they may even decide to bail out of their holdings. So in this respect, a false high or low *could* be a harbinger of (double) pressure in the other direction.

To see how this information can be useful, imagine a situation in which we are anticipating the market to turn bullishly around in an area of support, and so the idea is to participate in a break on the buy side; if the price action is currently forming a little cluster of bars going sideways in a tight span (buildup), wouldn't it be nice to see the bears first put in a break at the bottom of this cluster, only to get reprimanded by the bulls. This serves a couple of purposes that may prove beneficial to the prospects of a bullish turn: (a) seeing the bear break fail, sidelines bears may take heed and thus decide to stay where they are—out of the market; (b) bears in position may get the message also and their idea could be to bail out, if not immediately then possibly on the first bull break to come along (*confirmation* of the false low event); (c) at the same time, a number of sideline bulls will like what they see and their decision could be to act on the first bull break as well; (d) bulls in position, some of whom may have been on the brink of selling out their longs, may now breathe a little easier again (no selling pressure yet from these parties).

The more we can imagine these favorable forces to work in concert, the stronger the upside potential.

Understandably, false highs and lows gain in relevance when they show up at crucial levels in the chart. A false low in support will not easily go unnoticed, nor will a false high in resistance. To get a better idea on the mechanics in play, let us explore some hypothetical, yet pretty common chart situations, as depicted in Figure 2.5.

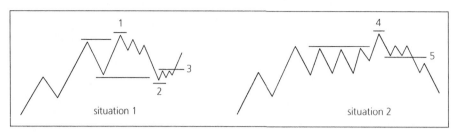

Figure 2.5. False highs and lows can have a strong demoralizing effect and often serve to announce a reversal of sorts.

In situation 1, we can regard the market as bullish (higher highs and higher lows on the whole) and for that reason the failed break at point 1 can be classified as a false high *in line* with the current directional pressure. Since all price swings at some point need to correct, a false high in a top doesn't necessarily portend the end of the bullish environment, but it is an indication of waning momentum. From it we can deduce that there is reluctance among the bulls to buy high up; or at least we can say that their eagerness is temporarily outmatched by the volume in the other direction, that of bulls taking profits and bears taking shorts. In other words, supply is currently toppling demand. But given the overall bullish conditions, bulls might very well return on the scene with renewed élan once prices have retraced to more "attractive" levels. Therefore, the false high at point 1 shows us valuable information regarding momentum, but it is not an indication of a major shift in dominance.

Note: It is essential to grasp that a break in line with dominance is hardly a guarantee for follow-through. In fact, in many an instance it produces the exact opposite effect. Savvy contrarians possess excellent understanding of pressure and momentum and their typical ploy is to counter whenever they feel a certain move has run its course. But not seldom they will deliberately refrain from action until the market has set a new break first—*then* they will counter. And they will be even more happy to do so when the break in question is set with little to no buildup (think false break trap).

As already stated, it is not always the contrarian who comes out on top in the tricky battle between failure and follow-through. The degree of double pressure on a break may very well have been underestimated and as a result, the contrarian may see his own stop triggered in turn. As a simple rule of thumb: the more extended the foregoing move and the poorer the break is set at the end of it, the bigger the chance the event will be countered with success, if only temporarily.

Let us now consider the false low at point 2. With the overall pressure still up and prices in an *area* of a former low, we can imagine plenty of sideline bulls to be on the lookout to position themselves for another leg up. Aggressive individuals may already fire long straight into the level of the former low in the hopes of an immediate bounce, but such eagerness is not devoid of danger, particularly when coming in with a tight stop. From where we stand, the preferred route is to monitor how the market handles itself in the level first. This not only buys *us* extra time in assessing the situation, our fellow traders can benefit from the extra information also. Always remember that we want both bull and bear to cooperate in our game and for this we need a certain degree of consensus.

Stalling action in the lows of a pullback in a level of support will surely strike attention among many participants. If nothing else, it provides a visible indication that sellers are no longer on top of the buyers and this could portend a revival of the bullish dominance anytime soon. But caution is still king because the skirmishes in the turn of a pullback can be quite choppy and in them a tight stop is easily found.

A development that could possibly work as a catalyst for the situation to resolve in favor of the bulls is when a *bear* break fails to extend the pullback and is then followed by a *bull* break soon after. After all, if the bears cannot follow up on their own break, and then suffer an upside break as thanks for their efforts, that provides a telling clue as to who is calling the shots in the turn.

While false highs and lows can indeed offer valuable information, by themselves they are no reason to act. In Situation 1, a good example of how to have incorporated a false low incident into a trading decision is to have entered long on the break of level 3. In this setup, the false low at 2 functioned as an excellent marker of an upcoming turn, but it was the subsequent *buildup* that provided the base for the actual trade.

When compared to the false high at point 1, the false high at point 4 in Situation 2 is likely to have a bigger impact on the bullish morale. The sideways buildup prior to the upside break indicates that this time the bulls had put a lot more effort into setting their break, only to see it fail soon after. Not a promising prospect. If prices cannot make much headway even after breaking out successfully from a buildup situation, then maybe there is more danger on the boil. The event may not necessarily portend a complete market turnaround, but it is a sign of trouble for the bulls and thus a good reason for all parties to monitor the following action with close attention for detail. Should prices fail to recoup from the false high incident and instead face another bear break, as was the case below the level of 5, the market is sending out an even stronger message.

To summarize on these theoretical yet very common examples, we could say that (a) a false break at the end of a swing in line with the dominant pressure could trigger a temporary correction (point 1); (b) a false break at the end of a correction could be a harbinger of the dominant pressure to soon resurface (point 2); and (c) a break that is built up properly by the current dominant parties but fails anyway could be an indication of a more serious power shift ahead (point 4).

Pullback Reversals

Should we conduct a survey among technical traders to get an idea of the most popular setups around, then any variant of the *pullback reversal* will probably rank high on the list. It is not hard to grasp the attraction if we consider how often this setup is glorified in trading literature and how easy it is to cherry-pick perfect examples from virtually any chart. But how rightfully earned is this reputation, really?

Before we try to answer this, let us examine the characteristics of the pullback first. In its most classic definition, it is a corrective price swing that travels somewhat diagonally against the prevailing trend. True as that is, there are many more variations of the pullback and probably the majority of them have very little to do with countering a "trend". The ranging market, for example, is flooded with seesaw motions and half of them are pullbacks, whichever way you look at it. And then there are the so-called "corrections in time" that hardly retrace in price at all, yet are pullbacks nonetheless. Furthermore, since the idea of superior and inferior moves is a matter of perception to begin with and highly dependent on the time frame of choice, we may rightfully ask ourselves who is actually countering who at any moment in time in the bigger scheme of things.

Naturally, it is always best to establish a view on these matters from one's own perspective and a trader's first task, therefore, is to recognize the line of least resistance in his chart. If there is dominance to be detected in the current technical picture, any decent retracement within it is worthy of attention. But there is always a tricky issue to solve: just when exactly have prices retraced far enough to "safely" anticipate a favorable turn?

In our discussion on the false highs and lows, we already touched upon a reversal technique, which was to trade the break from a small buildup progression in the anticipated lows of a corrective swing (Figure 2.5, Situation 1, entry above 3). In the following paragraphs, we will dig a bit deeper into the practice of turning point recognition.

In the wide array of pullback reversal tactics, two popular strategies stand out, both containing elements that can be implemented in our own plan of attack. The most universal approach is to measure the length of the dominant move and then wait for the pullback to retrace a certain percentage of it. If the trending move is, say, 10 points tall, many traders will wait to deploy their reversal positions until they have seen a retracement of about 4 to 6 points, so in essence the conventional retracement levels of 40, 50 and 60 percent.

Regardless of how this technique holds up statistically, it is easy to point out its most apparent drawback: with no further discretion built in, it needs a relatively wide stop to survive all corrections deeper than anticipated.

To counter the element of uncertainty to some degree, another popular tactic is to wait for the pullback to first reach an area of support or resistance within the trending swing—preferably residing at a correction level of 40 to 60 percent—and then fire in it, in anticipation of a favorable bounce. This technique can be referred to as waiting for a *technical test*. Since most trending swings will show some form of sideways activity on the way up or down, and not seldom halfway or thereabouts, corrections back to these levels are highly anticipated and can make for great bounce candidates indeed.

For a technical test to earn attention, there is no need for a classic trend/pullback situation. Any kind of correction that hits upon a former level of support or resistance, major or minor, can be referred to as a technical test and thus harbors within it a potential for a bounce. Should one insist on playing a reversal without waiting for buildup, firing into a technical test is certainly superior over firing into a void. But there is still a large degree of aggression involved.

A more conservative route, and the one we will explore in more detail later on, is not to buy or sell straight into a retracement spot, technical test or not, but to monitor how prices handle themselves in the potential reversal area first. This wait-and-see tactic is based on the premise that most pullbacks will not turn on a dime. On our 5-minute frame we often get to see at least one or two, if not many more bars that reflect a little bull/bear skirmish right in the anticipated end of the correction. This not only allows for extra time to assess the likelihood of the reversal itself, it builds up the required tension prior to it, and at the same time it tends to offer a better view on the exact level of the break.

Obviously, this is not to suggest that by showing a little more patience we will never get stopped out or tricked into a premature entry—or fully miss our ride, for that matter; but if we aim to play reversals with a tight stop, this more conservative route definitely deserves preference over blindly buying and selling into the market without waiting for prices to stall first. Let us examine some textbook examples to get an idea of how these tactics can be put into practice.

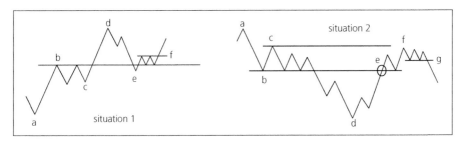

Figure 2.6. Pullback reversals are often initiated from a key level of support or resistance. Rather than trading into these levels straightaway in anticipation of an immediate bounce (both at point *e*), it may pay to allow the market a little extra time to set up the turn in buildup fashion.

In Situation 1 in Figure 2.6, pullback *d-e* represents a classic technical test in the level of *b*, which was a function of the earlier sideways activity within bull trend *a-d*.

It can safely be stated that the level of *b* plays a crucial role in this chart: (1) it built up pressure towards another leg in the trend; (2) it worked as a technical magnet for the pullback later on; (3) it provided a level for a technical test in a 40/50 percent correction; (4) it offered a platform for bulls and bears to fight it out in order to determine the "definitive" lows of the correction, thereby setting up a pullback reversal in buildup fashion (*e-f*).

As already hinted, by waiting for buildup, it is inevitable to occasionally miss a turn. In fact, it is quite a frequent occurrence. But it will save us also from many a quick shake. On balance, patience will prove a much better ally than eagerness, as countless chart examples will aim to demonstrate in the chapters ahead. In Situation 1, the buildup between *e* and *f* is a very common development, and a favorable one at that. It resided pleasantly in technical support of *b*, while building up tension below the level of *f*. Should the pressure escape on the bull side, this is very likely to trigger a double-pressure response.

Regardless of entry preference, however, it is important to note that the higher entry above *f* does not necessarily compare unfavorably to the more economical entry at *e*. First of all, the buildup below *f* shows more confirmation on the likelihood of the reversal, which is already a plus. But there is another issue to take into account that will affect the

23

clinical odds on both wagers. It regards the levels for protection and target in relation to the level of entry. If we assume both the bounce trade
at *e* and the break trade above *f* to have been protected "technically"
with a stop below the last distinctive low prior to entry, there are some
interesting things to point out.

On the trade above *f*, the last low of significance prior to entry resided at the level of *b*. A stop, therefore, could have been placed a little
below the latter.

On the bounce trade at *e*, a technical stop may have been placed
below the first low on the left, below point *c*. Let us further assume that
both traders had the high of *d* as a technical target in mind. Should it
have been met, the aggressive trader, since his entry was lower in the
chart, may have scored more pip on reaching target, but not necessarily
more profit in terms of percentage. To examine this, we have to consider
the ratio between risk and reward. For example, should the stop level
on the bounce trade have resided at, say, 16 pip away from entry and
the target at 32, then this particular venture would have yielded a ratio
between risk and reward of 1:2. It is not unthinkable, however, that the
conservative trader, despite his entry higher up, could also have applied
a ratio quite similar to this. The distance from *f* to the target level of *d*
may now only have been about, say, 24 pip, but the stop below *b* was
set at a smaller distance also. Should it have resided at about 12 pip
away from entry, then this too would have yielded a ratio of 1:2.

Even when adhering to a "more conservative" mode of operation, it
can be a fine line between acting prematurely and acting too late; the
market is certainly not always so kind as to grant us the most effective entry if only we be patient. There is little point also in arguing over
which approach is the statistically more viable, for all is a matter of
perception within the situation at hand. From where we stand, we can
generally label an entry more aggressive than conservative when there
is relatively little buildup involved prior to the break.

Situation 2 in Figure 2.6 nicely demonstrates what exactly it is that
we aim to avoid when waiting for buildup. The downtrend *a-d* is basically a mirror image of the earlier bull trend in Situation 1, but this
time the pullback reversal played itself out a little differently. Techni-

cally seen, the level of *b* once again presented itself as the most likely candidate for a possible turnaround (a 50/60 percent retracement in an area of former support, now resistance), but an immediate short at point *e* would have put an aggressive bull in serious trouble before the actual turn set in.

Take note of the fact that in this situation, prices once again put in a technical test before reversing, but instead of using a former level of support to bounce away from (*b*), the market opted for a former level of resistance to turn around in (*f* matches *c*). Both *e* and *f* are valid technical tests and equally common in occurrence. But since we have no way of knowing beforehand which level the market will pick in any one situation, the idea is to remain on the sidelines until more clarity comes along. Not always will the market offer us this extra information, but it will do so often enough to consider patience a vital ingredient in operating tactics.

As to the conservative short in Situation 2, an entry below the level of *g* and a tight stop above the level of *f* will certainly have suited many bears just fine.

Ceiling Test

In our discussions on the pullback reversal, we came to appreciate the technical test as a potential base for a bounce should prices hit upon it (*bounce effect*). Equally intriguing, however, is this level's ability, and tendency, to initiate the correction in the first place (*magnet effect*).

To see the logic in the magnet and bounce principles going hand in hand, let's imagine a bullish price move from A to B, some stalling in B and then another move up to C. If we were on the sidelines with bullish views on this market and then saw prices come down from the high of C, what would be a defensible play? Of course, we can only answer this in general terms, but it is fair to suggest that waiting for prices to hit upon the level of B makes for a decent tactic. This implies that we deem the level of B a "safer" zone to operate from, than say, a little *above* B, with the level yet to be hit. The point is, if *we* see reason within this approach, based on technical grounds, then so will many other players with us, and they too may postpone their purchases until the level of B is hit. As a logical consequence, this unanimous absence of buying enthusiasm is exactly what may cause the correction to carry on until the magnet in question is hit.

Needless to mention, this is not to say that the magnet *will* be tested, it merely suggests the potential; yet in the marketplace, the mere likelihood of an event often plays a major role in the development of it. Such can be the self-fulfilling nature of price action.

Observation has it that this magnet-and-bounce principle is not just the prerogative of the typical trend/pullback situation, it is basically present within *any* seesaw motion in the chart, even within in the tiniest of technical shapes. This then leaves us to discuss how we can put these mechanics to our benefit in regard to future operating tactics. For this purpose, let's have a look at the technical test's more subtle cousin, the *ceiling test*.

A good way to introduce its workings is to explore the ceiling test principle from the perspective of a range breakout situation. The reader may remember the three qualifications used to rank the likelihood of follow-through on these type of events: a terribly, poorly or properly built up break. Another way to describe these distinctions is to regard a break as either very premature, slightly premature or ready-to-go. Evidently, our purposes are best served by the latter, since this type will show the desired buildup prior to breaking out. The very premature break, however, is not likely to cause much problems either; this one is so devoid of buildup that we will simply decline it without much further thought. With this in mind, the trickiest situation usually regards the *slightly* premature break, which may show just enough promise to trap a trader into the market a little too soon.

When confronted with a break of this kind (a potential tease break trap), the best course of action, from where we stand, is to decline the offer; but we shouldn't take our eyes off the situation just yet—quite the contrary. Should prices indeed fail to follow through on the initial break, but not fully retreat either, we may soon see the attacking parties give it another shot. If so, an element that could play a telling role in whether or not we should participate in the subsequent breakout is the presence or absence of a ceiling test. Let's explore some examples.

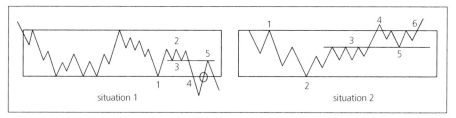

Figure 2.7. Principle of the ceiling test at work in a ranging market (both at 5).

First off, to grasp the concept of a ceiling, picture an arch-shaped formation in the chart and then zoom in on the series of bars that make up its top. In Figure 2.7, in Situation 1, progression 1-2-4 depicts a bearish arch. By definition, any arch, before rolling over from the highs to the lows, will show a little sideways progression in the top, even if it is made up of one single bar (pointy arch). The highs of it, obviously, form an intermediate top in the chart, but at the same time, the lows of this topping progression form a ceiling, basically a small level of support (3). Naturally, in a bullish arch, a U or V-shaped formation, this "ceiling" level would reside at the top of a bottoming progression (floor). For ease of use, we will refer to a floor as a ceiling, too.

By extending the level of 3 to the right, we can see how at some point a pullback came to test this mini barrier from below (5). This is a textbook example of a ceiling test following a tease breakout, and it is a highly anticipated event. In fact, the mere ceiling test *potential* is one of the core reasons why the breakout at 4 is regarded premature.

But tease break traders may not be the only parties at risk by the adverse magnet of the ceiling. Sideline bears who declined the initial breakout may get into trouble also should they too eagerly decide to take their chances on the first pullback to hit the range barrier from below (circle). This approach defies a price technical concept that is best not taken lightly when playing with tight stops: rather than turning around in the *most obvious* level of former support (resistance of the bottom barrier), a bullish pullback is known to gun for the *last level of former support*, even when less prominent within the bigger picture (the level of

3). We could say this is to "fill up" the hollow space between the range barrier and the ceiling test extension. This is essentially a function of the magnet effect described above, and by no means a rare occurrence.

Where eager players run a risk of an adverse magnet to work against them, patient traders stand excellent chance to benefit from it. Should prices indeed bounce back from a ceiling test and then go on to attack the range barrier second time around, this shows a persistence on the part of the assailers not likely to go unnoticed. As a result, the defending parties may now prove more intimidated, and possibly more willing to dump their holdings on a *subsequent* break.

Situation 2 in Figure 2.7 shows a variant of the very same principle. The arch of interest in this picture is progression 1-2-4. The range high is broken at 4, but not from a buildup progression *directly below* the top barrier; so that puts this break in the tease break category, too (regardless of outcome).

By declining the offer at 4, bulls may have had their suspicions about the potential for *immediate* follow-through, but not necessarily about the bullish prospects in general. It is therefore not unthinkable that they are actually hoping for this tease break to fail. After all, should prices indeed be forced to retreat, their typical tendency is to be sucked towards a level of support back inside the range (low of 5 put in a ceiling test with the highs of 3). And that could serve as an excellent platform from which to launch another upside attack.

Note that this particular "ceiling" (a floor in a V-shape) is not really located in the deepest part of the 1-2-4 arch; but since this level represents the *last* level of former resistance inside the range, it is the *first* magnet of interest to qualify as potential support on the way back from the tease breakout, and we can refer to this as a ceiling, too. Aggressive parties may already buy straight into this level in anticipation of an immediate bounce (5); more conservative players may want to see how the market handles the test first, and take it from there; others may decide to remain on the sidelines until they actually see the top barrier of the range broken second time around (point 6).

None of the above is to suggest that tease breakouts are merely a postponement of a superior break later on, but it is very common practice, especially when the dominant pressure is working in favor of the breakout. In the total of hints and clues with which to paint our view on the price technical picture, the ceiling test's presence, or absence, can have a major say in whether or not to accept a break. (Entry specifics are taken up in Chapter 5.)

Like most price action phenomena, the ceiling test principle is not limited to any particular market environment. It is present in both ranging and trending markets and can play a role in basically any type of reversal or break. Situation 1 in Figure 2.8 shows another textbook example of a ceiling test, when the low of 4 came to test the top of the bottoming cluster in arch progression 1-2-3.

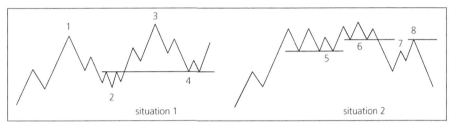

Figure 2.8. Some more examples of the ceiling test principle (4 and 8).

Note: If you scan your charts for *higher lows* and *lower highs*, major or minor, you will often find that plenty of turnarounds were initiated by a perfect ceiling test bounce. Especially when the chart shows strong continuation prospects, say, bullish, a correction may not make it all the way back to a former low, because bulls already buy the ceiling test level.

Another interesting variant of a ceiling test is shown in Situation 2. In this chart, the bullish dominance came under pressure when the lows of 6 were broken. As bulls fought back to undo the implications, a pullback emerged, which offered sideline bears an opportunity to take position from higher up. The parties who already fired short at 7, in the extension of the lows of 5, may have had good reasons to do so, but they did expose themselves to the danger of a ceiling test at 8. Since the lows at 6 represented the *last* level of former support, it was a more likely magnet for the pullback to gun for and possibly reverse in (all this in terms of probability, of course).

Round Number Effect

The directional effort of any currency pair is a big players game. The volume necessary to significantly move the currency markets is simply beyond the realm of the average home office trader, even if he were to operate on a scale that could be considered huge by whatever home trading standard. Corporate banks, central banks, institutions and hedge funds are the typical big parties competing heavily with one another in the Forex arena. There is no point in trying to figure out these parties' motives for doing what they do at any moment in time. They may be considering macro-economical releases, fundamental outlooks, interest rate decisions, chart technicals, you name it. Even if we knew what one big party was up to, most certainly there will be a bunch of other big players doing the exact opposite. In all cases, we best concentrate on the chart. After all, whatever is bought and sold, it should show up in the price action.

To complete the series of core price action principles, let us explore the *round number effect*. One does not need to observe the charts for long to find constant evidence of how the price action tends to work up to, and then revolve around, a notable round number of interest. Whatever causes these particulars, anything that shows up as a regular occurrence is always worthy of examination.

What is a round number level in a currency chart? Most pairs have a four digit quotation after the decimal mark (ignoring the pipette) and whenever the last digit shows a 0, we can consider it a round number. On a tiny scale, say a 1-minute time frame, a quote like 1.2630 can be seen as a relevant round number, and the next one in line would either be 1.2620 or 1.2640. On a bigger intraday frame, say a 2 or 3-minute chart, the relevant levels usually move up a notch and we often get to see the price action zigzag between the so-called "20-levels" (1.2600, 1.2620, 1.2640, and so on). But arguably the most notable round numbers in any currency chart, and the ones we will sharply monitor on our 5-minute frame, are the full and half cent numbers, for example 1.2600, 1.2650 and 1.2700. We will address them as the 00 and 50-levels.

In almost any session, sooner or later a 00 or 50-level will come into play. It is not uncommon to see the price action meander around these numbers for many hours on end. Parties will come and attack them, others will come and defend them. There is never any telling beforehand how exactly these skirmishes will play out, but we can rest assured that no trick or trap is shunned to fool and demoralize the opponent. Particularly in the early stages of a round number fight, it will certainly pay not to pick sides too eagerly.

Like any other tug-o-war, round number battles at some point demand a conclusion (not necessarily in our session, though). From the pleasant safety of the sidelines, it is our task to detect and assess the various hints and clues that may point in favor of one side more than the other, all of which will be covered as we go along.

Whether the direction of the market is indeed a result of superior contestants throwing their weight around, or just a consequence of all combined activity is basically irrelevant. For what it is worth, no party can ever have his way with the market like a neighborhood bully. Even the big players know very well that at any moment in time they might run into a bigger bully themselves and get hurt in the process. On top of that, they are only human and just as susceptible to follies, false perceptions and tactical trading errors as any ordinary trader trading from his home. Therefore, rather than being intimidated by these powerful parties, we should welcome their presence, for without their volume, prices are not likely to move substantially anytime soon.

A very interesting consequence of round number focus is that these levels, too, tend to work like technical magnets. If a trade sets up properly, in line with the dominant pressure, there is arguably no better ally to get double pressure going than a 00 or 50-level about 20 pip out. This too is a variant of the earlier mentioned *magnet effect*. By the same token, however, the pull of a major round number could work the other way around, to the detriment of a trade; we can refer to this as the *adverse magnet effect*.

Taking both mechanisms into account, one of our primary goals is to set up our trades in line with a favorable magnet, while trying to avoid the adverse pull of a 00 or 50-level as much as we can. (There will be no shortage of examples in the chapters ahead.)

In a normally active environment, the eur/usd pair shows an average daily range of over a 100 pip, meaning hardly a session will go by without at least one decent round number fight printed. To keep good track of these potential skirmishes, the 00 and 50-levels are best plotted thinly in the chart by default.

Note: In a low-volatility environment, which can be quite persistent, prices will have a much harder time swinging back and forth between 00 and 50; as a typical consequence, the market tends to shift its attention away from the 00-50 stretches in favor of the 20-levels. While none of this affects the nature of price action itself, or the way the round number battles are fought, it may indeed pay to adapt our own game to the tighter climate as well. In Chapter 11 we will examine this adaptation process from the perspective of a faster intraday chart on several popular markets.

This concludes our theoretical discussions on the most essential of price action principles. In our next chapter will expand on all these concepts further, but this time from the practical viewpoint of the 5-minute chart.

Chapter 3

Price Action Principles—Practice

Armed with the theory part of price action principles, let us now explore
how all this translates to real price action on the eur/usd 5-minute. In
no hierarchical order of appearance, each of the following charts will
show at least several examples of the core principles at work. We will
get to see the typical round number fights, false breaks, tease breaks,
proper breaks, pullbacks, technical tests, ceiling tests, false highs and
lows, and a whole array of practical hints and clues yet to be discussed.

It is important to realize, though, that historical studies can only
offer a representation of past market behavior. On the good side, time
and time again this behavior has proved itself extremely persistent and
a diligent price action student should have little trouble incorporating
the past messages of the market into a viable strategy for the future.
No studying effort, however, could ever bring across the true essence of
what it means to trade *live*, but that is never a valid excuse to ignore the
virtues of preparation.

One of the biggest mistakes the aspiring trader can make—and probably the most common folly at that—is to adopt a certain method that
seems doable and then immediately go out and trade it without properly
backtesting it first or fully making it his own. Another common mistake
is to utilize charts that come free with a trading platform, rather than
renting a superior standalone package for a small monthly fee. Bar the
occasional exception, free charts usually make for terrible backtesting
if only for the fact that not much historical data is provided. A good

standalone package will allow you to backtest at least a full year on the 5-minute. That's an incredible amount of useful information, all at the push of a button. Furthermore, professional charts are fully customizable, do not irritatingly reshape the price or time axis when you scroll through them and you can draw in them without ever accidently firing off trades. It is all up to the individual, but the importance of proper charts, the very tools of the trade, is best taken to heart.

In all of our studies, the 5-minute chart of the eur/usd pair will be the instrument of reference (with the exception of Chapter 11). The setting is classic candlestick, with the bullish bodies printed white and the bearish bodies printed black. As price action traders we have no need for bells and whistles in our charts, but allow me to suggest the luxury of one technical tool that takes up no space at all, yet can be a very useful asset: the 25 exponential moving average (25ema). Surely we can do our trading without this "indicator" plotted, but I have come to appreciate this average as an excellent guide and filter in both analysis and trading operations.

As the name suggests, the 25ema represents the average closing price of the last 25 bars, but with a small tweak in computation that favors the weight of the most recent bars. It is slightly slower than its more popular cousin, the 20ema, which is often plotted for similar guiding purposes. The exponential tweak itself adds very little, though, and when used as a mere gauge of market pressure, any average between, say, 18 and 30 would serve this purpose just fine. Sloping up, with most bars closing above it, the bulls are momentarily on top; sloping down, the bears have the best of the action. All this in relative terms.

In order not to compress the bars too tight horizontally, it is chosen to show about 6 to 7 hours of price action per chart, which should give an adequate view on the nature of the session at hand. When trading live, a trader could set up his charts with some extra hours in it. On the 5-minute, however, there is usually little benefit to be gained by plotting more than a day's worth of price action on the screen. Too much information may even start to conflict.

When setting up the horizontal stretch, keeping a tiny bit of space between one bar and the next will make for pleasant charting. As to the price scale on the right, I prefer to squeeze down my charts on this axis, thereby decreasing the height of all bars; this creates a calm, non-aggressive feel, quite opposite to a chart that has been stretched out vertically. And lastly, to keep the charts clutter free, there are no grid lines in them, just the thinly plotted round number levels of 00 and 50.

It is chosen to let these charts reflect the three session nature of the Forex markets in Central European Time (CET), starting with the Asian session at 00:00, followed by the European and London Open at 08:00 and 09:00 respectively, and the US Open at 15:30 (US stock markets Open).

The arrows in the chart call attention to the so-called entry bars (entry taken on the break of the forgoing bar), but since we have yet to address our entry techniques in Chapter 5, at this point they are just put in for future reference and to already give an impression of how a confluence of price action affairs can lead to powerful breakouts.

To minimize the disturbance of having to flip back and forth between chart and text, effort has been made to present the charts at the top of the left page (a few exceptions here and there). What will certainly aid the absorption of discussions below them as well is to spend a few moments to examine each chart example first, so as to already obtain a general idea on the technical topics ahead; this will surely get easier with every new chart that is introduced. Later on in our recap series in Chapter 8, with all the concepts and principles already well ingrained, the discussions will be shortened to fit a two-page format, which will keep the charts in view throughout. In Part 2, in the long series of con-secutive intraday charts, the commentaries are minimized even further and will appear within the charts themselves.

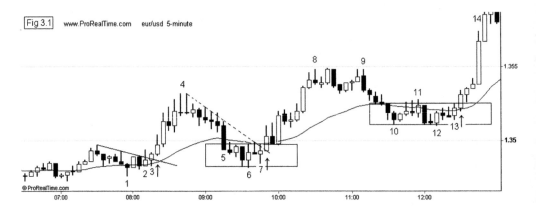

Figure 3.1 This chart serves well to illustrate the concept of the double-pressure pop stemming from a buildup situation (bull swings 3-4, 7-8 and 13-14). Without delving into details of entry and exit technique, let's find out if there were price action principles at work that may have hinted at the coming of these powerful breakouts.

A little before the European Open at 08:00, bulls had slowly taken the initiative (prices above the 25ema), but their dominance was far from outspoken. To their credit, they had managed to successfully fend off a bear attack in bar 1, which had put a mini higher low in the chart. A little bullish cue.

With prices back on the 25ema, a small pattern line may already have been plotted as depicted, but it wasn't a telling boundary by any means. The line did earn merit, though, when bar 2 briefly broke out on the upside, only to retreat and close below it. A point won by the bears.

Note: When plotting lines for visual assistance, there is no need to look for anything grand. Small boundaries (spanning about an hour of price action) can be very effective also. For bullish purposes, draw your lines either flat, or let them slope down across some descending highs, never up; vice versa for breaks on the bear side. But do keep in mind that any pattern line, big or small, is always a function of personal interpretation. If only for this reason, the mere perforation of a line may not make for the best of trading signals. The break of a 5-minute bar, on the other hand, is incontestable and the more crucial the position of this bar in relation to the neighboring price action, the bigger the impact of its break. This principle lies at the base of our operating tactics and the general idea will be to trade the break of such a bar more or less in conjunction with a pattern line perforation. On occasion, we may already enter before our pattern line itself is taken out, but more common is to hop along shortly after the event.

The first breakout situation is a good example of the latter. Note how bar 3 opened more or less on the pattern line (low of the white body), then went down a bit, only to close bullishly outside the pattern (high of the white body). This was a token of bullish resilience, but no crucial bar was broken yet. The very moment the high of bar 3 was taken out, however, bulls didn't waste time buying themselves in, leaving plenty of bears little choice but to quickly buy out. A classic double-pressure situation. (From what is shown on the left of this chart, it's hard to say whether this truly called for action.)

While there are countless ways to snap up prices in a pullback (4-6), the conservative route is to wait for the correction to hit upon a *technical* element in the chart (a test of support or resistance), and then see if prices can find some footing in it (buildup). If you take position merely on account of an attractive retracement level, say, a 50 percent correction of the foregoing swing, you are basically resorting to tactics of the hope-and-pray variety. Buying or selling straight into a technical test is not without danger either, for prices may very well march through it, if only to shake out the parties who came in with a tight stop. Hence the recommended approach of waiting for some bars to settle in the area first.

The 1-3 cluster from where the first bull swing had taken off is a good example of an *area* of technical support. On balance, the thicker such a block on the left, the harder it will be for prices to fully cut through it on their way down.

Quite like an angular line can help to mark a boundary of interest, wrapping a box around a cluster of neighboring bars can be very useful also, particularly when dealing with a potential reversal in the high or low of a pullback. A single horizontal line at the side of the anticipated break may suffice, but a box can really help to visualize the tension in the turn (5-6-7).

Underneath the dotted pullback line, bar 7 was a false low with its direct neighbor and a higher low inside the box. When this bar was taken out topside, so too was the resistance of the box pattern, the pullback line, the 25ema and the round number. Such a confluence of broken sweetspots present in a single breakout stands to work to the benefit of follow-through simply because it will have many traders focus their attention on the very same break; and contrarians are less likely to counter such event.

It took some pushing and pulling in the current highs of the market (double top 8-9), but once bar 9 was broken down, bulls finally let go and a bearish pullback ensued (9-10). Note that this correction only retraced about 50 percent of the foregoing swing 7-8, an indication that the bulls were keen on keeping the pressure up.

While conservatism in the markets is highly promoted, it is always a pleasant fact that many parties have no problem with aggression. For example, the typical buying of the proverbial falling knife on a 50 percent correction can be indirectly beneficial to the breakout trader's cause, for this kind of bravery is necessary to slow down the pullback's momentum, so as to set the stage for a sideways phase from where a more "conservative" trade may sprout.

A rather effective way to anticipate the break from this buildup is to monitor closely the current low of the pullback and the first high that follows it. The moment prices edge down from the latter, we can already wrap a box around both extremes and extend it to the right. (In this situation, the initial box could have been plotted around the low of bar 10 and the high of bar 11; prior to the actual breakout, however, I adjusted the top barrier a little to match the high of bar 13.)

With an empty box in place, the next few bars will usually start to pull and push within it—the first stage of buildup. There is no way of knowing, of course, how many bars will show up in the box, but each one will add to the pre-breakout tension. Prices could break out either way, but chances are good that the market will pick the side of least resistance, in line with the earlier dominant pressure. This implies also that there is a potential for a breakout trap at the "less favorable" side of the box.

At some point in a buildup progression, parties will have to step up to the plate and force their way out. But a mere break of a box barrier, even at the favorable side, may still not suffice to attract sufficient participation. Always preferable is to first see some *extra* tension in the box prior to the breakout; buildup within the buildup, so to speak. At times, this final tension can be subtle to detect, but it is never a matter of "feel". The bars will always guide the way.

Let's take a closer look at how this second box was built up. The 10-11 upswing was the first bull attempt to end the correction, but it didn't take long for bears to take over again and short prices back to the former low: a common seesaw motion in the potential turn of a pullback. Very interesting was to see bar 12 briefly break *below* bar 10, only to be bought up instantaneously, and quite aggressively at that. A textbook contrarian trap.

Not long after this false low incident, with prices pulling and pushing back inside the box, bar 13 provided another technical tell of significance. This bar, too, first surpassed the low of its little neighbor (technically a bearish feat) and then closed strongly up. This not only printed another false low in the chart, it put a higher low in the box. If we compare the implications of bar 13 with those of bar 7 earlier on, we can already see some nice price technical repetition at work.

The second box took twice as long to break as the first, but in many instances this only enhances the likelihood of a double-pressure pop. After all, the more trading done within the buildup, the more parties trapped on the wrong side of the market when prices finally break out, and their flights to safety can only add to the breakout pressure.

All this is not to suggest that the break trade above bar 13 was a guaranteed winner, but with (a) bullish pressure in the overall chart, (b) prices in a 50 percent retracement zone, (c) a false low at 12, (d) a false and higher low at 13, (e) an upside break of a box pattern, and (f) the 50-level magnet hanging above, at least the *prospects* for bullish follow-through were excellent. (Entry and exit specifics will be taken up in Chapter 5.)

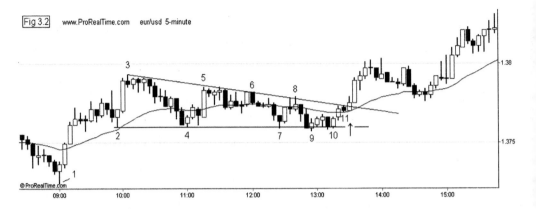

Fig 3.2   www.ProRealTime.com   eur/usd 5-minute

Figure 3.2 There are many ways to analyze price action but there is never any need to overdo it. Particularly when going the leisurely route of the conservative style there is seldom reason to strip the chart apart. This is not to suggest that some bars are not relevant. All of them are. But there's little point in busying ourselves with *every* skirmish in the chart. Always remember, it takes time for the market to set up a trade in high-odds fashion. Whether prices are currently trending or ranging, breaking away or pulling back, eventually things will work up to a boiling point in almost any session; that's the time to sharpen up the focus.

In Figure 3.2, the activity caught between the two pattern lines, more than three hours worth of price action, was essentially the market's way to absorb the bull rally that had protruded from the London Open at 09:00 (1-3). A quick scan tells us that prices never pulled back more than 50 percent from the high of this rally: this was a bullish sign throughout and the core reason also to shun all trades on the short side. Surely it may have been possible to scalp some pip on the way down within this pattern, but that is not the premise of the conservative style we're about to discuss. It's best to concentrate on the nondebatable high-odds ventures first. They do not come in abundance; maybe once or twice a session in any one market. But you need no more than that to prosper in this field.

Even among conservative breakout traders there will always be room for debate as to what exactly constitutes a *proper* break. Yet few traders will have questioned the bullish potential of the pattern line breakout above bar 11. Without bickering over the fact if this was indeed the best

trade of the session, let us simply explore if we could have seen this opportunity coming.

First off, if we consider the opening rally 1-3, there was no denying
the bullish pressure in it, but its starting point was somewhat uncomfortably located. Coming up from well below the 25ema and with no
buildup prior to breaking through, activity like this is known to raise
suspicion among a wide variety of participants. For this reason, these
rallies may not make for the best of continuation candidates on any
first pullback correction. This is not to promote rebellion against the
pressure itself, but before playing along, we better find out first how the
market handles this situation. Chances are, we are not the only ones
who need extra time to absorb and assess the implications.

Another element of concern was the fact that prices had taken out
the 50-level on the way up but not tested it back since. This doesn't
have to be an absolute deal-breaker, but on balance, the less built up
this initial perforation, the stronger the adverse magnet potential; just
an extra incentive to be a little more cautious on the bull side.

When the first serious correction set in (3-4), bulls successfully defended the intermediate low of 2, which created a double bottom at 4: a
praiseworthy feat in open defiance of the round number magnet. With
this supportive element in place, the bulls' next task was to get the bars
trading back above the 25ema again, so as to visibly reclaim their technical advantage (4-5).

The 5-6 progression is essentially a ten-bar skirmish over the possession of the average. Within it, bulls repeatedly bought themselves in
from the base of the 25ema, but as soon as prices headed out a little,
they were shorted right back. Something had to give. When yet another
strong bearish bar popped up (6), the bulls were the first to call it a
day, which then led to the 6-7 correction. From a conservative sideline
perspective, none of this may have set up a trade yet, but the series of
descending highs in the UK morning session did allow for a very fine
pattern line to be plotted and extended for future purposes.

Note: When putting in pattern boundary that spans at least several
hours, it is easy to plot it slightly off, particularly when the highs or
lows of relevance do not line up so neatly. Always try to get in as many

touches as possible and then extend the line well beyond the current bar in progress. Should the line maintain its value for an even longer period, just extend it some more. At times, you may have to adjust it a little along the way in order to find a better alignment with the follow-up action. If your pattern line has become invalid or redundant, erase it to keep the chart clean, but do not do so immediately when prices break away: the extension of the line could still play a role in a pullback situation. (Will be taken up in Chapter 5.)

Since we shouldn't have been looking to short this chart, there was no real reason to put in the horizontal line here. It is plotted to show a textbook example of a false break trap (7). As we can see, bulls may have given up on the 25ema support below bar 6, they were quick to return when bears came to pierce the double bottom lows of 2-4. Recognizing very well the absence of buildup, contrarian parties simply responded by doing what they love to do most, which is to counter the non-buildup break. This tactic worked out wonderfully well and now left a triple bottom in its wake (2-4-7).

Ironically, just a few bars after the failed break through support, bulls let themselves get trapped in almost identical fashion, in the high of bar 8. Although more in line with the overall pressure, this break was of poor quality also. Now prices had come straight up from the lows, only to break out with virtually no pausing (buildup) underneath the pattern line: not a great way to set a break either. Once again contrarian parties stepped in, this time anticipating a failure of the bulls. As trapped bulls hurriedly sold out, this added to the bearish pressure of the 8-9 swing.

Failed perforations at either end of a pattern are very common indeed and they clearly illustrate the danger in playing breaks without the backup of buildup. How about another false break at 9.

Obviously, these stand-off situations can't last. Sooner or later, one side will force its way through the defense of the other. But how can we tell a tradable break from a potential trap? By following closely the pressure in the bars. A situation that definitely warrants attention is when prices tighten up in cluster format while pushing up or down against a pattern line of interest.

One of the most telling clues to obtain that a breakout is near is when a *strong* bar gets printed on the right of a cluster progression. Bar 10 is a good example (and so was bar 6 earlier on). Granted, when bar 10 was broken topside, prices were still trapped within the bigger pattern, but the event did let on that the bears were once again beaten in support, and this time *with* buildup. That basically put the overhanging pattern line next on the agenda. Time for a conservative breakout trader to sharpen up the focus some more.

There is another form of buildup that can really put the pressure up. Whenever prices in a potential breakout area are capped on one side by a pattern line and on the other by the 25ema, we have what can be referred to as a *squeeze* situation. Although this chart is actually not the best candidate to introduce this highly effective form of pre-breakout tension, it does show us, prior to the breakout, one tiny bar squeezed tight between the pattern line and the average (bar 11). Preferably, squeezes contain at least two or three, if not many more bars, which can really make the tension coil up like a spring. We will see plenty of examples soon enough.

Very interesting also was to see the break above bar 11 stem from a *W-pattern*, progression 8-9-10-11. When such a potent pattern is positioned favorably within the price action, it is widely known to portend a breakout on the bull side (as is its bearish counterpart, the *M-pattern* on the bear side). W and M-patterns come in many different shapes and sizes and they can serve a very useful purpose in both entry and exit technique. We will take up their appearances and implications in more detail in the discussions and chapters to come.

To top it off, this pattern breakout found itself assisted by a very powerful ally. Have a look at how the round number of 1.38 literally sucked prices in from the moment the "proper" break was set. Not a bear in sight until the level was hit upon. Such can be the power of a favorable magnet.

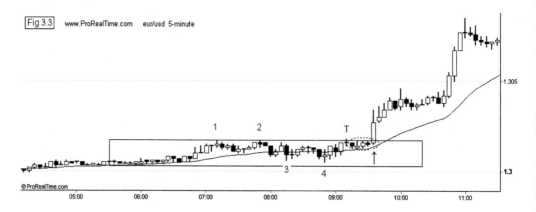

Figure 3.3 Whenever the action goes more or less sideways for a number of hours, we can generally identify the market as traveling in a *range*. In most such cases it shouldn't be too hard to wrap and extend a box around the activity. Aside from establishing a clearer view on the barriers of interest, a box will help to visualize the pressures and the buildup within the range itself. It is certainly possible to do all of your analysis without ever drawing a single box or line on your charts; but just by looking at the picture above, it's hard to deny the benefits of a little visual assistance.

Note: Before delving into the range breakout, let us briefly discuss an interesting characteristic of the eur/usd market: with the big UK and US traders absent, and news and incentives often scant, it makes sense that there isn't much firework to be expected during the latter half of the *Asian* session. Understandably, Asian traders aren't particularly keen on taking positions that will probably travel relatively flat for the rest of their day. How is this useful? Without carving things in stone, we can generally state that when the latter half of the Asian session contains a pretty tight range, it is highly prone to be broken when volume picks up, first thing in the EU/UK morning. A good indication of volume revival is the way the bars immediately grow in length, usually from 08:00 on (EU Open), but almost certainly in or around the more powerful UK Open at 09:00. As a result, not seldom the first decent trade of the new session is found within this voluminous hour and it will pay to be alert when trading in this time zone. As for other markets, it could never hurt to check your instruments for similar kind of particulars.

Figure 3.3 provides a fine example of a UK morning breakout. The box may already have been plotted when the high of bar 2 had put in the double top with bar 1. With the bars currently traveling above the 25ema, the bottom barrier was of less significance and could always be adjusted later on.

From 08:00 on, the activity did pick up a bit, but the bars remained very tight in span. Prior to the UK Open at 09:00, bears had managed to take out the low of bar 3 in bar 4, but then failed to reach the obvious round number magnet. Already a telling clue. Not only did this show bullish resilience (or bearish weakness, if you wish), it put a false low in the chart. And since the low of 4 undercut the low of 3 by a mere one or two pip, it pretty much resembled a double bottom also (3-4). Not much later prices were trading back above the 25ema again. All very bullish.

Have a close look at progression 2-3-4-T. This shows us another W-pattern, a flatter version of the 8-11 variant in Figure 3-2. By tracking the bars from left to right, it is easy to see why these patterns harbor such strong breakout potential: with a double bottom built in and the right leg swinging up, the pressure definitely points north.

From the false low at 4, eager bulls immediately pushed on to set the bull break at T (tease). This can be seen as a little premature (not much buildup prior to the break), but the situation definitely called for attention. We already addressed the fact that attacking parties can be very persistent, even when forced to retreat on first try. The more they have the chart's pressure working in their favor, the bigger the chance they will give it another shot in the bars to come.

Note that the retreat from the tease breakout was very modest. The next few bars simply kept pushing up against the top barrier, a definite sign of bullish determination. In fact, these four bars in the ellipse represent a textbook squeeze: not only did they push up against the top barrier (ignoring the tease high), the 25ema at the other end was lending a supportive hand, gently squeezing the bars out of the box. To a conservative breakout trader, this is one of the best setups in the field, and it gets even better when the buildup hangs from the right leg of a W-variant. The bullish response to the breakout may have been a bit over the top, but the mechanics in play are evident: bulls buying in, bears buying out.

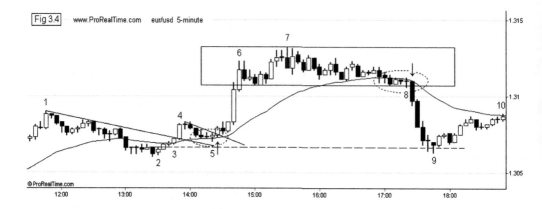

Figure 3.4 Squeeze progressions do not solely occur in the top or bottom of a range; they can just as well form above or below an angular pattern line, with the 25ema pushing at the other end (first ellipse).

A little before this took shape, bulls had broken through a bigger boundary in bar 4. The buildup leading up to this break was a bit on the thin side, but the overall conditions were definitely supportive. While not visible in the snapshot above, we can grasp the bullish nature of the forgoing action by monitoring the uptrending slope of the 25ema on the far left. That tells us a bull rally had preceded the 1-3 progression. The latter pattern is often referred to as a bull-flag formation (only the flag showing).

The general consensus on a favorable flag pattern is that (a) prices tend to break away in line with the pole from which the flag is hanging, and (b) the follow-through on the breakout tends to mimic the length of the flagpole. Naturally, such fine prospects make these flag patterns interesting candidates to be *traded for continuation* (trading a break in line with the earlier dominance).

Understandable also is that when prices break away from a flag (or any other pattern) with relatively little buildup preceding the event, plenty of breakout traders may be left empty-handed on the sidelines. But there is hope for these parties still. After all, it is quite common for prices to briefly revisit the pattern they broke away from. We can refer to this type of pullback as a *technical test of the breakout*; in many a chart this is a highly sought-after event for it could offer an opportunity to catch the breakout in "second instance".

We can tell by the small bars in progression 4-5 that the pullback was calm and orderly, devoid of bearish aggression. To those who aim to hop on, this is a favorable development. The more subdued the contrarian pressure in the correction, the better the odds for a turnaround once the pullback's momentum peters out. Opinions may differ on how to best position oneself for the ride, but two elements are likely to play a role in the tactics; the first is a pullback line (if one can be drawn neatly), the other is a break of a crucial bar in the lows or highs of the correction.

Sometimes the most "useful" slope of a minor pattern line becomes evident only at the very last touch before its perforation; still, with every bar taking five minutes to complete, in most cases there is ample time to experiment with the angle, even when using the high or low of the current bar in progress.

Interesting also was the subtle false low of bar 5. This bar had briefly dipped *below* its two neighbors but closed back above the 25ema. To bulls lying in wait to buy themselves in on a pullback reversal, a false low, even when seemingly minute, is always a welcome feature, for it shows weakness on the part of the opponent. When bar 5 was taken out topside, this "technically confirmed" the false low incident (bear break followed by a bull break), while coinciding pleasantly with the break of the pullback line, if plotted as depicted.

Looking closely, the perforation of the pullback line was in fact another bull-flag break (swing 2-4 the pole, progression 4-5 the flag). It is very common indeed to see a pullback transform itself into a little flag variant on top of a bigger broken pattern. Should these smaller flags get broken in turn, away from the bigger pattern, not seldom that is when prices pop for real. This chart really shows a textbook example.

Bar the occasional exception of a very stale session, at some point either a 50 or 00-level will become the topic of a more lengthy fight. Since many parties tend to focus their attention on these round numbers, it is easy to understand the many clashes around them. A tricky feature of a typical round number skirmish, however, is that the initial perforation of the level frequently takes place without much protest. It is when prices start to run out of steam above or below the broken level that the true fight begins. This tendency of prices to retrace to a broken round number is what we have termed the adverse magnet effect. There is no need for the market to immediately put in this test on any first correction, but it can play a nagging role in the coming action and possibly keep many traders on the sidelines.

Like the EU/UK morning, the early US session is another voluminous environment. It is often referred to as the UK/US overlap, which more or less starts an hour before the major US stock markets open for the day and ends shortly after the close of the London markets (14:30-18:00 CET). In the event of a strong rally leading up to the US Open (as was the case above), the overlap is known not for its compliance *with* but more for its rebellion *against* this pre-Open pressure. If aware of these mechanics, bulls sitting tight on their profitable positions will surely have kept a sharp eye on the action. With no correction of substance yet, and with even a small bull leg added to the 5-6 breakout, the current situation was practically untenable. Note the sneaky false high in bar 7, and the way the bar spun bearishly around, right in the US Open at 15:30.

Technically seen, the total box progression was the market's way to absorb and assess the 5-7 bull rally. Although no significant lows were broken yet, the gradual succession of lower tops clearly indicated that bull parties were no longer so keen on buying in the highs of the market. Or else their enthusiasm was easily curbed by whatever supply came forth (including that of fellow bulls selling out).

In the few bars that preceded the collapse of the box (second ellipse), tension had been building up in a textbook squeeze: the bars, though tiny in span, were jammed tight between 25ema on one side and the box barrier on the other. An interesting cue, favoring the bear side, was the tiny false high in bar 8; in an attempt to escape the bearish implications of the squeeze, bulls had taken a shot at an upside break, only to see their efforts attract no follow-through whatsoever. Such failure may appear almost nondescript on the chart, but it can have a big impact on the bullish morale a little further down the line.

Ironically, prior to the box collapse, bears were dealt a little trap of their own: within its 5-minute span, bar 8 had broken below the range barrier also, only to close above it again. Such can be the fickle behavior in a pattern barrier skirmish.

Without delving yet into details of how exactly to have traded this, if at all, we can imagine the break of the range to be somewhat compromised by the round number level directly below it. Although the number itself possessed little technical value in this chart (no prior fight around it, and thus no *technical* support offered), the earlier price action had been very bullish, which may still have left a lot of buy orders lying in wait to get filled on a pullback to 1.31, or even a little below it (common contrarian practice). On the other hand, with the UK/US overlap already in its final stage, would bulls really want to step in against a downside break of the box, knowing that volume would probably be thin in the hours ahead?

Although we can never be sure of how a break will play out, it is essential to always look at the situation from *both* sides of the field prior to taking position. By also reflecting on the vantage point of the opponent, as opposed to merely looking on the bright side of our own intentions, we may obtain a better take on the true prospects of the wager at hand.

As it turned out, bulls ostentatiously threw in the towel on the break of bar 8. The dotted line is put in to mark the near perfect ceiling test with the high of bar 2. Whether it was a ceiling test, a double bottom or even a false low that would have stopped this decline is basically irrelevant (we shouldn't be trading there anyway). But to bears in position, this level provided an excellent marker to cash in some or all of their windfall profits from the mini crash; at the same time, it offered heroic bulls an opportunity to take their chances on a double-pressure pullback to the 25ema (9-10; not recommended).

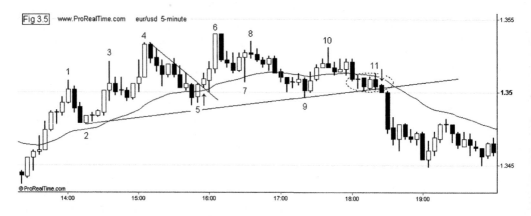

Figure 3.5 Examine for a moment what happened to a bull who bought
himself in when bar 3 surpassed the high of 1, bar 4 the high of 3, and
bar 6 the high of 4. These breaks may all have been in line with the
current dominant pressure, but that doesn't necessarily make for great
opportunity. There was no buildup prior to any of them and the moves
that led up to each breakout were already quite "extended". That makes
these breaks very prone to (temporary) failure.

Of course, it is not our business to comment on the tactics of our
fellow traders in the field. Maybe they are tiny scalpers cleverly aiming for a couple of pip as stops are hit above a previous high or low;
or maybe they are trading from a much bigger frame, with their stops
safely placed well above or below the market. But from where we stand,
trading such non-buildup breaks as mentioned above is a losing proposition on the whole.

Pullback 4-5 came to test the broken round number (adverse magnet), a feat that coincided with the first touch of the 25ema since the
start of the bull rally—always an interesting development to monitor.
Prices may have sunk a little through, but they held up well in the area
of the big 1.35.

While it usually requires quite some buildup to set up a barrier break
of a range (at least a small cluster of bars), pullback reversals, on the
other hand, can be very swift. Sometimes it takes no more than a single
"turnaround bar" in the 25ema to set up the reversal in tradable fashion
(5). In a bull trend, a popular practice is indeed to trade the break of a
bullish bar in the low of a bearish correction, with a stop below the low

of the pullback. When going this route, however, traders are well advised to make distinctions between a highs-odds turn and its low-odds counterpart. Bar 7, for example, may have been a classic turnaround bar also (a so-called *doji,* showing a very small body on a long tail), but it set up very poorly for breakout purposes. First off, an entry above it would have been very close to the high of the foregoing swing (6), leaving prices little room to "reverse" before running into potential resistance. Second, the tall span of bar 7 would have demanded a rather wide *technical* stop. And third, this stop would have resided quite unpleasantly on the path to the 00-level adverse magnet. When compared to the break of bar 5, the break above bar 7 was of much lesser standing, if not plain unsavory.

The 25ema by itself never provides support or resistance, it is just an average. Yet in the continual seesaw motions of price action it is extremely common to see a pullback of about 40 to 60 percent coincide with the average closing price of the last 25 bars—and not seldom with some form of technical support as well. The *low* of bar 7 is a good example: it tested both the 25ema and the high of bar 5 and this simultaneously represented (a) a ceiling test (floor in the 4-5-6 arch), (b) a technical test of a former breakout and (c) a 60 percent retracement of the forgoing swing 5-6. This type of "obvious" support will surely have contributed to the aggression with which the low of bar 7 was bought (a popular scalper's tactic). No such aggression came forth, however, on the *break* of bar 7.

On the way down, pullback 8-9 undercut the low of bar 7, but the more prominent low of pullback 4-5 stood its ground well. This may have kept the bullish pressure up for the moment, but it was hard to ignore the magnetic power of that round number level; prices kept coming back to it.

If an initial pattern line had been drawn to connect the turnarounds of 2 and 5, bar 9 will have fallen below the extension. This doesn't automatically warrant adjustment, but we best keep the perforation in mind. Should future price action better line up with the new low, perhaps it is wise to adjust. Considering the squeeze progression in the ellipse later on, the line is indeed best plotted as depicted.

Before we take up the ellipse situation, let us first address the bull swing 9-10. This leg headed out quite happily but suffered a nasty blow when prices approached the former high of bar 8. Try to imagine how bar 10 must have shown a tall white body at some point, only to do a full turn and close on its low. Bearish dojis in the high of a bull swing (8 and 10), like bullish dojis in the low of a bear swing (7), can be somewhat intimidating. They are often looked upon as *reversal bars*, but by themselves these dojis do not deserve such status. To judge their potential impact, we should always regard them in the light of the overall picture.

Things indeed had started to look a little less promising for the bulls. Despite their repeated efforts to leave 1.35 behind, the adverse magnet never lost its pull. With now two lower tops standing (8 and 10), it was evident that supply kept coming in at lower levels. If this continued, it wouldn't take long before the bears would start to sink their teeth in the round number itself.

On the other hand, let us not overlook the fact that the three major lows of 2, 5 and 9 were all put in at higher levels, which was still a sign of underlying demand. Neutrally regarded, the chart showed a standoff situation with descending tops on one side and ascending bottoms on the other, in essence a triangle pattern. As with all triangular patterns, at some point they demand a conclusion.

The four bars within the ellipse set the stage for the chain of events about to unfold. With prices stuck between pattern line support on one side and resistance of the 25ema on the other, this was a make-or-break situation. As long as the line held up, there was hope for the bulls still, but it wasn't hard to imagine the consequences if they failed to defend it properly.

The bears, obviously, had a task of their own. With the bars caught in a classic squeeze, they now had their opponents in striking distance of defeat. It was crucial not to let them escape.

What will certainly help your understanding of price action is not just to look at the bars from a technical perspective but to really try to grasp the extent of psychological forces at work. In the marketplace, hopes and dreams are built and shattered by the minute and in this emotional rat race it is never sure to anyone which side the axe will fall. One thing *is* certain, though: the losses of one party will pay for the profits of the other. Arguably no technical development better illustrates the pivotal line between victory and defeat than a little squeeze progression in a critical level of support or resistance.

As prices flipped back and forth between the pattern line and the 25ema, ultimately the market had no choice but to pick sides. For a brief moment in time, bulls may have felt a sweet tingle of victory when bar 11 managed to break the high of the bullish bar before it. But alas, as is often seen in a squeeze, follow-through appeared nonexistent and the break turned out to be a trap.

This is a yet another fine example of how a tiny false break on one side of the price action can be a harbinger of a major break on the other. If you were a bull in position and you saw bar 11 produce that upside break only to fully turn around and end on its "lows" (lower region of the bar), how would you feel? And as the market then proceeded to take out this bar at the bottom, breaking a major pattern line and round number in the process, would you still stick around in hopes of sideline assistance? Or would you rather let go of the rope and sooth your aching hands. Or better still, take position on the short side yourself!

The total progression on top of the pattern line shows the typical features of a market slowly turning around from bullish to bearish. It is interesting to note also that throughout this pattern, plenty of bulls had taken position on bearish corrections to the round number, and they even bought a little below it. But the very moment this support caved in from a *buildup* situation, the chart dropped 50 pip without a bull in sight. This shows us most evidently that in the marketplace, it is never about price, it is all about pressure.

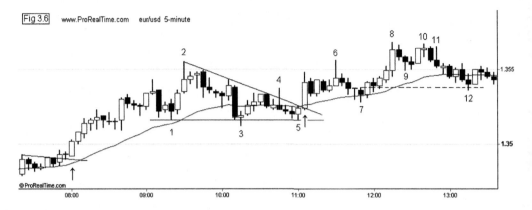

Fig 3.6 www.ProRealTime.com eur/usd 5-minute

Figure 3.6 From the start of the first bar in the EU Open at 08:00, bulls had shown their intentions quite unambiguously, which had left little room for bearish opposition. As prices moved higher, bears repeatedly tried to squeeze out a pullback of substance, but they were all cut short even before the 25ema was reached. These failed counterattacks resulted in a number of false lows during the opening rally, of which bar 1 was probably the most distinctive. That was indeed a terrible break to open up a short and it didn't take much bullish prowess to shake out the bears involved in that wager.

As is often seen when the market puts in a strong rally, contrarians of the clever variety tend to back off until at least a former area of support or resistance is touched upon. If no such level is found within reasonable distance, round numbers tend to make attractive substitutes. It is seldom a smart idea, though, to short or buy straight into a round number in the hopes of an immediate bounce. As much as you can "expect" these levels to put up a fight, not seldom they are taken out more than a bit before the defenders come in. In that respect, the perforation of the 50-level in bar 2 was actually quite modest.

Pullback 2-3 ate back about 50 percent of the opening rally, which we know is very common even in the best of trends. Note how bar 3 slightly undercut the low of bar 1, but then was quickly bought up. An interesting false low. As prices moved up again to reclaim their position above the average, they soon ran into resistance of a pattern line coming down from former highs. The initial perforation of this boundary, despite being in line with dominance, was poorly built up and thus a likely candidate to provoke contrarian aggression (4).

The horizontal pattern line points out the triple bottom features of the 1-3-5 progression. Being so common an occurrence, we may almost take for granted that prices tend to bounce on a 50 percent correction of an earlier rally, but let us not discard the bravery involved to make this happen. After all, plenty of pullbacks do move on to deeper levels. By comparison, the task of the breakout trader is not nearly as heroic, for he will not meddle with the forming of the buildup itself. His job is simply to piggyback the breakout, should one come forth in tradable fashion. So how about the break of bar 5?

It's not hard to see why bar 5 was a crucial bar. The low of it helped to form the triple bottom element and the high ran up against an over-hanging flag line (squeeze variant). With both pattern lines converging sharply, a break, either way, was practically unavoidable. Considering the bullish dominance from earlier on, and not to mention the bullish close of bar 5, the odds definitely favored a bull-side breakout.

Bar 6 was a false high with bar 2 and another sign of round number resistance (note the topping tail). Leaving also a double top behind (2-6), this development was likely to produce a pullback of sorts; but not every bull in position will immediately have feared the pending adverse pressure. In fact, a modest correction can indirectly favor the trend-side prospects, for it offers sideline parties a chance to join the trend more economically, which could serve to put new life in it. Of course, not all pullbacks will "help the trend along", but it is not for nothing that so many strategies are specifically designed to exploit the *corrective* motions of the market.

Shortly after the 50-level was broken in the 7-8 bull swing, prices fell prey to the pull of the magnet (8-9), but confident bulls quickly retaliated with another upside attack. This time, however, they failed to take out their former high. And this put in a lower top at 10.

With nothing but higher lows on the board and with most prices trading well above the 25ema, there can be no debate as to the bullish supremacy in this session. In such an environment, conservative traders are much advised to shun all bets on the sell side. As to the prospects for further advance, however, there was a notable indication present that the market had entered a zone of stronger resistance. Have a look at the 7-8-9-10-11 progression, and particularly the part on top of the round number. It is an interesting variant of the classic double top and we can refer to it as the *M-pattern*. Earlier on, we already came across its bullish counterpart, the W-pattern. Both are very potent buildup formations and seldom hard to detect; but their breaks are best traded *in line* with dominance. When broken the other way around, as with the M-pattern here, the market's response can still be quite powerful, because the event could prompt many parties to *exit*. We should never take these patterns lightly.

The dotted line is put in to point out a classic ceiling test example (low of 12 tests high of 7), but with the M-pattern block now hanging ominously above, there wasn't much room for a serious bounce.

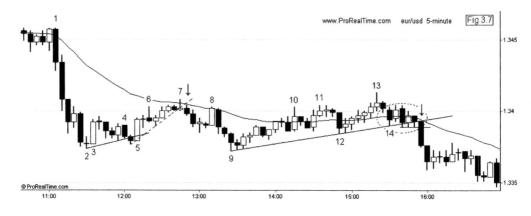

Figure 3.7 It took the bears a mere five candles in the UK morning to produce a vicious 80 pip rally that would put its undeniable mark on the rest of the session (1-2). Once the action calmed down a bit, bulls tried to regain some of the territory lost, but all they could manage, re-ally, was to stem the decline. This formed what is generally referred to as a bear-flag progression (2-4). Common perception has it that a flag pattern builds up to a break in line with the pole from which it hangs (continuation break). This is indeed a regular occurrence, but some im-portant distinctions need to be made; when acting on the implications of our technical patterns too eagerly, we may end up getting hurt more than benefit from them.

A first major factor in the way a break is received is its location in relation to the 25ema. On balance, the "further away" entry is taken from the average, the more riskier the trade, particularly when using tight stops. Even in a trending market, prices will always try to correct towards the 25ema, which basically turns the average into a perpetual magnet. With this tendency in mind, one of the most effective filters you can build into you trading method is to allow prices, in the vast majority of cases, to reach the average *first* before participating on a venture away from it. Such simple selectivity stands to improve the odds for a successful start of your trade most dramatically.

Another issue to take into account is the shape of the flag in relation to the size of the pole. When a relatively small flag hangs from a relatively large pole, participants may view the relation between the two as a bit "off" and thus be reluctant to trade the break of the flag. This concept is related to the principle of *harmony* and we will take it up in more detail in the section on our entry techniques in Chapter 5.

A flag break of the poisonous variety is shown below bar 4. Not only did this break originate from a rather small flag (in relation to its pole 1-2), just look at the distance away from the 25ema—that is huge!

Another thing that strongly contributes to the danger of trading a premature break is that contrarians are always on the lookout for them and, rest assured, they do possess a very keen eye for their favorite play. In other words, next to finding few companions to get his poor break going, the premature trader stands to encounter lots of participants of the dreaded other camp. Further adding to his troubles is the often treacherous behavior of his fellow traders at the first signs of faltering follow-through. Consider the 5-6 maneuver. That was not just the doing of powerful bulls, bears were toppling over one another in their hurried flight to safety.

Interesting to note also is that it took just one bar to fully crush the prospect of bearish continuation (5). We can refer to a bar of this caliber (in relation to the average size of neighboring bars) as a *powerbar*, meaning that it opens at one end and then closes strongly at the other. Looking closely, we can detect a virtual copy of this bar at 3. That, too, was a strong powerbar in defiance of the bearish pressure, but since it was the first to show up, its intimidating presence possessed less of a bite. Bar 5, on the other hand, showed up after a *sideways progression* had already stalled the bearish momentum (buildup), and it confirmed a failed flag breakout to boot. Understandably, this time around more bears will have taken heed of the adverse implications, not in the least since progression 2-5 bore all the characteristics of a W-reversal break.

To visualize the full W-pattern, start out with the left leg at 1, follow the up/down motions in the bottom of the bear rally and then imagine the upside break of bar 5 to provoke a bull rally all the way up to the level of 1. In practice, however, such symmetry is quite exceptional, and not very relevant either. In the vast majority of cases, the element of most significance in the W-pattern is not the right leg, but the *middle-part* progression following the left leg (2-5). The blockier this cluster shows up, the more likely that bears will bail out on an upside break of it. Moreover, when this block shows a powerbar on the right, as was the case with bar 5, bears with tight stops may not even wait for the middle-part's high to be taken out; they may use the break of the powerbar to exit immediately. (Naturally, in the highs of a bull swing, the same thing applies to an M-pattern situation.)

Do bear in mind, though, that when set against the dominant pressure, a middle-part break may still fail to attract *substantial* follow-through, or could even be a trap. In most cases it is recommended not to jump in on these breaks, but to use them mainly for exiting purposes when already *in* position. (See Chapter 6 on Manual Exits.)

On the way to fill the gap with the average, the 5-7 pullback had encountered little bearish opposition. But the tiny bars in the top of the correction let on that the bullish enthusiasm was wearing awfully thin. Surely the round number zone will have played its part here as well; sooner bears would short from that level than get out of the way above it. There are multiple ways to have traded this turn, but the conservative route is to wait for a decent sell signal first. This came presented when the bull break in bar 7 failed to attract any follow-through whatsoever and then was followed by a bear break in turn (false high confirmation). An added bonus, for the bears, was to see the break coincide with the perforation of the dotted pullback line.

On the way down again, suddenly a mean bullish powerbar came to attack the round number from below (8). It is never a pleasant sight to see a strong adverse move defy a fresh trade, but it is good to remember that the markets are not designed for comfort. By remaining calm and attentive, a bear could assess that none of the favorable elements on which his position was based had been overthrown by that bullying bar. The trend was still down, prices were still below the 25ema, the round number could work as resistance and so could the ceiling test with the low of bar 7, which was also a technical test of a former breakout.

Given all the violence from earlier on, it may seem a bit odd that no further follow-through came forth in the *new* low at 9, but it is actually quite common. We very often see the UK morning put in a strong rally in no more than a handful of bars, only to then absorb that action in a sideways meandering motion until the US Open at 15:30 CET. In these slower phases, breakout traders tend to be more picky and this usually sits well with the contrarian game. Their favorite practice, however, is to counter a break *against* dominance in a 40/60 percent retracement area (seen from the viewpoint of the rally). For example, notice the typical contrarian response when bar 11 had surpassed the high of bar 10, or when bar 13 had come to take out the high of bar 7. True, contrarians hadn't back away from the break in bar 9 either, if only for its total lack of buildup, but this had required more bravery to pull off, simply because the break through the session low was set *in line* with dominance.

There are bear and bull opportunities in any market, but when it comes to finding *substantial* follow-through (say, at least 20 pip), it is much advised to position oneself in line with the dominant pressure. In a lengthy sideways correction, it may take quite a while for a break to set up in high-odds fashion, but do not let this discourage you from staying put. In almost any session, sooner or later an opportunity will come. Always handy is to already put in a pattern line across the highs or lows of most relevance and then extend it to the right for future purposes (9-12-14 plus extension); with a fine line in place, it is then merely a matter of keeping good track of the buildup.

Note how the bars immediately fattened up around the US Open at 15:30, as is often seen also in the EU and UK Open. The five bars in the ellipse represent a pattern line battle. Although the 25ema was running flatly *through* this progression, this was a squeeze variant too, because the bars were now caught between support of the pattern line and resistance of the round number. Despite an initial perforation of the pattern line, bulls did their best to prevent the break from following through (note the three identical lows outside of it), but ultimately were forced to throw in the towel.

Figure 3.8 We can tell by the slope of the 25ema on the far left that there had been a decent selloff in the early Asian hours. What followed was a 50-level fight that lasted all the way to the start of UK session. Around 07:00 there was still no denying the bearish dominance, but with the EU and UK Open coming up shortly (08:00 and 09:00), it remained to be seen how this Asian trend would stand its ground against the often rebellious thrusts of the new morning volume.

Pullback 2-3 was the first bull attack to emerge, but as soon as the charge petered out, a little above the round number, the market sold off again (3-T). The subsequent barrier perforation at T, however, was a break of the poor variety. It is kindly annotated as a tease, but we might as well classify it as a false break trap (no buildup whatsoever). This left the bears very exposed, right in the EU Open at 08:00. The T-4 bull response is the textbook answer to such situation.

Note: Even before the low of 6 had come to match the low of 2, the bottom barrier of the box could already have been plotted as depicted.

Whenever there is a false high or low involved (T), here's a tip: sooner place your range barrier at the level *before* the perforation. On subsequent touches, the market tends to show more respect for the earlier high or low (6 matches 2 instead of T). As a technical rationale, we could say that a false perforation sooner acknowledges the foregoing level than invalidates it. For another example, have a look at how the high of bar 9 lined up with the high of bar 1, thereby ignoring F. (For an earlier variant, check Figure 3.6 and the 1-3-5 situation.) Although applicable in basically any box situation, this principle of barrier preference may come in real handy when having to plot a box over a much wider span, so as not to lose track of the level of most relevance when buildup starts to form. Of course, when the current price action starts to line up more neatly with a level of a false perforation, we should see no problem in adjusting our barriers accordingly.

When the high of bar 4 hit upon the low of bar 3, a ceiling test was a fact and it was now up to the bears to take advantage of it. It took a little skirmish in the round number, and a mini false high at 5, but then the bulls were forced to retreat, and not much later prices were pushing down against the bottom barrier once more (6).

At this stage, we can imagine the bears to have felt pretty content with the way things were going. Not only had they successfully fended off the first bull attack in the EU Open (T-5), the overall pressure still pointed pleasantly south and prices were now favorably positioned in the low of the market again. Little did they know they were in for a rude awakening.

Ironically, even though the powerful 6-F bull surge had crushed all bearish hopes for further decline, it ended with a classic bull trap of its own (F). Notice also that the F-8 response was a virtual mirror image of the T-4 response at the other end of the range.

When confronted with a failed breakout, the attacking parties basically face two options: they could either retreat in full or give it another shot. Apart from market pressure, an element that tends to have large say in this matter is whether the initial break was set with or without buildup. In case of a non-buildup failure, as shown at T and F, chances are good that the attackers will want to give it another try.

Always a strategic base for prices to recoup from a false break reprimand is a level of support or resistance back inside the range. In this regard, bulls had no reason to complain with what was offered. When the low of bar 8 came to test the 4-7 cluster (technical support), this favorably coincided with a touch on the round number and the 25ema; on top of that, the correction had hit upon the 50/60 percent retracement level of the 6-F swing. If we further take into account that the UK Open volume poured in at that very same instant (8), this harbored all the ingredients for a swift bull attack on the top of the range, perhaps followed by a break soon after.

Granted, all this may have been in defiance of the earlier Asian bear pressure, but that is seldom a deal-breaker in the powerful UK Open. To further examine the market's change of heart, have a look also at the elongated W-progression—and the triple-bottom element within—stretching itself throughout the second half of the box (1-F); this was already a major hint regarding the shift in consensus from bearish to bullish. And how about progression 3-F, a W-pattern within a bigger W-pattern. And lastly, hanging from the right leg of this pattern was a two-bar squeeze progression, building up pressure between the 25ema underfoot and the barrier overhead (8-9).

Since the latter element contained only two bars, and not very tight in span, we cannot blame a conservative bull for deeming the break above bar 9 a little too aggressive; it would have been nice indeed to have seen the squeeze fatten up a bit with maybe one or two extra bars, preferably getting a smaller in span. The UK Open is known to speed things up a little, though.

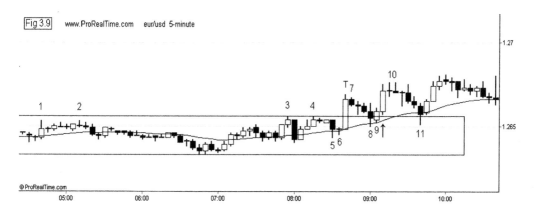

www.ProRealTime.com   eur/usd 5-minute

Figure 3.9 Let's take up one last example of price action principles at work before digging into the finer mechanics of our trading method.

Initially, the top barrier of this range may have been plotted across the highs of 1 and 2. That would have turned the high of bar 3 in a false high, or a tease break if you wish. But when not much later the high of 3 was hit again, and prices retraced from it, a new double top was a fact (3-4), which allowed us to experiment with the barrier as depicted.

With all the bars closing above the 25ema, bulls had kept the best of the action since the start of the EU Open at 08:00, but prior to the UK Open at 09:00 their dominance was far from outspoken. Their task was evident, though: to get prices trading away from that round number. Let's examine how it was done.

Following the double top of 3-4, bar 5 had dipped briefly below the 25ema but managed to *close* above it; a little sign of bullish resilience. It was also a higher low in the box.

From the tiny base of bar 6, bulls had forced their way through the top barrier in powerbar fashion (T). These tease breakouts can be a bit tricky at times. On the one hand they lack solid buildup, but they may not be completely devoid of appeal; this could leave many breakout traders confused on whether to hop along or decline. From where we stand, tease break perforations are best considered premature, but we should never lose track of the follow-up action.

Earlier on we addressed the authority of the powerbar and its powerful implications when broken; equally interesting is this bar's little cousin, the so-called *inside bar.* By definition, this is any bar that neither takes out the high nor low of its predecessor. When showing up next to a tall neighbor, even an inside bar can have a sizable span, but on the whole they are quite small and thus easily recognizable within the chart.

Like the powerbar break, the break of an inside bar, too, can have a serious impact on the price action. Particularly when the bar is situated at a crucial spot, its break is known to trigger quite a few traders in and out of position. With this tendency in mind, another way to look at the inside bar is to regard it as a one-bar buildup progression.

Although the majority of bars in this chart were all of modest span, there were some interesting inside bars to be detected. How about bar 6, as a prelude to the powerbar breakout at T; and bar 7, from which downward break the market responded with a pullback to support. And how about bar 9, which set up a pullback reversal in the top of the broken range.

Bar 9 was indeed an interesting bar. It presented itself bullishly next to bar 8, which had just performed a very telling feat of its own: the low of bar 8 had put in what we can refer to as a *triple*. This is a simultaneous touch of a pullback on the 25ema, a round number and a technical test of sorts. Since the low of bar 8 hit upon the high of bar 6, the technical test here was a ceiling test.

In a bullish chart, a triple represents threefold support, and plenty of bulls love to buy straight in it. In a bearish chart, a triple is likely to get shorted. However, it is the element of the technical test more than that of the 25ema and the round number that earns the triple's true bounce reputation (principle of support and resistance). This is why we very often see prices fail to bounce "properly" in a *weak double* (25ema and round number), where the technical test is missing. A double of, say, a 25ema and a ceiling test may already hold up much better because of the technical test within (*strong double*). But triples are definitely the most potent of bounce generators. For a recent example of an excellent triple, check the previous chart, Figure 3.8: the triple is found where the low of bar 8 hits upon the 25ema, the round number and a technical test with the highs of the 4-7 cluster.

When there is no round number involved, but instead the pullback hits upon a 50/60 percent correction of the foregoing swing, that represents a triple, too (provided it coincides with a touch on the 25ema and a technical test). We will see countless more examples in the pages and chapters to come.

For more inside bars, have a look also at the two little dojis at 10. Although the second doji was basically an inside bar to the first, they were both inside bars to the big powerbar on the left (actually, they stuck out a bit, but that hardly mitigates the implications). Naturally, if one of them already builds up tension, then two will do so even more. The break below the second doji represents a popular contrarian entry to scalp some pip on the way down to support (10-11).

Although this chart was far from trending, it is still relatively easy to identify the party in charge. From 07:00 on, the session had printed nothing but higher lows and higher highs, a clear indication that bulls were prepared to risk their capital at gradually higher prices. This is not to suggest that we should simply play along for the ride, but it does mean that we should be extra cautious when aiming to trade in the *opposite* direction (or best shun it altogether).

Note how bulls twice used a correction to the top barrier of the box, in conjunction with the rising 25ema, to buy themselves in.

This concludes our introductory discussions on the core principles of price action. Throughout all coming chapters, all of the above will find our attention again, since no chart ever gets printed without these essential building blocks in place. Our task now is to examine how we can put our understanding of these principles into a practical trading method.

Chapter 4

Orders, Target and Stop

If you search the internet for information on position sizing and trade management, chances are you will soon find yourself flooded by an endless stream of possible techniques, one more exotic than the other. Some traders prefer to scale in, others jump in fully packed; some scale out on flexible targets, others strongly advocate preset objectives; many traders trail their stops for protection, while more others just use a bracket and be done. In short, there are myriad ways to go about entering and exiting and most likely there is something to be said in defense of each and every technique.

This guide will offer some ideas on the matter as well, but do take note that none of it is ever carved in stone. I firmly believe, though, that the more a trader adheres to a strict set of entry and exit rules, the less likely he is to fall prey to challenges of the emotional kind. The first suggestion, therefore, is a popular management technique specifically designed to keep things very simple. At a later stage, we will dig a bit deeper into the finer subtleties of trade management.

Most trading platforms will offer a wide array of order types, but for our purposes, two standard settings will do: to enter the position, a *market order* will be fired by hand. Once in the market, a *bracket order* will automatically spring to life to close out the position at preset levels for either a profit or loss.

The market order is a logical choice. When the chart calls for action, agility is a must. By firing "at the market" no opportunities will ever be missed due to a *limit order* not being filled (the limit order has a specific price attached). The moment we spot our break, one click on the buy or sell ticket will ensure position in the market.

For exiting purposes, the market order is an option, too, but this would require a constant tracking of the open position and there is always the possibility of a connection failure to consider. More user-friendly and safer also is to use the bracket order option. As the name suggests, the bracket encloses an open position by having both a target and a stop automatically attached to the level of entry. Both sides of the bracket can be set to any desirable distance and each will close out the position when hit. A nice feature of this order type is that when one side gets hit, the pending order at the other end instantaneously gets cancelled. Hence the bracket also being referred to as an OCO (one-cancels-other).

Following are the suggested settings for a standard bracket on the eur/usd 5-minute in accordance with the trading method to be discussed in the next chapter. The target side is set at a distance of 20 pip from entry, the stop at a distance of 10.

These settings are not merely chosen for their ease of application. In a normally active eur/usd session, a 20 pip target complies fairly well with an average double-pressure pop from a buildup situation that is likely to have our interest. As to the 10 pip stop, to some readers this may seem awfully tight, but it is thoughtfully chosen as well: it allows a trade some room to breathe, but not to the point of hope-and-pray. Observation has it that if we position ourselves on a break in line with dominance, carefully selected and stemming from a buildup situation, there is usually little to be gained by setting protection at a level further out. Hundreds of trade examples in the chapters ahead will aim to validate this bold premise.

To ensure a protective exit at all times, the stop-side of the bracket is a market order too; when hit, this order will close out the position no matter what. Inherent to the use of a market order is the occasional issue of *slippage*. This happens when an order gets filled at a price worse than intended due to the fact that the market moved disadvantageously in the split second it took the platform to work the order request. This is best accepted as a little cost of business. In relatively normal conditions, slippage will be minimal, maybe one or two pipettes (tenths of a pip); in faster conditions, it may cost some more to get in or out of a trade. On occasion, slippage may even work to one's advantage.

In any case, never consider swopping the market order for a limit order to cheapskate on protection. This could turn out to be a costly mistake if no counterparty is found to fill your trade at the desired exit level: prices could march straight through your stop without ever taking you out. For this reason, most platforms do not even provide a limit order option at the stop side of the bracket. At the target side, a limit order will do.

With a 10 pip stop and a 20 pip target in place, spread and/or commissions included, these settings are said to show a ratio between risk and reward of 1:2. In other words, if we get stopped out twice for each time our target is hit, this will yield a break-even result over time. More encouragingly, if one winner is pocketed for every one loser incurred, things are progressing in very promising fashion.

Note: Certain bracket order settings can hold up for ages, but it is wise to evaluate at regular intervals whether the *current* market conditions still justify the settings of the past. For example, should intraday activity significantly pick up, or even go haywire like in the height of the euro crisis back in 2008/2009, it may very well be that the standard 10 pip stop would no longer suffice. A simple solution could be to set the distance for protection at a wider level (while taking off some volume to compensate). Should we adjust the target level more or less proportionally, we can even maintain a similar risk/reward ratio as before. (For instance by setting the stop at 13 pip from entry and the target at 26, and so on.)

Variations on the bracket order theme are easy to implement. It is certainly not a requirement to have the target level at all times double the level of the stop. Should a 20 pip target be deemed acceptable but a 10 pip stop too tight, setting the latter a little wider is always an option, even on a discretionary basis. Of course, this will affect the risk/ reward ratio.

As an alternative to a preset target, a trader could decide to let the price action determine when it's time to cash in a profitable trade. Theoretically, such flexibility makes perfect sense, but it may not serve all traders equally well. Anyone even vaguely susceptible to spur-of-the-moment paranoia, or greed for that matter, is probably better off putting faith in his bracket rather than in his own perceptions. It is not for nothing that this type of management is so popular among traders of *all* levels.

Since we have yet to discuss our entry techniques in the coming chapter on Trade Setups, let us not busy ourselves too much at this point with the finer subtleties of exiting. This is not to imply that the discretionary method does not deserve exploration—quite the contrary. We will have a closer look at some of these techniques in Chapter 6 on Manual Exits.

If we embrace the standard bracket order model, we will put on a full position on entry and take off all units on exit. The actual unit size (trade volume) with which to enter the market is of course a personal choice and very much dependent on the current level of competence as well as the amount of capital in the account. At this stage we need not bother with it, but the virtues of what is commonly referred to as *compounding* do deserve the utmost attention from anyone who is serious about his trading business. In Chapter 10 we will address this matter of unit sizing in detail.

When it comes to spreads and commissions, in Forex there are two kinds of broker models to choose from: the first, generally referred to as the retail model, charges no commissions but adds to the spread; the other usually offers a lower spread but adds a commission on top. On the eur/usd, both models should work out more or less to the same cost of business per trade (round-turn). The retail broker will probably offer a 1 pip spread during the active phases of the session; the commission broker may offer a 0.5 pip spread, or even less, but on top will charge a commission of about 0.5 pip round-turn.

When still in the learning stages, it is highly recommended to keep the volume very low and thus not worry too much about where to find the tightest spreads. Rather than trying to save a couple of pipettes on entry, way more effective, in these early stages, is to work on your price action knowledge and trading techniques. With no less than a 100 pipettes in a single 10 pip stop, avoiding just one unnecessary loss per week will more than offset a few extra pipettes paid in the spread.

That being said, as you progress over time and your volume goes up, and you would like to trade multiple markets as well, a commission type broker is probably the best way to go; most popular pairs will be offered at a reasonable spread and commission. Retail brokers may charge a slightly bigger spread on some of the other pairs; but over the years, the costs of business have gone down considerably with all parties, and may go down further still. In any case, always do your due diligence when it comes to choosing brokers and never take for granted what they offer on their sites. Best to apply for a free trial first, just to see how their spreads hold up in real-time, particularly in the hours of your time zone.

Chapter 5

Trade Setups

With the bulk of price action essentials now under our belt, it is time to sharpen the eye for combat. Recognizing the market's lust for repetition is one thing, it is quite another to take advantage of it. Without some specific rules of engagement, even the price action specialist is merely at the mercy of his own perceptions. Especially when coming in with a tight stop, there can be no such thing as trading on a hunch or shooting from the hip just because a situation has merit. Every single entry in the market should always be justifiable from a technical perspective and defensible in terms of protection as well.

From where we stand, there are three core requirements to meet on any one trading idea, two of which we have already addressed quite extensively: to trade in line with dominance and to take position on a break away from a buildup situation. The third requirement is a function of the buildup progression itself: within it, we need to look for a development that sets up the trade.

The interesting thing about trading breakouts is that despite the endless ways in which price action can manifest itself, there aren't that many ways for buildup to break. In this chapter we will cover four specific trade setups, three of which designed to take on a pattern breakout of sorts, the last to tackle the pullback reversal (which is often a pattern break variant as well).

The fact that a pattern can "break" implies the presence of a boundary of sorts. On this point, we already took up the benefits of curbing a progression of interest with a line or a box; these tools can indeed provide excellent assistance in detecting the pivotal levels in the chart from where prices might break or bounce. But let us be mindful not to clutter our charts, and our view, with all sorts of graphics that bear little relevance in terms of future purpose. In most instances, a single line or a box is all it takes to stay focused on the development at hand.

Once we have established a visual on a boundary of interest, our next task is to monitor how well this barrier holds up when raided. As we know, a mere perforation may not call for action yet (think tease and false break traps), but things always get interesting when attackers and defenders start to battle it in a tight group of alternating bars pushing up or down against the barrier. Within this buildup we then need to identify a *crucial* bar—the bar from which break to take position. In a textbook example of a bull-side breakout, this will be a bullish bar positioned at the end of the current cluster, with a close against the pattern barrier. When a subsequent bar takes out this bar at the top, the pattern defense is now considered broken and we can enter long at the market. On a bear-side trade, the situation is simply reversed (shorting the break of a bearish bar). We can refer to the bar that sets up the trade as our *signal bar*, and to the breakout bar in which position is taken as our *entry bar*.

Note: Although not an absolute requirement, Forex traders are recommended to use a chart that prints prices in increments of a *full* pip. This way, the highs and lows of neighboring bars, or those within a box pattern, can line up more neatly, which can only improve clarity on the barrier in question. Unfortunately, quite a few trading platforms print prices they way they quote them, in *pipettes*. In this setting it takes a mere pipette for a crucial bar to be broken by another, but this break may not yet surface on the more widely consulted "one-pip" charts, potentially leading to premature entries. Trading from a pipette chart is not *undoable*, but the advantages of the one-pip setting are hard to dismiss. If this is not available on the charts that come integrated with your broker platform, renting a standalone charting package for a small monthly fee solves the issue (highly recommended anyway, if only for studying purposes). By the way, the one-pip setting should regard the chart only, *not* the way prices are quoted on the order tickets.

In a perfect world, a pattern gets broken in a four-step fashion: (1) aggressors attack the boundary line, (2) defenders fend off the initial charge, (3) a little cluster of alternating bars builds up tension in the boundary region, and (4) prices break out and follow through.

In numerous instances, however, it will take a lot more pulling and pushing and tricking and trapping to see a pattern boundary give in (if at all). On the good side, there is no need for the market to behave "perfectly" in order to set up a tradable wager.

For example, when forced to retreat from a tease breakout on the bull side, prices may hit upon a level of support back inside the pattern from where a new attack on the boundary may be launched (think ceiling test and the re-break follow-up). At other times, a pattern is broken somewhat sloppy, with the next few bars freezing up outside the barrier; even though this may not look very promising from a follow-through perspective, the fact that contrarians can only stem the breakout but not undo it may ultimately work in favor of continuation. In other cases, we may see a pattern get broken quite substantially without much buildup, but then prices pull back to put in a technical test with the broken boundary line. These examples are clearly not representative of the "ideal" break, which may prompt us to decline the initial event. But the follow-up action *could* still set up a playable wager one way or another.

Pattern breakouts can be very choppy also, with little clue as to the ultimate resolution. In such cases, we may have to adjust the position of the pattern barrier, or perhaps erase it completely and take it from there.

All in all, trading pattern breakouts is a pretty straightforward practice, but things can get tricky if unaware of the finer mechanics. As far as our entry techniques are concerned, we will make a threefold distinction between all variations by either naming the setups a *pattern break*, a *pattern break pullback* or a *pattern break combi*. Each version will be introduced below, with detailed explanation on its typical appearance, accompanied by a number of chart examples to get the idea. After we have addressed one last setup, the *pullback reversal*, we have all the weapons needed to take on basically any chart from a conservative yet highly effective breakout perspective. In Chapter 7 we will expand our range of breakout techniques somewhat further with the powerful but slightly more advanced *trade-for-failure* setup.

Pattern Break

Despite the many variations, not to mention the tricks and traps, a very straightforward pattern break is still a regular occurrence. During the process of pattern formation, things may start out a bit fuzzy, but usually not much tweaking is needed to define the "pattern of the moment" with a respectable line, or box, on a 5-minute chart. Generally speaking, the more touches involved to form a pattern boundary of relevance, the "harder" this barrier, and the more buildup needed to push the defenders out of the way.

In a tradable scenario, this buildup materializes as a small cluster of alternating bars, known also as pre-breakout tension and in some cases referred to as a squeeze. Within it, there are strong psychological forces at work. If it is a level of support that is currently attacked, bulls in position can only hope that their sideline companions will come to the rescue on this level of last resort. But bears in position face challenges of their own. To see the bullish defense cracked, they, too, are in need of assistance, which may not be so easy to come by in a level of support. Surely many sideline bears would want to short *below* support, but who then is to do the dirty work of cracking it first.

Granted, these hopes and fears may be present at any random level in the chart, but whenever prices build up in an area of support or resistance, at least we have a clear visual on a particular level under stress—and plenty of parties, both in and out of the market, are likely to have their eyes cocked on the very same boundary as well.

Do understand that the way the break is set is only one part of the total of elements to be consulted prior to taking position. Always demanding attention is the chart's overall pressure; equally essential is to scan for potential obstruction on the way to target, as well as for adverse magnets that may work to the detriment of the intended stop. All this will be addressed shortly.

But even when the situation sets up relatively well in terms of general conditions, patience is still key. To justify our tight stop, of utmost importance is to allow the price action the time to set up our trades *properly*; we either step in on a break that fully complies with our entry requirements, or we do nothing at all. It is never our task to meddle with the forming of the buildup itself, nor to participate in breakouts that can be deemed premature or otherwise suspect.

Our first discussions on entry technique regard the standard pattern break setup. A small series of charts will serve to explain the tactics involved, but do realize that in the endless variety of price action patterns, this can only offer a snapshot of practical implementation. Throughout all coming chapters, though, we will see countless more examples of each breakout technique; so whatever is not fully palpable on first introduction will surely fall into place at some later point.

Before exploring the accompanying text, again take a brief moment to assess the global nature of each chart first. See if you can already detect the hints and clues of most relevance—like the line of least resistance, round number fights, obstructive elements, cluster progressions, crucial highs and lows, and so on. This practice will not only playfully activate your price action senses, it is likely to ease the absorption of the technical discussions below the charts as well.

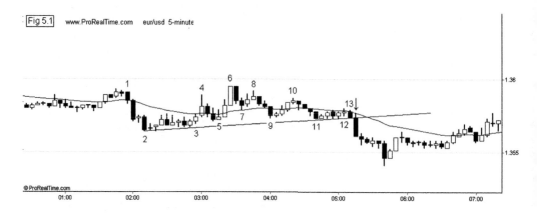

Figure 5.1 A typical characteristic of a sideways market is the way prices tend to alternate above and below a rather flat 25ema. In the early stages of it, in the absence of a dominant party, there may not be much telling who will come out on top. But by patiently monitoring the way the price action revolves around the average and by carefully tracking the highs and lows along the way, we can usually obtain a pretty good idea on the side of the market that is slowly getting the upper hand.

The first notable event in the session above was the sideways "correction" 2-3, hanging from the pole 1-2. Horizontal pullbacks are the market's way to absorb the implications of a foregoing move. Inevitably, at some point, prices can only do one of two things: they either break away in the dominant direction (think flag), or they break away at the other end, possibly setting up a reversal of sorts (think M and W-pattern middle-parts).

Bears will not have been amused to see the latter outcome come about (4). Just moments before they had been well on their way to the 50-level below, only to suddenly see their opponents aim for the round number above. (Note the completion of the W-pattern in the 3-4 swing.)

Following this countercharge was a lengthy skirmish over the possession of the 25ema, which ultimately resolved in favor of the bears. A development that may have played a decisive role in this victory was the fact that bulls, despite repeated attempts, had proved unable to reach, let alone retake, the round number of 1.36. At some point these misadventures were bound to affect their morale.

But let us zoom in on the initial bull attack first (4). When the average is perforated from below, and the next so many bars manage to close above it, we can refer to this as *bulls retaking possession of the average*. From here on, prices may still have a hard time reaching higher, but they do stand a pretty good chance of getting picked up whenever they hit back on the average, particularly on first touch; and even more so when this coincides with an element of technical support.

In a rather slow and compressed session, support or resistance is never far away. For example, when the low of bar 7 hit upon the high of bar 5, this was a spot-on ceiling test that coincided with a touch on the 25ema and a 50/60 percent correction of the 5-6 maneuver. In an earlier discussion, we referred to this threefold collision as a triple: a strong turning point candidate. Scalpers in particular love to take advantage of these little pullbacks to support, if only to rake in a handful of pip in the initial bounce. But for prices to head out more authoritatively, or lastingly, decent sideline assistance is usually required. In the session above, this never convincingly materialized for the bulls. Not long after taking possession of the average, they were twice forced to retreat below it (8-9 and 10-11)—and then failed to recoup third time around.

Note: As previously noted, there is no point in overanalyzing every little skirmish in the chart; most of the time there are no trades near and it will do to sit back with just an overview perspective on the open session. Yet always interesting to monitor in any chart are the attempts of either side to reach the next round number in line. Both parties have their own level to gun for, and these pursuits, in the end, will either fail or succeed. Of course, these levels do not have to be reached on any first try. But whenever we see one side *repeatedly* fail to make it to their magnet and then lose the initiative, a power shift is likely at hand. Put differently, *the failure of one side to reach their round number very often sets the stage for a successful attack on the number at the other end.*

This is essentially what happened in the chart above. Moreover, the failed attempts to reach the 00-level—at 1, 4, 6, 8, 10, and finally at 12—will not only have had an impact on the bullish morale, they will have boosted the confidence of the bears with equal prowess.

Initially, the pattern line may have been plotted slightly more ascended to connect the 2-3 element with the low of bar 9. But when the 11-13 progression took shape later on in the session, the situation called for a little adjustment. When drawn as depicted, the seven bars caught between the pattern line and the average represent a textbook squeeze. Whenever prices break away from such a "trapped" progression, the double-pressure response can be very powerful.

Textbook in it also was a failed attempt of the bulls to break away from the bearish grip (12). You may not think much of such a tiny false high, but it can be a great harbinger of bullish capitulation further down the line. Just try to imagine the predicament of the bulls: so far all their upside attacks had failed and now they were being reprimanded yet again, and in support of a pattern line to boot. If not even an upside break in support could tempt a sideline bull to come to the rescue, then what is a bull in position to think.

With a bear break now seriously on the boil, this leaves us to discuss our pattern break entry technique. Despite its excellent tip-off, bar 12 itself did not qualify as a signal bar. Should we have shorted below it, our entry would have been straight into the support of the pattern line. On certain occasions, a trader could decide to apply a little more aggression (we'll take it up later on), but this is seldom a smart idea in a relatively slow chart. Best to give the market a fair chance to set up the trade properly.

There were at least five reasons why bar 13 fit the description of a valid signal bar: (1) it was part of a solid squeeze; (2) it nicely filled the space between the 25ema and the pattern line, leaving virtually no room for another bar to get printed in the squeeze; (3) it confirmed the false high at 12; (4) it closed bearishly, in line with the anticipated break and right up against the pattern line; and (5) there was a highly favorable 50-level magnet waiting about 25 pip below. What more does a bear want to see to get ready for action.

In the vast majority of entries, position is taken the very moment the entry bar surpasses the high or low of the signal bar by a pip (fire short below bar 13). When this moment draws near, get ready with your cursor on the buy or sell ticket, but never front-run the event; fire only when the signal bar is truly taken out.

The very moment position is taken in the market, a preset bracket will automatically spring into action to eventually close out the trade for either a profit or loss. As already stated, there are countless ways to set these orders, but let us for now agree on the suggested 10 pip stop and the 20 pip target. As we will come see many times over in the pages and chapters ahead, this is an excellent bracket to work with on a "normally active" 5-minute frame. Should you prefer to manage your trades on a more discretionary basis, if only on occasion, this is of course heartily encouraged, but at this stage of our studies our purposes are best served by keeping things both simple and unambiguous. (Alternative management techniques will be taken up in Chapter 6 on Manual Exits.)

Note: In most breakout situations, and this regards all setups, we should only step in if the close of our signal bar is in line with the direction of the anticipated break. This means we will short below a bearish bar and enter long above a bullish one. At times, though, neutral dojis can qualify as signal bars as well, and on occasion we may even accept a short below a small bullish bar or go long above a small bearish one (think inside bars). But at all times it is highly recommended not to short below a strong bullish bar, or to enter long above a strong bearish one. These type of entries are less likely to provoke an *immediate* follow-through response and thus more likely to present the trade with a bad start. And that is a situation best avoided, especially when working with tight stops.

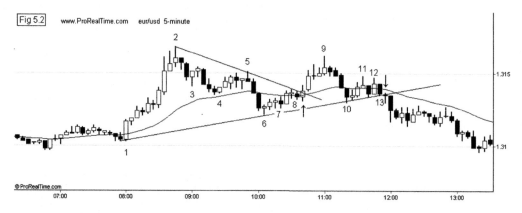

Figure 5.2 There's no denying the pressure was up from the moment the European opening bell rang at 08:00. Just look at that bull swing 1-2, not a bearish bar in it. Savvy contrarians may have smacked their lips at the sight of it, but from where we stand, there will be no selling such an opening rally.

Bar 2, and the two bars before it, show what is referred to as *topping tails*. In Japanese candlestick analysis, a tail is the part of the bar outside the body (can be a *bottoming tail* also). If rather tall, it indicates that in the course of bar formation, prices reached a certain high or low but then closed significantly away from that level (price rejection). Tail bars in the current highs or lows of a rally can provide valuable information indeed, but to take a reversal position merely on account of their presence can be a very dangerous practice. Aspiring contrarians should take note.

Even so, no rally can last forever and all have to face a serious pullback at some point. Yet if the trending move was any good, we can almost be certain that there will be many parties on the lookout to pick up prices on a correction of sorts. If so, the key question is, how far will prices retrace?

We have already voiced the dangers of trying to simply guess the turning point of a pullback. Arguably, a safer approach would be to wait for prices to stall first and then try to hop on. Unfortunately, that can be tricky also; many times the initial stalling is only temporary and the pullback may retrace a little deeper still. For example, bulls who entered long in bar 3, or above it, were the first casualties to fall in the failed pullback reversal. Those who stepped in on the break of bar 4 (better already) may soon have regretted their purchases also.

Troubling the bulls here was the fact that the 1-2 rally had been so one-sided (no stalling on the way up) that it failed to offer a decent level of support for a pullback to gun for and turn around in. In such cases, there is usually less consensus on where to pick up the reversal, even when plenty of bulls are aiming to buy. And as the buying thus comes in less unanimously, prices tend to respond less unanimously also. The 25ema can sometimes help out, as it tried to do at 4, but without a *technical* element to coincide with its slope, the supporting powers of a moving average are usually little more than an optical illusion.

As it turned out, it needed a deeper pullback for the bulls to come out and defend the opening rally with a little more verve (5-6). Even though the tiny bottoming tail of bar 6 was not a great marker of bullish enthusiasm yet, bears did take heed of this bar's message, if only for the fact that prices now resided in the notorious 60 percent retracement zone of the 1-2 rally: a last resort for the bulls to keep the pressure up.

To the careless eye, progression 6-8 may seem like a nondescript set of little doji bars; but if we examine the action more closely, these bars tell us the interesting story of how the bulls and bears fought it out in the lows of that pullback. Note that within this progression most bars closed away from their lows, already a fair indication that bears were slowly being pushed aside.

Let's zoom in a little further. With the two doji bars at 8 together taking ten minutes to complete there was ample time to plot the descending pattern line as depicted. While the highs of these dojis were thus curbed by the resistance of a pattern line, their lows found support in the highs of another doji duo, the two bars at 7. Perhaps not a perfect squeeze, but there was little room to move without breaking out either way, and this always adds to the tension.

A development that favored the bull breakout was the fact that the entry bar (above the arrow) had first taken out the low of its direct neighbor only to reverse strongly up (false low). From this still picture, though, we cannot tell with certainty whether this took place before or after the pattern line was broken, but if we consider the opening price of our entry bar, it is fair to assume that the false low was put in first. While this particular break may have been accepted either way, given the bullish prospects, the false low scenario *prior* to entry is of course the preferable order.

Next to examining the conditions that favor a positive outcome, we should also scan the chart for elements of potential obstruction on the road to target. When doing so, it is good to realize that a free path out is probably more rare than common. A former swing high or low may not pose too big a problem; double tops and bottoms can be a little tougher to crack but need not necessarily be feared when not *too* prominently displayed in the chart. Never pleasant, though, are fat, blocky clusters of price action not too far to the left that need to be eaten through to get to target. (We will see plenty of this soon enough.)

As to the bull trade in question, there was little call for pessimism when aiming for a 20 pip target; in fact, there were two eventualities likely to help the trade along: first there was the magnetic pull of the 50-level to get prices going, and then there was the former high of 2 to finish off the job. Recalling our discussions on price action principles, former highs and lows can be strong magnets also.

In this instance, resistance may have kicked in just a pip shy of target (9). Since few trades will reach destination without suffering at least a little setback on the way, it's best to stay calm when this happens and just wait for the trade to recoup. Of course, never pleasant is to see a pullback suddenly eat back all the open profits on a trade and then even go on to challenge the stop. But it is vital to accept that this is an inevitable part of the trading game and best taken in stride. Cleverly pulling away a stop in the hopes of a favorable bounce (at 10?) *may* occasionally save a trade from annihilation, but it is a terrible practice to engage in and a losing proposition on the whole. Regardless of style and technique, one of the first tasks in trading, for any trader, is to learn how to take a loss gracefully.

Bulls did come out to defend their pattern line (1-6-10), but few were prepared to join higher up. We can imagine the round number overhead and the now prominent double top a little above it (2-9) to have played their part in this lack of buying enthusiasm.

A development of attention is progression 10-13; even though the 25ema is running flatly through this buildup, this is a squeeze variant, too, with the bars now caught between pattern line support and 50-level resistance. Whenever a cluster of bars shows up between two opposing elements, of whatever kind, this always raises the tension—and sooner or later demands a conclusion.

Let us zoom in on this seven-bar squeeze to find out if we could have seen the break below bar 13 coming. To begin, the buildup had started out with the 10-11 bull swing, which was a perfect ceiling test with the 8-9-10 arch, and also a failure of the bulls to reach the 50-level magnet. As prices fell back to the pattern line, bulls quickly responded by swinging them back up (higher low). But before the high of bar 11 was reached, prices fell back to the pattern line once more (lower high). With now two false highs in the squeeze, and prices closing bearishly on the pattern line as well (13), the situation had reached a critical phase. Should bar 13 be broken at the bottom, not only would this *technically confirm* the false high in bar 12 (bull break followed by a bear break), it would show that sideline bulls were no longer able, or willing, to defend their pattern line support. And that left the bulls *in* position highly exposed, possibly prompting many of them to bail out to keep their damages small. Couple that to the bearish outlook, and we indeed have all the ingredients here for a nice double-pressure pop on the sell side (enter short on the break of bar 13).

Notice that our entry bar, below the arrow, did not sell off right away. Evidently, even in the face of a solid break, contrarian parties can be very resilient. But do not let this disturb you. A bit of pulling and pushing in the breakout area is all part of the game for dominance. Whatever you do, avoid exiting in the entry bar itself. Nine times out of ten that will be a fear-based exit, and a poor one at that. Also, with a stop safely in place, what is there to fear? This is not to suggest that an open position cannot be validly exited before either the stop or target is reached, but bailing out in the *entry bar* is seldom a valid display of such technique. For now, let's just stick to a rigid application of the 20/10 bracket and see what that brings.

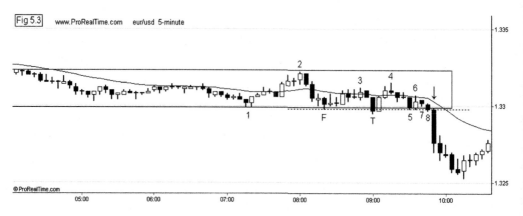

Figure 5.3 To avoid trading against dominance, our first task in any session is to examine the bigger picture. An excellent starting point is to monitor the directional efforts of the 25ema. Is the average sloping down, with most bars traveling below it, we are currently dealing with a southbound market and our trades are best chosen in line with this slope (lengthy flag-type corrections may form an exception).

Another way to get a dependable idea on the pressures in play—and very handy also when the average is running more or less flat—is to track the last so many arches in the chart and see how they relate to one another. Figure 5.3 demonstrates how this can be helpful. Starting from 07:00, we can count four arches standing in support of the round number of 1.33: progressions 1-2-F, F-3-T, T-4-5 and 5-6-7. As is often the case, the first arch is the biggest of the series and the rest gradually goes down in size. Sometimes an arch in the middle will be the most prominent, as in a head-and-shoulders variant, but whenever there is a smaller arch following, the implications are basically the same. Naturally, the last arch is the one to observe with most attention for detail, particularly when compressed. Not seldom this arch is so flattened out, as was the case with the 5-6-7 progression, that it is hardly recognizable as an actual arch (think squeeze). Needless to say, all this applies to a bullish chart also, with U-shaped arches hanging below a barrier, working up to an upside break. Furthermore, we will not only find these arches standing on or hanging below a horizontal barrier, they can just as well reside beneath or on top of a tilted pattern line. Have a look again at our previous chart, Figure 5.2, and check out the three arches standing on top of the ascending pattern line. Note also that the last arch was a squeeze progression leading up to the break below bar 13.

The great benefit of these arch progressions is that they are very easy to track and seldom demand a high level of attention when still in development. When dealing with a multiple-arch formation in the making, we usually get fair warning as to when to sharpen our focus. For example, even though the false break at F, the tease break at T and the false highs at 3 and 4 were all interesting elements to detect, none of them got us anywhere near a trade at the time. In the end, all we had to do was keep a half eye on the action until things called for a little more attention, probably somewhere around bar 5.

Although in most sessions we can usually tell the bullying party from the underlying one in little more than a glance, we should never make assumptions on the outcomes of their battles. What we can do, however, is promise ourselves not to trade in favor of the oppressed for as long as their underlying status has not been set straight. In the chart above, the down-sloping 25ema and the shrinking arches clearly let on that the bears currently had the best of the action; in fact, bulls could do little else than bravely defend themselves against the repeated attacks on the round number of 1.33. Without thinking short yet, this tells us that all bets on the buy side are off for the moment.

As is very common in a round number fight, there were incidental perforations below the level but they did not lead to immediate collapse. Always keep in mind that round number defense can be very tenacious and perforations seldom follow through without at least *some* form of buildup backing up the charge.

Notice that the false break at F was no cause to redraw the box yet (its falseness validated the prior low of 1); but when later on the lows of 5 and 6 came to match the low of F, the barrier could have been lowered to the level of the dotted line (now ignoring the break at T). It remained to be seen, though, how indicative a mere break of this "tricky" barrier would be with the round number still very much in play. While it could never hurt to put the level in, this is one such situation in which we should be extra cautious not to get trapped into a premature break; a careful tracking of the buildup in the round number *area* is paramount.

Progression 5-8 was a four-bar squeeze caught between the barrier and the 25ema; but prior to its bearish close, bar 8 had already perforated the dotted line by a pip. Perhaps a less conservative bear may have deemed this a good enough signal to have fired short straightaway, as opposed to waiting for bar 8 to close and be broken by another bar. But that would have left the squeeze rather thinly built up. In most similar situations, and in the tricky environment of round number defense in particular, my advice would be to sooner wait for an extra bar to fatten up the squeeze than to act on a somewhat premature break in fear of missing out. In this view, the entry *below* bar 8 is the more textbook pattern break short.

If fear of missing out is an issue in your trading, causing you to act before your turn a little too often, consider concentrating on indisputable breakouts only; a great benefit of this approach is that you can now *validly* skip all breaks that do not qualify as such, without feeling upset if they do follow through.

Granted, since there are no absolutes in trading, at times there can exist a thin line between a "proper" break and its premature counterpart. As a rule of thumb, the bigger the total pattern and the stronger its relevant barrier, the more work to be done by the assailers to crack it convincingly. There is never a specific minimum of bars required, but the fatter the buildup (say, at least four bars), the better we can form ourselves an idea on who is likely to come out on top in the squeeze. In a pullback reversal, on the other hand (as opposed to a bigger pattern breakout), the break in the turn may set up much faster and it may take no more than a single bar for a setup to earn validity status. (Will be taken up later in this chapter.)

Situations like the one above show us also that it isn't necessary to always work with a nondebatable pattern line and a perfect signal bar to match it. The general idea is to trade off the *most crucial bar in the barrier area*. Sometimes we may even find our entry before the pattern boundary is visibly broken, but more common is for the signal bar to either line up with the barrier or reside slightly out, as was the case with bar 8.

Note: When trading off a signal bar that is sticking out, we do not want this bar to be overly tall, or produce an entry too far away from the broken pattern line. While nothing is ever carved in stone, always a preferable condition in a pattern break scenario is to have the stop reside inside the pattern; this will allow for a pullback to test back the broken barrier without immediately getting shaken out.

Countless charts in this guide will show that if you trade from build-up, it is absolutely doable to come in with a 10 pip stop and a 20 pip target. Surely, in the early stages of your price action journey, it may not always be so evident to tell the difference between an indisputable entry and one that can be deemed a little premature still, but this is hardly your immediate concern. Way more crucial to your bottom line— at any stage, really—is to learn to recognize the wagers of the *unsavory* kind. In other words, rather than aiming to maximize the positive, more essential is to minimize the negative. And it is an easier task as well. Protect your account from unnecessary setbacks and chances are good it will grow pleasantly over time as you grow along with it.

Let's check out some more examples.

Figure 5.4 The first half of this chart shows another triple-arch formation on top of a pattern line. The short below bar 10 represents a rather
straightforward pattern break venture, but there is an element involved
that deserves some extra attention; it is the issue of the adverse round
number magnet.

The three bullish turnaround bars (1, 2 and 3) perfectly illustrate
the pull of a round number magnet. Bears may have had the best of
the action in terms of overall pressure, this had not kept the bulls from
putting in this triple-bottom variant. To understand the concept of the
adverse magnet, and the dangers involved, consider for a moment the
fate of a bear who had opened a short, say, somewhere around 13:30.
But check out also what happened to a bull who let himself get trapped
into longing the re-break of the round number, for example in bar 4 or
5. Both parties fell prey to the pull of the adverse magnet (adverse in
terms of their positions taken).

The point is that we need to be extra cautious when aiming to trade
away from a round number level. It is quite different from trading *towards* one. Especially in the early stages of a round number fight, the
price action can be very fickle and this can be a dangerous environment
to pick sides, even in line with dominance. Should these skirmishes
persist, at some point the price action will probably start to tighten up,
possibly showing more failures on one side than the other; that is a
good sign to start paying more attention again.

What were the giveaways that led to the short below bar 10? First
off, the chart was rather bearish on the whole (25ema sloping down,

most bars closing below it), which meant there was work to be done for the bulls should they want to change things in their favor. Very indicative, therefore, were the four consecutive failures to retake possession of 1.33 (4, 5, 7 and 9). Equally interesting was the triple-arch formation on top of the pattern line, progressions 2-5-6, 6-7-8 and 8-9-10. The last arch represented a squeeze variant, with bar 9 and 10 caught between pattern line support and round number resistance. Thus, the bearish close of bar 10 not only highlighted the failure of the latest bull attack in bar 9, it also rounded a lower top in a triple-arch formation, while setting up as a signal bar right on pattern line support.

From all this, it was fair to deduce that the magnetic pull of the round number was wearing thin and that prices were about "ready" to move away from it. But do note that it had taken several hours for this to materialize.

Despite the perforation of the pattern line, bulls came out to defy the break below bar 10. Because of this counterpressure, our entry bar (underneath the arrow) closed right back in the pattern line level; and the next bar, too, managed to keep both bull and bear in suspense for another five minutes (11, a tiny inside bar). Was it fear of the pending US Open (15:30) that kept the bears from aggressively playing the sell side here? Reasons are never relevant. It is interesting to see, though, that once bar 11 was taken out at the bottom, bearish reservations were promptly cast aside and the market quickly tanked (inside bar break).

It didn't take long for bears to find out that this victory was one of the shorter variety. On the good side, it looks like our trade may have reached its 20 pip target before the sudden bullish turnaround took place; as much as this demonstrates the benefits of working with a set target that isn't over the top, we cannot dismiss the element of luck in this particular venture. It is important to grasp, though, that all trade examples in this guide merely serve an educational purpose in context of probability; an individual outcome by itself, good or bad, is essentially irrelevant.

Although we will take up the particulars of unfavorable conditions in more detail in Chapter 7, it will probably not surprise the reader that the tiny bull-flag 13-14 made for a poor continuation setup on the bull side. After all that pulling and pushing in the round number earlier on, it just wasn't very likely that bears would now give up on the area without a good fight first. Not favoring the bull side either were the small features of the flag in relation to the rather big pole (12-13). As to the flagpole itself, since this move had emerged quite "suddenly" from well below the 25ema, the prospects for *immediate* bull-side continuation were already not that great to begin with (no buildup to back up the shift in dominance).

Obviously, not all charts comply with "technical logic". It takes little experience in the market to understand that anything *can* and at some point *will* happen and for this reason all suspicions regarding price action are basically out of line. Very important, though, is not to get carried away by the game plan of others when our own is being defied. In other words, it is one thing to accept that a non-buildup turnaround can indeed flip a chart around without much protest, it is quite another to trade such a move for continuation. And certainly so when aiming for 20 pip, which is a substantial move on the 5-minute. In this light, it requires little contemplation to skip the long offer on the break of bar 14. We just don't trade that.

But how about two hours down the line. Considering the length of progression 15-18, a much bigger bull-flag, the action clearly let on that bulls had taken control of the chart. But there is something odd about this flag, too, and that is the total absence of bearish aggression. There had been exactly one brief contrarian attempt to gun for the round number magnet (15-16), a plan that was quickly abandoned at the first signs of support. From that moment on, bears had not even tried to challenge the 25ema for over an hour, which then led to the forming of the flag.

In a strong trending market, flat and lengthy flag progressions are very common and we should definitely try to trade them for continuation when given the chance; but how bullish was this chart, really? Or to put it differently, if we decide to pass up on the offer above bar 14, for a lack of technical backup, but accept the trade above bar 18, then where exactly is it that the line between skipping and trading a break is drawn?

Alas, there can be no single answer to this puzzle. Since no chart situation will ever show up exactly as before, each breakout event is always a matter of personal interpretation. When confronted with a "borderline" case, probably one of the hardest things to do is to trust your eyes and trade (or skip) what you see—not what you think. This chart provides a good example. Technically seen, the bearish pressure had been fended off successfully by the bulls, but the chart itself still wasn't very bullish. And for as long as that obnoxious round number magnet had not been properly tested back, our fellow participants may have cherished similar reservations regarding the upside potential. With such reasoning in mind, it is only logical to at least have felt a pang of discomfort when confronted with the break above bar 18.

On the other hand, if we look at the facts, the 15-18 progression certainly was a decent flag hanging from a decent pole (12-15) and it had lasted long enough to prove the bulls dominant. Furthermore, the bars in it had built up considerable tension prior to the upside break. In the final stages of it, there had been two bear attempts to escape the dreaded squeeze, and both had instantly failed (false lows at 17 and 18). With the pattern line sloping down, the 25ema sloping up, and prices caught in-between, what else can a breakout trader do but pay his respects to price action and thus fire long on the break of bar 18.

But this is definitely not my favorite setup. (Note also that the flag break came about in the often slow and tricky US lunch-hour doldrums, 18:00-20:00 CET.)

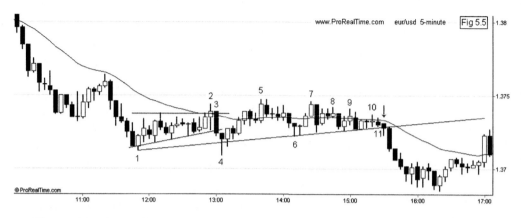

Figure 5.5 Charts like this do not leave much room for argument as to
which side of the market to shun. By the time prices hit the low of 1,
the environment had sent out a clear warning that bulls had no place
defying this tide for at least some hours to come. That is not to say that
profits cannot be made on the long side in a bear market, but it is no
easy chore to rake in 20 pip targets. And why swim against the tide
when you can surf along with it.

An excellent example of how to get yourself in trouble is depicted
by the false high at 2. By forcing an upside break, bulls tried to defy
the implications of the bear-flag progression 1-2. Not a good idea in a
bear market, and right in the 25ema to boot. Bears didn't waste time
destroying the bullish dreams (3).

Countering the bull break at 2 is a well-known contrarian tactic that
we can refer to as *trading a break for failure.* It rightfully leans on the
premise that a break against dominance is sooner reprimanded than
respected. In Chapter 7 on Skipping Trades and Trading Breaks for
Failure, we will have a closer look at how to take advantage of these
"foolish" breaks, but at this stage, our first priority is not to get trapped
in one ourselves.

But trend traders, too, need to pay attention to detail. False breaks
at the "poor" side of the market do not necessarily make for great wagers at the other. Bar 3, for example, the bearish powerbar that had
crushed the bullish breakout, positioned itself as a terrible signal bar
for sell-side purposes. It was way too tall to set up a high-odds break
of its own, right in the lows of the market: even a "harmless" pullback

to the 25ema magnet (very common) would already have taken out our stop.

This shows us also that even when the market has one-way pressure written all over it, it still takes careful planning to trade along the path of least resistance. Looking for a continuation break in the low of a bear rally (or in the high of a bull rally) is seldom a smart idea. On balance, the best follow-through potential is found either in the turn of a substantial pullback, or on the break of a lengthy sideways range (1-11)

When anticipating a break of a bearish pattern, always handy is to run a pattern line beneath the lows of most relevance. In this chart, the false bear spike in bar 4 (bottoming tail) is ignored in favor of later touches. And what a beautiful line it was. In pattern break tactics, these indisputable boundaries are always a big plus because they leave virtually no room for debate as to when they are broken.

Of equal beauty were the numerous arches on top of it. The three most prominent were progressions 1-2-4, 4-5-6 and 6 through 11. In its entirety, this was a giant bear-flag hanging from the tall pole of the UK morning bear rally.

If we zoom in on the last arch, we can see that the 6-11 progression contained a number of smaller arches itself. And notice also how all of them gradually went down in size until things finally worked up to a boiling point in the apex of the pattern. With the bars caught between the pattern line on one side and the 25ema on the other, the last mini arch was a textbook squeeze. Do we need more giveaways as to the bullish predicament?

But there were more clues to be found. Earlier on, starting with the false high at 5, bulls had failed to reach the round number magnet and then kept on failing at 7, 8, 9 and 10. Such a series of lower tops will not likely have boosted the confidence of bullish sideliners anytime soon, nor that of bulls already in the market. The last failure, the false high at 10, was particularly interesting, since it was a failed attempt to break away from a bearish squeeze. By now we have already seen plenty of evidence that if such an attempt fails, it is often a harbinger of utter demoralization.

Bar 11, a tiny inside bar with its false high neighbor, filled up the remaining space between the pattern line and the moving average. Something had to give.

Looking closely, we can see that the actual entry on the short below bar 11 may not literally have broken the pattern line yet; in fact, the entry was right on it. However, with the break setting up so well and considering the "ripeness" of the bear-flag, I truly believe there is no reason to postpone entry on a short like this and run the risk of missing the collapse. Of course, since nothing is ever set in stone, an alternative tactic could be to wait for an extra pip or so to see the pattern line broken first, and then fire short. But it would have been overly prudent, if not a mistake, to have waited for another bar to fatten up the squeeze. In an earlier discussion concerning Figure 5.3, the latter tactic was suggested (waiting for bar 8), simply because the situation asked for some more buildup to set up the trade properly. Not so in the chart above.

As to the low of our signal bar (11), pleasant also was to see it match up with the low of bar 10, allowing this short to take off from a *double-bar* break. Evidently, a double-bar setup shows more tension than a single-bar setup, since the low or high in question holds up not for five but for ten minutes. Any extra tension preceding a breakout will sooner help follow-through along than obstruct it. Furthermore, to take out our stop on this short, bulls had to crack the squeeze progression on the upside again. In the light of all their earlier failures, that would have demanded quite some bravery to pull off. All this rendered prices highly vulnerable to bearish aggression. To top it off, let us not forget to mention the favorable magnet of the 1.37 round number, about 25 pip below.

I hope that most of what we have addressed so far regarding the regular pattern break setup has been quite easy to follow and that it radiates a certain *technical logic*. The main thing to take away from these examples is to understand the importance of *sufficient* buildup, particularly when trading breaks with tight stops.

Pattern Break Pullback

While a regular pattern break setup is certainly not a rarity to come across, plenty of breakouts take place without offering an acceptable entry on first go. Sometimes there is just too little buildup prior to perforation; at other times the pattern line is debatable, the signal bar uncomfortable, or maybe the price action too feverish or lackluster. Whatever the reason, in many an instance we have no choice but to step away from the initial break. Yet this doesn't necessarily render the event totally untradable. By keeping close track of the post-breakout action, we may still be offered a chance to hop on board in second instance.

Two such situations deserve our full attention. The first is when prices, after breaking out, start to cling around the broken barrier, not knowing whether to follow through or prove the break false; obviously, this is an indication of defender's resilience, but at the same time it shows that the attacking parties are not so easily demoralized either; for as long as this fight persists (buildup), there is still a reasonable chance for the market to break away in line with the earlier break.

The other situation of interest is when prices do follow through on the original breakout, but then pull back to challenge the area of the broken barrier.

Either situation knows many subtle variants and all *could* set up a trade in line with the original break. Our task, therefore, is to see if we can locate within the post-breakout action a valid signal bar from which break to take position. We can refer to this entry technique as trading the pattern break pullback setup.

Figure 5.6 The short below bar 9 completes the total concept of a skipped break, a pullback, a ceiling test and a second-instance entry based on the pattern break pullback setup. Before we examine the details of the trade, it may be interesting to briefly compare this chart with the previous one, Figure 5.5. Despite the striking similarities on the whole, the differences between a tradable and non-tradable break (in first instance) couldn't be better illustrated. In the foregoing chart, prior to breaking down, prices had built up tension on top of the pattern line and this allowed us to play the break upon occurrence. In our current chart, prices broke away from a cluster formation that resided well away from the pattern boundary (progression 6-7, middle-part of an M-pattern). Due to the "sudden" collapse, the break in bar 8 did not allow for a regular pattern break entry. But our chances to participate were not lost.

The price action on top of the pattern line shows the unmistakable features of a bear-flag formation: a slightly tilted progression hanging sideways from a strong bear pole (1-2). In such a pattern, a series of ascending lows may give off an impression of demand. But the buyer beware; if the trending pole from which the flag is hanging is any good, we can rest assured that bears won't sit idly by and watch their dominance undone. A popular ploy is to wait for the bulls to run out of breath in the higher region of the flag and then unleash upon them a quick wave of selling. Fine examples of this contrarian practice can be spotted at 3 and 5 (false highs).

There is a widespread notion among technical traders, and not without merit, that the extent of follow-through on a flag breakout often mimics the length of the pole from which the flag is hanging. We can refer to this as the *pole-flag-swing* principle (a lightning symbol, if you wish). Whether or not one fully abides by this premise, the break of a decent flag pattern is always worthy of attention. So let's have a look at how this one came about.

Ironically, just prior to the event, after four hours of pushing and pulling within the flag, bulls had finally managed to stay on top of the 25ema for a number of consecutive bars (6-7), but then the tables suddenly turned (bar 8).

Note also that it was a false high in bar 7 that set the stage for the flag breakout at the other end. As bears jumped in and bulls jumped out, powerbar 8 completed the right leg of an M-pattern reversal (4-5-6-7-8). With the 6-7 middle-part hanging ominously above, sideline bulls no longer bothered to defend the pattern line as done on previous touches. Prices sank straight through.

This leaves us to examine the details of the pattern break pullback entry below bar 9. For starters, pullback 8-9 had retraced about 50/60 percent of the breakout swing 7-8. In doing so, bar 9 had not only put in a triple with the pattern line extension, the round number and the 25ema, the high of this bar had put in a ceiling test with the lows of the 6-7 block. Notice also that even though bar 9 had bullishly perforated the pattern line from below, its close was back *outside* of the pattern, and very bearish to boot. This clearly let on that both bull and bear had cleverly made use of the 8-9 bounce, the former to sell out, the latter to sell in.

In technical terms, bar 9 set up a valid second-instance short, but there is one little issue here that almost spoilt the fun. This signal bar stood relatively tall, which meant that the entry was offered quite a few pip away from a potential retest of the adverse round number magnet. That can be tricky for our stop. However, let us not discard any such offer too easily. When the technical picture speaks highly in favor of *immediate* continuation, as it did above, it is perhaps a risk worth taking (a personal call, of course). After all, should only one out of three such wagers follow through as anticipated, this would still yield a neutral result on balance (when applying a risk/reward ratio of 1:2).Needless to mention, such reasoning is defensible only when the odds for follow-through are indeed excellent at the point of entry.

Note: At a later stage, you may want to spice up your range of entry techniques with a little more aggression. If so, consider the short below bar 7, an M-pattern middle-part break. For a bullish example, check the break of bar 10 in Figure 3.2 in Chapter 3. These sharper entries can be very effective, but are deemed more aggressive because they are taken in front of a bigger pattern breakout. Apply with care.

Figure 5.7 A little after 07:00, prices had broken out of a thin Asian range in what can be considered a tease break variant (T). Bulls had shown little interest, though, in countering this break, or in defending the round number a little below it. This had prices slowly trailing south into the EU Open at 08:00.

The first few bars in the Open favored the bull side (2-3), but with the box extension and the 25ema blocking the path, bears had little trouble curbing the incoming demand. Note the five consecutive topping tails in pullback 2-3.

It is very common for a smaller pattern to form itself outside of a broken bigger pattern. If it is a very fat, blocky cluster of bars that rebelliously hangs below a broken box, this usually indicates strong resistance to the bearish implications of the breakout. Much less so when this smaller pattern is a relatively gentle, *angular* pullback. In fact, we could look upon progression 2-3 as a bear-flag hanging from the pole 1-2 (a continuation pattern in technical terms).

Within its 5-minute span, bar 3 had bullishly penetrated the box barrier from below, only to collapse and finish as a bearish doji away from the box. This already had all the makings of a pattern break pullback setup. But before any bar deserves signal bar status, we should always check first whether the surrounding conditions are supportive of the venture.

What were the hints and clues available? How about: (a) pullback 2-3 had retraced about 50 percent of breakout swing 1-2; (b) bar 3 set up as a reversal doji in the top of a pullback; (c) the bar had perforated the 25ema but closed below it; (d) the break below bar 3 allowed for an entry favorably close to the box barrier extension and the 25ema (no adverse magnets); (e) the entry on this short pleasantly coincided with the break of a pullback line.

Against all this, bulls had little to bring to the table except maybe for a thin sliver of hope that the round number of 1.37 would still hold up. From all that was offered, though, it was fair to deduce that the odds favored the short side way more than the buy side. Hence the pattern break pullback short below bar 3.

Note: In a pattern break pullback situation, it is highly preferable for the signal bar to set up not only in the broken barrier area but in the 25ema as well (bar 3); many times, both coincide. Should we spot a turnaround bar in a pullback *before* the average is reached, in most cases it will be wise to wait for a stronger setup. Chances are, the correction has not run its full course yet.

After taking the short to target in a matter of just two bars, prices reversed with similar prowess (4-5). Upon arrival in the box barrier extension, resistance kicked in once again, as is evident by the bearish close of bar 5. This basically set up another signal bar, but there is a dissonant in this picture that was not present in the situation on the left. It is the powerful V-shape response of pullback 4-5.

Although we will take up the particulars in more detail in our section on the pullback reversal later in this chapter, the attentive reader may have noticed that next to the *length* of the pullback, the *strength* of it is also an important element to monitor. As a rule of thumb, the stronger the pullback presents itself, the more fighting (buildup) necessary to force its turn. In fact, some pullbacks can be so powerful in appearance that we best abandon the idea of a reversal setup altogether. (See Chapter 7.)

In a more borderline event, it can sometimes hinge on a tiny detail whether the scale is tipped in favor of skipping or trading a break. I believe this was the case also with the short below bar 6.

First off, progression 4-5 had retraced about 100 percent of swing 3-4 and had done so quite aggressively (three bullish powerbars); this alone already put the potential reversal in the less desirable corner. A favorable element, though, was to see bar 5 trapped between resistance of the box extension and support of the pullback line (squeeze variant). When the pullback line was then broken by bar 6, the low of bar 5 was not. Instead, bar 6 formed an inside bar with an identical low. This set up a potential double-bar break.

Before we go there, let us imagine the low of bar 5 to *have* been broken by bar 6 straightaway. With now only one bar in the turn of a pretty aggressive pullback (5), this would have offered a weaker entry for a sell-side bet, and perhaps one better skipped. In the actual situation, with bar 6 setting up as an inside bar to bar 5, the tension in the turn had doubled, and this considerably improved the odds for follow-through on the bear break. Can one bar really make such difference? Depending on the situation, very much so.

A turnaround bar followed by an inside bar at a crucial spot in the price action can be a very potent setup. We will look into this more closely in the coming section on the pattern break combi. But let us explore some more pattern break pullback examples first.

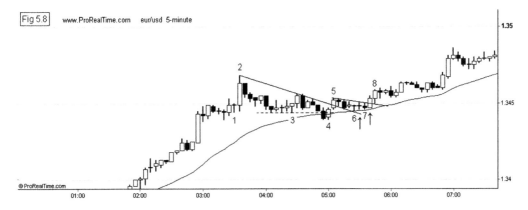

Figure 5.8 A strong uptrend that manages to keep all bars well above the 25ema is not something to be taken lightly, not even by powerful parties with bearish views on the bigger picture. But even when the overall pressure is unmistakably one-sided and all signs point in favor of continuation, it still takes careful planning to hop along for the ride, especially when working with tight stops.

When aiming for continuation, the principle of *harmony* between trend and pullback is a crucial element to examine and this will be taken up in more detail in the section on our fourth setup, the pullback reversal. For now, as a simple rule of thumb, and this basically regards all our breakout ventures, we should avoid to enter well away from the 25ema. Since the average often acts like a magnet too, we have much less to fear from these habitual corrections when trading from its "base" (for lack of a better word). The bull breaks above bar 1 and 3, for example, were both set in line with dominance and not devoid of buildup either. But both entries suffered strong risk of the adverse 25ema magnet, and went up against the adverse pull of the round number as well.

Despite the need for caution, there is one undeniable advantage of the trend and that is that it clearly tells us which side of the market to shun. Either we wait for a setup to trade in line with the trending pressure, or we do nothing at all. This is a vital concept to grasp and we can only hope that the unfortunate bears who got caught in the false break below the dotted line will have taken note (4). Of course, it were not only bears who got trapped in that false downward break. Some bulls, too, will have been tricked: either into exiting their profitable longs, or when forced protect themselves from further loss on whatever they bought higher up.

It may seem contradictory that there can be danger in trading a break when the opponent is likely to be forced out on it, since this implies a double-pressure situation. But that is hardly a guarantee for follow-through. Particularly when the break is set straight into a *trending* 25ema, as was the case below the dotted line, double pressure against dominance can be very short-lived, if forthcoming at all (mind the contrarians!). In other words, while a bull can be forgiven to have exited his long, this was certainly no place for a bear to play short.

Recalling the principle of false highs and lows, a failed break on one side of the market could be a harbinger of a successful break on the other, especially when the latter is set in line with dominance. With this in mind, it is hardly surprising to see new bulls come in when bar 4 was broken topside. Earlier on, we referred to this technique as *trading a break for failure* (see Figure 5.5). In a favorable chart, this can be a very lucrative practice, but is best explored with solid breakout experience under the belt. (More on this in Chapter 7.) For now, the break of bar 4 can be rightfully skipped in anticipation of some more pulling and pushing in the round number area.

Whenever a pattern boundary gets broken (2-5), traders need to make up their minds on the validity of the event, in essence, whether to hop along, counter, or let the situation pass. When consensus appears divided, but the break itself is not undone, not seldom this leads to the forming of a smaller pattern outside the broken bigger one (5-7).

In contrast with the foregoing pattern break pullback examples, progression 5-7 was much less angular, almost flat, and quite nondescript; but it was a pullback nonetheless and its purpose was to test the validity of the bigger pattern breakout. Well supported by a bullish triple (round number, barrier extension and 25ema), the first bullish bar in this mini flag could already present itself as a signal bar for another breakout. So attention is key.

The first bar to be taken out on the upside was the one at 6. Although small as a bar can be, this was a valid signal bar. It originated in the lows of the pullback and in the presence of the bullish triple as mentioned. Furthermore, bar 6 was a miniature false low with its neighbor on the left, a feat that was technically confirmed when the next bar (our entry bar) came to take out its high (first arrow).

Once again prices were reluctant to move out, but they did not retrace much either. When caught in a noncompliant trade right after entry, always stay calm, trust your stop, and give the market a fair chance to work things out. As a rule of thumb: at least for as long as the 25ema holds up in line with your trade, the odds to see prices take off favorably are very good still. And in this stalling phase, tension can only build up. In many such scenario, at some point we may even be able to anticipate the *exact* spot for the market to resolve the situation; for example, when bar 7 showed up, there really was no more space left in the squeeze between the overhanging flag line and the 25ema. Something had to give then and there.

In retrospect, an entry above bar 7 is probably superior to the one above bar 6; after all, the buildup was now extended with two more bars and there was a flag line perforation to help the bull break along. Needless to say, there is never any way of knowing that a few bars down the line a "better" setup will show up. But then again, if good is good enough (and it is), that is irrelevant also. Standard operating tactics dictate that we have to accept the first *valid* offer to come along.

Shortly after the small flag was broken, bar 8 briefly tested back the breakout, which was also a touch on the round number magnet. If for some reason not yet in position, a bull could make use of this mini correction to quickly buy himself in, *without* waiting for another bar to be taken out first. Since this practice overrules standard procedure, it is to be used sparingly and as a last resort only; we could look upon it as a belated entry on a break that was somehow missed just moments before; it is definitely not recommended as a clever way to cheapskate on a fill, for example by deliberately skipping a valid break in the hopes of finding a more economical entry on a slight pullback reaction. Even though this "trick" may work out here and there, saving yourself a pip or so each time you get away with it, you only need to miss an entry once on what could have been a pleasurable 20 pip ride and you can start all over again being smart.

Note: A continuation trade in the highs or lows of a rally can be a tricky proposition, but need not be shunned by default. Whenever a pullback fails to materialize in *price*, a correction in *time* could set up a valid offer as well. Generally speaking, the lengthier such action the better, which is why it is much advised to at least wait for prices to meet up with the average.

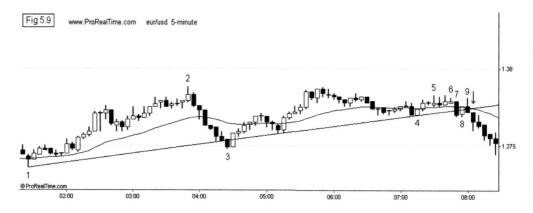

Figure 5.9 Apart from the price action itself, the degree of slope of any pattern line is largely a function of how the chart is set up both horizontally and vertically. For visual guidance, it is highly recommended to set up the ratio between both axes as default. By always looking at the same setting, your eyes will become more easily accustomed to the beat and drum of your chosen instrument and it will be much easier also to tell a pattern line from a *trendline* (usually steeper and stronger). This implies that there is a certain threshold regarding a line's angle beyond which a break would no longer meet the requirements of tradability. Unfortunately, there are no hard-and-fast rules on this matter, but if you set up the ratio between the time and price axis as a constant, regardless even of the actual setting, this can only benefit the way you gauge the action on your instruments and time frames of choice. Personally, my advice would be to sooner squeeze down the charts vertically and stretch them out horizontally than the other way around—pretty much as depicted in this guide. Anyway, always keep in mind that the steeper the pattern line (in relation to the average slope), the stronger the market and the bigger the chance this dominance will prove resilient when attacked.

Even though there may appear to be plenty of "room" in the chart for prices to correct, it remains to be seen how well a tight stop would hold up in a breakout wager that is likely to attract some tenacious defenders. All of this is dependent, of course, on the situation at hand and on how flexible a trader is when it comes to his entry and exit techniques. There is certainly no law that says you always have to trade your breaks with a 10 pip stop and a 20 pip target.

Figure 5.9 shows a multiple-arch formation on top of a respectable pattern line (arch 1-2-3 followed by head-and-shoulders 3-7). Progression 4-7 was the flattest arch in the range so far; in the top of it there resided a small series of topping tail dojis, a clear token of resistance (5-6). Maybe it was too early to already think short, but it was evident that bulls had run into strong opposition. Bar 7 certainly didn't change their situation for the better.

This chart example shows a third application of the pattern break pullback setup. In the first version, we covered the angular pullback to the broken pattern line (Figures 5.6 and 5.7). In the second, we saw prices stagnate a little outside of a broken pattern (Figure 5.8). In this final version, we now have prices stalling in the breakout level itself, with the pattern line running straight through the buildup. This could be the result of a line being plotted slightly off, but is a regular occurrence also even when dealing with a nondebatable slope. As to the line in question, it looks okay the way it is drawn (overruling the low of 3 in favor of more touches further up).

Bar 7 left little to the imagination as to the bears' intentions, but the lack of buildup on the pattern line rendered the bar invalid as a signal bar. The low of this bar held up anyway, since bulls immediately retaliated with a counterattack in bar 8. While deserving credit for curbing the initial breakout, bulls now faced the resistance of the 5-6 bear block above; this left them quite exposed and in need of assistance.

Right in the opening bell of the EU morning (08:00), help did arrive and for a brief moment in time bar 9 must have shown a brave and victorious bullish body. But alas, five minutes turned out to be too long for this bar to preserve its bullish features.

By forcing bar 9 not only to retreat, but to close below the pattern line as well, bears again hit hard on the bullish morale. It then took a mere break of this bar to bring capitulation about.

Isn't it nice that we can watch all this unfold from the pleasant safety of the sidelines. By letting the other parties do the fighting first (buildup), all we have to do is time the entry on the break, should one come forth in tradable fashion (enter short below bar 9).

Note also the favorable position of the 50-level magnet. Provided entry is taken away from buildup, a round number about 20 pip out can be a very powerful ally in the total concept of a trade (it surely isn't counterproductive). Of course, round numbers can make for nasty opponents as well (3). It's all a matter of perspective.

Pattern Break Combi

The pattern break combi harbors many features of both the regular pattern break setup and the pattern break pullback variant. The suffix *combi* is referring to a two-bar pattern, a *powerbar* followed by an *inside bar*. The possible combinations that make up this duo are plenty, but the message is essentially the same in all: the powerbar displays directional pressure, the inside bar builds up tension next to it. In conditions that favor the direction of the powerbar, it is the inside bar that functions as our signal bar.

Even though a combi breakout is often acted on in relative isolation (inside bar tactics), the follow-through response is generally the strongest when the combi is part of a bigger breakout of sorts. Hence the *pattern break combi.*

Figure 5.10 shows a number of standalone combi setups; the first three are bullish, the last three bearish. Note that the last example shows a *reversed* combi, meaning the inside bar came before the powerbar; interestingly, this doesn't have to affect the implications of the pattern itself. To see why, imagine the taller doji on the right to be broken at the bottom by a third bar: that would technically confirm a false high (bull break followed by a bear break), which harbors bearish implications of its own.

Figure 5.10 Typical combi setup examples.

Less common, but no less powerful, is for a combi to contain two tall dojis standing next to each other, both closing in the same direction away from their center. Yet another version is to see the small inside bar replaced by a powerful doji.

Preferably, the color of the inside bar's body, if not a neutral dash, is the same as that of the powerbar. Favorable also is when both bars share the same high or low at the breaking end (double-bar break). But these features are not a specific requirement for a combi pattern to earn setup status. For example, it doesn't have to be a deal-breaker to see a bearish inside bar alongside a bullish powerbar, as long as the inside bar is still situated in the higher region of the powerbar.

And lastly, should a second inside bar pop up next to the first, this can only add to the tension; therefore, all else equal, the implications of a three-bar combi are the same as those of a regular two-bar combi (perhaps even stronger).

In the majority of combi breakouts, position can be taken on the break of the inside bar, but on occasion it may be an option to postpone entry until the powerbar is taken out also. Whether this would indeed provide a "stronger" signal is up to the assessment of the situation at hand. Always keep in mind, though, that the presence of a combi pattern by itself is never a reason to think long or short. It is just a tool with which to time an entry in a breakout situation.

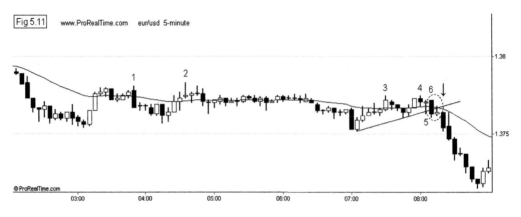

Fig 5.11   www.ProRealTime.com   eur/usd 5-minute

Figure 5.11 When it comes to the eur/usd instrument, the first few hours of the Asian session may show some decent price swings still, but it usually doesn't take long for prices to enter into a stale, lackluster phase that can last all the way to the European Open. Caution is always recommended when volume visibly dries up. In Figure 5.11, the phase between 05:00 and 06:30 shows the classic features of a market lying dead in the water. It is very important not to mistake this kind of price action for buildup. Whereas a little cluster of sideways bars in an active environment can already build up tension fairly well, a lengthy phase in a dead market is often no more than a pointless set of price bars trading into nothingness. Not surprisingly, such a climate sits much better with the contrarian game than that of the breakout trader.

On the good side, no price action is ever lost on the careful observer and even a stale Asian session can provide valuable hints and clues that can be of help later on. Let us therefore establish an overview on Figure 5.11 first before zooming in on the details of the pattern break combi setup in the ellipse.

Telling by the slope of the 25ema on the far left, bears were the dominant party in the early Asian session. In the sideways hours that followed, bulls repeatedly tried to make a stand, but they weren't very convincing and never really made it past the 25ema defense.

The fact that the bulls could not reclaim possession of the 25ema was a strong bearish clue to obtain. After all, how on earth were these bulls to topple the bears if they couldn't even stay on top of the average. Great markers of bullish failure were the false highs at 1, 2, 3 and 4:

instead of triggering follow-through on the upside, these breaks invited bears to play short.

Since we have no way of knowing how exactly our breaks will come about, if at all, it is best not to entertain any preset notions or preferences on the event itself. With multiple setups at our disposal, we can simply sit back and see what the market has in store. For visual guidance, maybe we can put in a pattern line or a box, but most of the work is done by simply watching the bars get printed in a buildup area of interest.

By putting in a powerful doji in pattern line support (5), right in the EU Open at 08:00, bulls had given it one last shot, but to little avail it turned out. If this bar was capable at all to rekindle hope in the bullish camp, we can imagine the next bar to have crushed all further illusions then and there (6). From where we stand, this was a clear sign to get ready for combat.

In a way, we could look upon the inside bar in the ellipse as a one-bar mini flag hanging from the powerbar pole. Note also how this tiny bar, before closing near the bottom of its powerful neighbor, had managed to put in a subtle "double" with the pattern line extension and the 25ema. However insignificant in the bigger scheme of things, this little upstroke had already taken care of two adverse magnets *prior* to entry, meaning there was now a smaller chance for these elements to get tested *after* entry.

Looking closely, this particular inside bar showed a "bullish" close, but on such a tiny body that is not an issue of concern. We can take position on the sell side the very moment the low of the inside bar is taken out.

Figure 5.12 Traders familiar with Japanese candlestick analysis may have heard the combi referred to as a Harami, a Knight-with-Cross, or maybe a Spinning Tops setup; who knows what other fancy names have been coined to acknowledge this very potent pattern. Of course, the actual names are all irrelevant, and in many instances so is the pattern itself.

Zooming in on the action in the chart above, we can detect a number of combis that may have been playable on a tinier scale but didn't really set up well for anything substantial. Nimble scalpers may have taken their chances on the breaks of combi 2, 5 and 7, if only to extract a handful of pip in the wake of each break. An offer to have declined for sure, was the break of combi 3 at 4: this breakout appeared right in the level of a previous high, quite a few pip away from the 25ema, and suffered the adverse magnet of the round number to boot. A poisonous combi to trade, even for a quick scalp.

To minimize the danger of getting caught in a noncompliant break, always a mandatory routine is to monitor first how well the environment favors the wager at hand. Prior to taking position, we should check the pace of the market, the dominant pressures in it, the thickness of the buildup and the presence or absence of adverse magnets and obstructive elements on the way to target. With a little experience, such a checklist should take no more than a few seconds to run. But it can do wonders for your bottom line.

Granted, the ways to perceive price action are countless and what may seem a wholly unsavory proposition to one may very well represent a textbook opportunity to another. While all is indeed a matter of perception, there is never much reason to get caught in a very conspicuous *trap*, as in the bull break at 4, or the bear break at 6.

The breaks of combi 2, 5, and 7, stemming from buildup, all possessed merit, yet it seems fair to have questioned whether they set up thick enough to have anticipated a 20 pip break.

To understand the distinction between "thin" and "fat" setups, let us compare for a moment the cluster progressions 1-2 and 6-7 with the buildup leading up to the combi in the ellipse (8-10). The latter definitely showed a lot more substance. Note also that prior to breaking away in the ellipse, bulls had taken possession of the 25ema first, meaning their buildup resided favorably *on top of* the average, which wasn't the case yet at 2 and 7. Within this cluster, another interesting tell was the aggressive way the bulls had responded to the bear break at 9, which had left a strong false low on the chart.

Since bar 10 showed up bearishly in our squeeze, it did not serve well as a signal bar for the bull-side breakout. So we can skip the offer above it, but we should not lose track of the action here; after all, with the combi setup in our toolbox, it may only take one extra bar for a *valid* break to set up (fire long above the inside bar in the ellipse).

Note: If your trading hours include the UK Open (09:00 CET) and the market sets up a solid trade right in it, don't be shy to accept. While opening activity can be dangerously fickle, it does tend to respect a *properly* built up break. As will be demonstrated in the long series of consecutive charts in Part 2, the first decent trade of the EU/UK morning is likely to be found in and around the UK Open, when there is usually sufficient volume being pumped around to back up the break. However, do avoid shoddy breakouts or anything that sets up as a *continuation* trade in the high or low of a swing *leading up* to the UK Open. These type of breaks are more likely to provoke rebellion when the first wave of volume pours in.

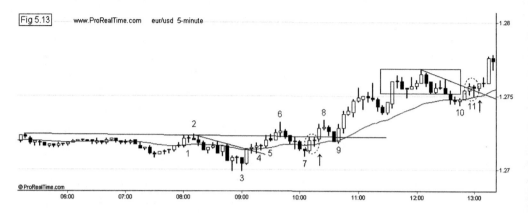

Figure 5.13 Reversal formations come in many shapes and sizes but there is one version that has earned quite a reputation for itself: the head-and-shoulders variant. In its most textbook appearance, this pattern shows a triple-arch formation standing on a horizontal or slightly tilted pattern line, often referred to as a neckline. The arch in the middle is the most prominent (head), but it is the shoulder on the right that warrants the most attention. Should it start to build up pressure on the neckline, a serious bear break may follow. As is the case with all patterns, inverse versions are equally common. Figure 5.13 shows a bullish variant: the triple-arch progression hanging below the pattern line from 07:00 up to the first ellipse.

It is one thing to be able to identify these "classic" patterns, it is quite another to trade their breaks with acceptable odds. At least two conditions demand attention in all situations: the break of the pattern should not be set against explicit dominant pressure, and there should be sufficient buildup prior to the break.

To understand the dangers of unfavorable pressure, have a quick look at the box progression on the far right, around 12:00. Although a lot smaller than its more elongated counterpart hanging below, this box represented a head-and-shoulders variant too (three arches), but we can immediately see why the bear break stood poor chance to succeed: it clearly defied the dominant pressure in the chart. It's nice to know your patterns, but without a respectful eye for the bigger picture, such "knowledge" may do more harm than good.

Before we take up the combi setup in the first ellipse, let us briefly discuss a couple of combis of the tricky kind. Combi 1, for example, represented a typical bull trap, quite like combi 3 in our previous chart, Figure 5.12. Before stepping in on a thin break like this, it may help to ask and answer two essential questions first: (a) does this look like an offer that many other bulls would want to accept? And (b) how demoralized are the bears at this point; would they rather throw in the towel on the break at 2, or open up new shorts?

As always, the true answer will only be known after the fact, but we can usually gather a fair view on the most likely outcome simply by following pressure, conditions and buildup.

How about the break of combi 4? Small as a combi can be, this one possessed a little more merit. Not only was the combi favorably positioned in the base of the 25ema, it found technical footing in a small pattern line extension. Even so, since the market had only just sprung up from the lows, it would have been rather optimistic to have anticipated *immediate* continuation at this point. And there was overhead resistance to deal with as well (pattern line extension of former highs).

An offer to have declined for sure was the break of combi 5. If we now consider the preceding bull swing 3-5, which had come up from the lows with little pausing on the way, this pattern breakout had all the makings of a tease break trap.

Combi 5 did possess an interesting feature: the high of the inside bar resided slightly higher than the high of the powerbar. This is actually quite common in a combi setup and does not have to affect the implications of the pattern itself. The reason for declining the break was simply the poor buildup preceding the event.

The market did manage to break out for a handful of pip (6), but then follow-through dried up and a correction set in. On the way back, it was only when prices had reached a 60 percent retracement of the 3-6 swing that bulls came in with more verve (7). Note the ceiling test bounce when the low of bar 7 hit upon the high of bar 3.

This brings us to the combi setup in the first ellipse. The powerbar in it already betrayed the eagerness of bulls to position themselves for the head-and-shoulders breakout. Should this bar have been broken straightaway, however, that would have qualified as another tease (from where we stand), on account of the meager buildup involved.

When considering a breakout but deeming the current buildup too thin, always welcome is to see the market *not* break but instead put in an extra bar of pre-breakout tension. In this case, the extra bar was an inside bar and thus formed a combi setup with its powerful predecessor. An added bonus here was to see both highs in the combi line up, which set up a double-bar break.

In the meantime, the 25ema had come to support the inside bar from below, basically turning the latter into a one-bar squeeze. With the right shoulder of the head-and-shoulders pattern now "rounded", and prices pushing up against a pretty straightforward neckline (ignoring the tease breakout), it wasn't hard to locate the sweetspot of the moment. Should we ask ourselves again whether an upside break would be reason for concern for a bear in position, I believe it is now justified to answer that affirmatively. Perhaps an extra bar of buildup would have been nice (think three-bar combi), but it would have been overly prudent to decline this offer. Hence the long as depicted (first arrow).

Note: As much as we all want our trades to dash for their target from the get-go, in plenty of instances this will not be the case. Next to the inevitable struggles right from the start, a common occurrence is to see prices first take off nicely, only to then turn around and confiscate all of the earlier gains (8-9). Although unpleasant to witness, it is crucial to train your mind to withstand these mishaps gracefully without the need to do anything silly, like bailing out at break-even to prevent the trade from turning red. Nine times out of ten, if you cast your dread aside and look at things neutrally, all you see is a pullback to test the validity of the break. And frankly, if the pullback ranks so high on the wish-list when still empty-handed on the sidelines (think pattern break pullback setup), why be freaked out by one when already in position? Particularly on a *first* correction after a fresh breakout, one of the worst things you can do is not allow your trade a chance to recoup in a technical test. Apart from occasionally saving yourself a full stop-out, this nervous practice stands to abort a multitude of trades that may have otherwise worked out. Furthermore, the 8-9 correction here was not just a test of the breakout; it also touched upon the 25ema in a 50 percent correction of the 7-8 swing. And we all know the powerful implications of such a bullish triple.

The second tradable combi of the session, in the ellipse on the far right, serves well to demonstrate the resilience of a trending market, as well as the dangers of trading against it. The first parties forced to bail out on the break of combi 11 were no doubt the unfortunate bears who had shorted the bear break of the little box a few bars earlier.

Psychologically, the bull break of combi 11 may have been harder to accept than the head-and-shoulders break earlier on, if only for the fact that the market had already rallied quite a bit and that bears had shown themselves rather defiant above the 50-level. But if we consider the trending slope of the 25ema, this shows us most evidently that the market was still very strong, and thus likely to find new buyers in the base of the average.

This particular setup holds the middle between a regular combi and its reversed counterpart in which a powerbar comes second to the inside bar. But the bullish implications are practically the same. Furthermore, before closing high up and outside the pattern line, the low of combi 11 had found support in the high of bar 10, while touching on the round number and the 25ema (bullish triple). A very nice setup indeed—but it did lack the favorable magnet that was present on the earlier trade; and not insignificant either, the break was set in the often less voluminous lunch-hour doldrums (12:00-14:00). In a normally active environment, however, as above, this is generally of minor concern and perhaps not a good reason to skip an otherwise valid offer; in a staler climate, the lunch-hour aspect definitely adds a con to the prospects of a continuation break. Best not to worry about this for now; we will have a closer look at the pros and cons of conditions in Chapter 7.

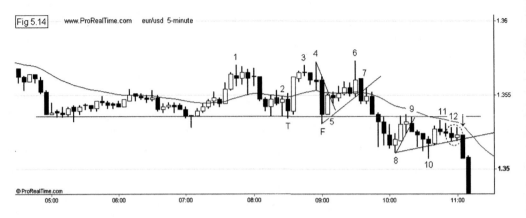

Fig 5.14   www.ProRealTime.com   eur/usd 5-minute

Figure 5.14 Few charts better illustrate the fickle nature of a round number fight. Prior to the pattern line's collapse, there were repeated attempts to trade away from the 50-level center, both up and down, but the magnet effect kept kicking in, pulling prices right back. In such an environment, both bull and bear can get trapped multiple times if they do not pay close attention to what the market is saying. And even more caution is warranted when the bars start to exceed their average span while feverishly alternating between bullish and bearish. More often than not, this indicates a big player clash and in it, a tight stop is easily found.

The horizontal pattern line may have had few connectors to be drawn in nondebatable fashion, it was still a useful tool to mark the barrier between bullish and bearish territory in the early UK session. Of the four arches standing on top, the last three had evolved into an unmistakable head-and-shoulders progression (07:00-09:45).

Before this reversal formation had fully materialized, early-bird bears had to pay the price for stepping in too eagerly on the breaks at T and F, a tease and false break trap respectively. The latter venture in particular (a terribly built up break in the UK Open) was just begging for a contrarian whack. As to the tease (T), the price action there did contain elements of a squeeze (a few bars caught between the pattern line and the 25ema), but this is not the kind of buildup we should be looking to short; prices had not tightened up below a slowly descending average, and the level of the pattern barrier wasn't too clear either. On top of that, the "signal" bar in question was a *bullish* doji (2). Not a great short setup by any means.

On the other side of the round number, bulls suffered troubles of their own. Each time they had come to attack the highs of the session, they were forced to retreat almost instantaneously. Bar 3 was a double top with 1, and bar 4 a false high with 3. A similar fate befell bar 6 when it came to take out the high of 4. But was it any wonder? Look how poorly built up these bull attacks on the highs were deployed.

If a single former high or low can already form a technical magnet, then range barriers can do so even more. It is therefore not just the breakout trader who runs a risk of getting trapped in a false break event; any player who trades within the range with a protective stop a little outside of it can get trapped in equal fashion. Consider the predicament of a bull who had "safely" placed his stop a few pip below the low of T. And what about a bear who had placed his stop above the high of 3 or 4. The message is clear: when the action shows a high degree of fickleness, it is best not to pick sides until things truly build up.

Seen in this light, the bull break of combi 5 was best left alone, and so was the bear break of combi 7, although of better quality in terms of pressure.

Taking into account the length of breakout swing 6-8, pullback 8-9 was just too shallow a correction for bar 9 to set up a valid pattern break pullback short. Not only would the break below this bar offer an entry far removed from the 25ema, lurking above was a ceiling test magnet with the low of combi 7, if not a round number test a few pip higher up. Whenever there are conspicuous adverse magnets still on the radar, traders may be less willing to play the turn of a pullback in fear of the correction not having run its full course yet. This is why it is so preferable to have these magnets "out of the way" *prior* to taking position, the 25ema touch in particular.

From 10:00 to 11:00, the market formed what can be referred to as a bear-flag variant (flag 8-12 hanging bearishly from the pole 6-8). So, not only had the bulls to weather the implications of the broken head-and-shoulders formation, now adding to their troubles was the danger of a pole-flag-swing situation: the flag breakout could trigger a response equal to the span of the 6-8 swing. And the almost tangible pull of the big 1.35 level certainly didn't help their cause much either.

Considering the nature of their predicament, we do have to give the bulls some credit for standing up to the bears below the broken head-and-shoulders. In an act of utter rebellion, they had even successfully fended off the 00-level magnet by hammering out a double bottom of sorts (8-10). But alas, this only provided the bears with more economical levels to short from. As a result, prices never put in that ceiling test with the low of combi 7, and they never made it to the 25ema.

As much as the bearish dominance was evident, the activity within the flag didn't really build up in a very compressed fashion as seen in some of our earlier flag break examples. Nor was the flag line itself of very fine quality (arbitrarily drawn). In most such instances, when sticking to conservative tactics, this would render participation invalid. On occasion, however, the odds for follow-through on a certain break can appear attractive enough to justifiably deviate from standard operating procedure. But do take heed that this is best applied sparingly and with appropriate attention for detail.

As to the prospects of the flag breakout, I believe a little aggression here was called for. Granted, the 25ema had yet to be properly tested, but with no less than four consecutive bearish dojis building up tension in the flag (combis 11 and 12), it is fair to deduce that the bullish defiance was wearing awfully thin. Think of it this way: if you were a bull in position, would *you* sit tight and hope for the best below combi 12—or would you gracefully accept defeat and get out of the way?

Conservative traders can of course skip, but it's hard to argue with a bear for taking a chance on a short like this. As it turned out, the very moment combi 12 was broken, the pole-flag-swing principle kicked in with not a contrarian bull in sight. It's just an outcome, though.

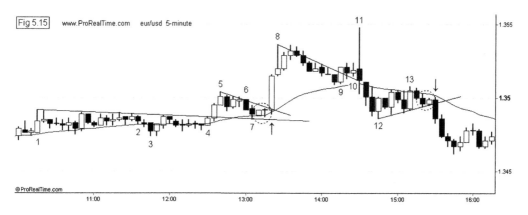

Figure 5.15 Squeeze progression 1-2 may have favored the buy side, it still needed volunteers from the bullish camp to initiate the break. As this failed to come forth, bears had tried to take over at 3, but with little to show for it in the end. During the forming of progression 3-4, bulls had slowly managed to take control of the situation again, demoralizing bears and building up tension while at it.

The break above bar 4 represents a valid pattern break entry, but let us assume to have missed it for whatever reason. This means we would now have to follow the coming action closely to see if we could possibly catch our ride on the bandwagon still. For this purpose, we have at our disposal the pattern break pullback setup and its equally powerful cousin, the pattern break combi.

It took 45 minutes, nine bars, for a combi setup to show up (ellipse). If we take into account that the combi appeared at the end of a pullback to pattern line support, this qualified as a pattern break pullback setup, too. Of course, it is totally irrelevant how we name our setups.

In a way, the market's initial response to the break above bar 4 couldn't have been more textbook. First there was the pop towards the round number magnet (5), then a little stalling in that level for a hand-ful of bars, followed by a pullback to the pattern line extension. On arrival, the low of bar 7 had hit upon the 25ema while correcting about 60 percent of the breakout swing 4-5 (triple). How many times have we not seen similar post-breakout activity.

By running a line across the highs of the pullback, we can see that when the combi was added, the blocky features of the 5-6 cluster had transformed into a more angular-shaped flag formation. This illustrates a concept that we have touched upon in an earlier discussion: the forming of a small flag outside the boundary of a bigger pattern. Should this smaller flag be broken as well, this shows a failure of contrarians to undo the break of the bigger pattern and thus sends out a strong continuation message.

Note: Not all traders adhere to the *breakout* strategy. A very popular play is to buy or sell straight into a technical test. For instance, sideline bulls may have liked the outlook enough to already have bought themselves in on the low of bar 7 the very moment it touched upon the triple. This tactic differs strongly from our own but is not necessarily without merit. In fact, in this particular case one could argue that if an entry above bar 4 was valid but missed, the breakout trader, too, could now pick up an entry in the low of bar 7, so as to correct the mishap of missing his break at no extra cost. Although it is hard to battle the logic within this reasoning, any entry is always best judged in the light of the *current* circumstances. In that respect, before progressing into a flag pattern, the 5-6 cluster had shown the bearish features of an M-pattern middle-part. Therefore, for us to have bought the low of bar 7 would have been in defiance of this bear block development. So yes, it *can* sometimes prove beneficial to have missed an entry on first go: instead of being positioned in a noncompliant trade, we are offered a chance to re-evaluate the situation from the safety of the sidelines. (In the long run, of course, missing our breaks will surely backfire.) But this then brings up another issue. What to do in bar 7 when already *in* position on the initial break above bar 4? After all, by declining entry in bar 7, we basically suggest that the original bull wager above bar 4 had lost validity. And that implies that we should have scratched the trade below bar 6. Frankly, that may indeed have been a valid option, but we will look at this in more detail in Chapter 6 on Manual Exits.

To summarize on the above, if the market shoots away from a missed break and no *immediate* second instance entries are offered (like a mini pullback in the entry bar itself, or maybe in the bar after), the best way to deal with the mishap is to simply accept that it happened and not look upon it as something that needs to be corrected. Just regard the situation with neutral eyes again and take it from there.

As we can see, when a blocky pullback is not that extensive (5-6), it may only take a few extra bars to transform it into a continuation progression (5-ellipse). The combi in the ellipse was reversed, meaning the "powerbar" came second to the inside bar, but such order does not affect the implications of the setup itself (enter long above it).

Was it an option to already have taken position above the first bar of the combi, the bullish inside bar? Opinions may differ, but that would have set up the break quite thinly; although residing in the pleasant support of the 25ema and the pattern line extension, that little bar was the first to defy the blocky pattern overhead, and not too intimidating at that; not a great marker of bullish enthusiasm yet. With the doji bar added, the situation had definitely changed for the better. Notice also that this bar had first taken out the inside bar at the *bottom*, only to turn around and close high *up* (false low). Always a favorable element when thinking long.

About an hour later there appeared another interesting combi setup, a three-bar variant (9-10). The two inside bars following powerbar 9 set themselves up outside of a broken flag progression (8-9), while building up tension towards another bullish pop. In strict technical terms these bars were not really inside bars (sticking out a bit), but they did build up tension and set up a nice double-bar break. But what about the surrounding conditions? Were they as favorable as they had been on the first combi trade?

To answer this, let's start out by comparing the technical support underneath this setup with that of the earlier combi on the left. Immediately we can see a major difference in backup. The combi in the ellipse rested on the fat cluster of progression 1-4, while being guided along by the 25ema. Beneath the three-bar combi 9-10, on the other hand, there was no support to be found, at least not within the range of our stop. Instead there were two adverse magnets that stood good chance to meddle with the trade: the 25ema about 12 pip below entry and the 00-level a few pip further south. A touch on the latter was certainly not unthinkable considering the fact that the number had been broken earlier on but not yet tested back.

But there was another issue of concern and telling enough to skip the trade altogether. Looking closely, we can see that the break in bar 11 was presented right at 14:30 CET, which is the time of major US news releases, if on the agenda (one hour before the US stock markets open). By the look of that huge bar, it is safe to deduce that this particular bull spike had come about as a result of such a release. It takes little time in the markets for any trader to understand that these events can really tear the technical picture apart, and cause great slippage on both entry and stop. (We will take up the news report issue in more detail in Chapter 6.)

The high of the news spike nearly touched the 50-level magnet (11), but then the notorious counterstrike set in and down the market went again, taking out every bull brave or silly enough to stand in its path. The drop did not halt until prices had exhausted themselves in the earlier highs of progression 1-4, which again acted as support (12). As it turned out, the low of bar 12 matched the low of bar 7 to the pip: a good spot for a happy bear to cash in his windfall profits from the mini crash, or for an aggressive bull to take his chances on a bounce away from support (not recommended).

Next up was a bull/bear skirmish that bore all the makings of a bear-flag hanging from the news spike flagpole 11-12. A flag line underneath this progression was easily found and turned out to be well respected until there was virtually no more room left for another bar to get printed in the pattern. During flag formation, there were several bull attempts to break away from the bearish grip, of which bar 13 was the most notable failure (false high in a squeeze).

It is quite common for a combi to set up a break from a squeeze progression (second ellipse). Note that the inside bar, our signal bar, showed a bullish body, which isn't preferable when aiming short; but on such a tiny bar, that is hardly an issue of concern.

Even so, it should be noted that this trade, too, was not of the same quality as our first combi long. The trade on the long side could boast of excellent support and really had the market's pressure working in its favor. The flag break on the short side was more a result of a midsession change in environment, which in turn was initiated by a news spike collapse. Not the most exemplary conditions for a continuation bet. But then again, we do not necessarily need the *best* possible odds to justify participation, *reasonable* odds can do equally well. Seen in this light, the bear-flag breakout is probably worth a shot—one winner pays for two failures. Such optimistic reasoning, however, is best not applied when dealing with a *news* break event, simply because the maximum risk on the trade cannot be guaranteed (adverse spike potential). Hence the earlier skip above bar 10.

Pullback Reversal

Given the abundance of seesaw motions in any chart, it is no wonder that pullback reversal strategies rank high on the list of popular trading techniques. However interesting the general premise involved, aspiring traders would do well not to think of these tactics too lightly. Always a reason for caution is the contrarian element within. For even when the reversal itself is traded in line with the dominant pressure, there is still the pressure of the pullback to reverse.

Pullbacks come in many shapes and sizes, but all can be classified into one of two categories: they are either a correction in price or in time. In the time variety, the pullback often resembles a horizontal or slightly tilted flag. In many such cases we can trade the "reversal" as if dealing with a regular pattern break setup (or a variant of it).

The correction in price is usually more diagonally shaped. To qualify as a reversal candidate, this type of pullback should correct about 50 to 60 percent of the dominant swing. (In a very strong trend, 40 percent might do, provided the turn sets up well.)

But rather than measuring the amount of retracement in absolute terms, perhaps an even better marker is to wait for the correction to reach the 25ema first, preferably even perforate it a bit, and *then* look for a turn. In fact, adhering to this one filter alone may already prevent the majority of pullback reversal traps.

It gets even better if, prior to turning around, the correction manages to put in a test with an element of support or resistance, like a pattern line extension, a ceiling test, a previous high or low in the dominant swing, or even a round number level.

Our standard entry on the pullback reversal is taken on the break of a signal bar, too. This bar may represent the high or low of the pullback itself (one-bar turnaround), but probably more common is for the anticipated turn to show at least a few bars of pushing and pulling before the pullback appears to be ready to "roll over".

It should be noted that the specifications listed above are best seen as guidelines with which to gauge the ripeness of the correction and the readiness of the turn. Reversal tactics are always a function of the bigger picture and best applied accordingly.

Figure 5.16 In earlier discussions we touched briefly upon the virtues of proportion in the trend/pullback relation. We can refer to it as the harmony principle. Although somewhat prone to personal interpretation, within it there are quite a few elements present that can be put to good use without much room for debate. A first sign of harmony, and rather easy to detect, is a favorable degree of retracement. Another thing to monitor is the *way* the bars in the pullback get printed. They do not have to be all white or all black, but their average span should not exceed that of the bars in the dominant swing. On balance, the best reversal candidate is a pullback that appears to travel almost "reluctantly" against the dominant pressure.

To estimate the percentage of reversal, it is best to start out with the point from where the latest dominant swing took off (1). In this manner, pullback 3-6 had retraced about 50 percent of 1-3; and so had pullback 9-10 in relation to the 7-9 swing. This picture demonstrates also why the 25ema is such a great average to plot in the 5-minute chart; in a relatively calm trend, it tends to "lag behind" just enough for a pullback to collide with it prior to reversing.

Take note of the bear trap below bar 5. At least four reasons come to mind why this mini break did not deserve entry signal status: (a) the break was directed against the pressure of a little bull block to the left (4); (b) it went up against the resistance of a pullback line; (c) the 25ema had not been *properly* tested (no buildup in the turn); and (d) no technical tests were hit upon in the high of the pullback yet.

None of this may have called for aggression on the buy side, but these were valid reasons to lay low on the sell side.

Equally poisonous was the perforation of the pullback line a few pip further south. When aiming for a reversal, it is crucial to realize that the pullback will possibly do everything in its power to postpone, if not fully fend off, the moment of the turn. This is why we see so many false turnarounds on *first* try; rather than stepping out of the way on the initial break, contrarians tend to come in again to take advantage of the pullback's temporary weakness. If only for this reason, a broken pullback line, by itself, does not make for the most reliable of entry signals, and even less so when the correction has yet to run into an element of support or resistance.

As to the latter, the more conspicuous this obstructive element the better, but even the high or low of a seemingly insignificant bar could do. For example, in bear swing 1-3, bar 2 represented a tiny one-bar "hiccup" in the downtrend, essentially a bullish reversal attempt that had failed. Insignificant as this may have appeared at the time of occurrence, ultimately it was this bar's low to which the high of the pullback was drawn (high of 6 tests low of 2).

As we know, when a 50/60 percent correction meets up with a trending 25ema and a technical test (triple), things always get interesting. Any moment now, plenty of reversal strategies *could* spring to life, and as a consequence, contrarian parties may be forced to bail out (double-pressure potential).

It took three bars in the high of the pullback to set up the turn in tradable fashion (6-7). Technically seen, this was also a pattern break combi setup. Even though both the powerbar and inside bar of combi 7 were equally nondescript, their timing and placing were superb; and the equal lows allowed us to short from a double-bar break. Note also the favorable 50-level magnet about 25 pip below. This was a high-odds reversal setup in all respects (could even qualify as a pattern break pullback setup).

Another element that contributed favorably to the prospects of the reversal was the fact that this was the *first* pullback to defy the 1-3 breakout. Subsequent corrections can still set up a tradable turn (as shown in this chart also), but the first pullback to hit upon the 25ema in a newborn dominant swing is generally the one most eagerly countered.

About an hour later, the second pullback showed strong similarities with the first. Once again the correction had retraced about 50 percent of the dominant swing, and in the top there appeared another technical test with a former "hiccup" on the left (high of bar 10 hit upon bar 8). Perhaps a ceiling test with the lows of combi 7 may have represented a more notable magnet, but that would have required a serious breach of the 25ema and a near full retracement of the 7-9 swing. This pullback was fine as it was, and thus a reversal candidate.

Bar 11 was the first bearish bar to show up in the highs of the correction. Was it equally poisonous, as a signal bar, as bar 5 had been earlier on?

Let's examine the pros first: (a) the pullback had corrected about 50 percent of the 7-9 swing; (b) prices had pierced the 25ema a bit and then were stalling in it, building up pressure while at it; (c) the pullback line was already broken and could not block the path; (d) bar 11 was a bearish turnaround bar and set up favorably close to the average (no adverse magnet); (e); the high of the correction had put in a technical test with bar 8; (f) the market was still in bearish mode.

On the downside, bar 11 was a very modest turnaround bar in relation to the relative strength of the bullish pullback, and also the first bearish bar to show up in the turn (not necessarily a deal-breaker, though). And the pullback itself was the second to appear against the bearish pressure. To a very conservative bear these elements may have raised a little red flag still.

At the risk of missing the turn completely, always an option is to wait for one or more bars to bring more clarity about. Should bar 11 have been discarded as a signal bar, bar 12 would have made for a good replacement. Following the earlier break of bar 11, this was the *second* break in the turn to favor the bears. In countless turnaround situations, it is the second break that triggers the desired double-pressure response.

Note: To understand the advantage of a second break over a first, we could look upon the turn in a bullish pullback as an M-pattern variant. (And upon the turn of a bearish pullback as a W-pattern variant.) To visualize this, simply track the price action from the start of the pullback to the start of the second turn. For example, in a bullish pullback, the action first goes up to reach the 25ema, then goes down on a first break, then goes up again in defiance of this break, and then goes down again (second break). That is an M-pattern turn.

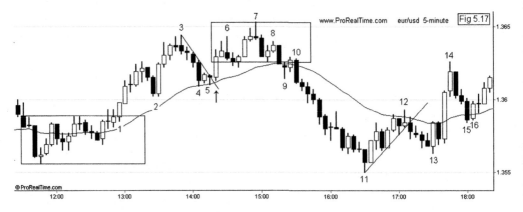

Figure 5.17 Next to the dominant pressure, another thing to assess in pullback reversal tactics, and no less significant, is whether the market is currently trending or ranging. A pullback reversal that needs to surpass the barrier of a range to get to target is likely to meet more opposition. The session above shows reversals of either kind.

The trend variant came about as a consequence of the 3-4 correction. This pullback was diagonal and orderly (black bars only), had retraced about 50 percent of the 1-3 swing and was the first to reach the 25ema since the break of the box in the left hand corner. Since the foregoing turn at 2 had been rather swift on our 5-minute, the chart failed to provide a *textbook* ceiling test (no floor to bounce off), but the 3-4 pullback had found support nonetheless, which formed a higher bottom. The indisputable pullback line was a welcome bonus too, and so was the lovely combi setup squeezed tight beneath it (5).

A nonfavorable element may have been the adverse magnet of the 00-level; although the lows at 2 had come real close, the actual test was still left open. However, with both the environment and the setup speaking in favor of continuation, this was of minor concern only and certainly not disruptive enough to skip the trade (enter long on the break of combi 5).

How about the 7-9 retracement. This was another pullback to the trending 25ema, but we can immediately see that the conditions in which it showed up were not nearly as favorable. First of all, the progression was not a neat, one-sided diagonal retracement to the average (the bullish upstroke at 8 had turned the pullback into a two-legged swing), but more worrisome was the fact that the correction was now part of a head-and-shoulders topping formation (6-7-8). As a matter of fact, the neckline of this progression (low of the box) was broken by the very same bar that treacherously posed itself as a signal bar for a pullback reversal long (9).

When we have both bearish and bullish elements in place (reversal element in a trending market), the general consensus on the situation is likely to be divided. A problem this is not, because we do not *have* to trade. Nine times out of ten, the best side is neither short nor long, but outside of the market (skip bull entry above bar 9).

But how about pullback 11-12. This retracement wasn't as gentle as the 3-4 correction earlier on, but when compared to the powerful bear rally before it (10-11), the countercharge wasn't overly aggressive and as such may have qualified as a reversal candidate. However, there was a good reason also to decline the offer below bar 12: the *surrounding* conditions were unsupportive.

If we solely concentrate on the bear rally preceding the pullback, the trend was unmistakably down and maybe there was more of this to come. Yet if we zoom out to address the bigger picture, we can see that prices were actually residing in the lower part of a much wider range. In fact, the low of bar 11, a spot-on round number test, represented a double bottom with the low of the box on the left. In other words, even though the collapse of the earlier bull trend was beyond dispute, with prices now in the lower region of a range this was not the best environment to look for bearish *continuation*. To better understand the dangers involved, let us briefly recall the typical forces in play in the lower region of a range: bears take profits, sideline bears stay away and contrarian bulls might come in any moment.

This is not to suggest that we cannot trade a pullback reversal within a range, but we do have to be more picky about it. Particularly when prices plummet straight down from the top of the range to the bottom (7-11, or 10-11, if you wish), we definitely shouldn't be too eager to play for more continuation near the lows.

While nimble scalpers may have been able to extract some quick profits in the turn below bar 12, or thereabouts, powerbar 13 depicts a perfect example of the dangers involved. Granted, this trap scenario is not unthinkable even in the best of reversal breakouts, but it is all the more common in a nonfavorable environment, and with the pullback already not the prettiest to begin with.

For future purposes, it is recommended to examine for a moment how this trap came about. Note that contrarian parties didn't immediately come out to counter the bearish intentions below bar 12. Instead, bears were "allowed" to enter the ring and even enjoy some follow-through on the way to their 50-level magnet: so far, all quiet on the southern front. Until suddenly, somewhere around the *halfway* mark of the 11-12 swing (very typical), contrarians came in full throttle with a merciless powerbar that singlehandedly set the stage for the upcoming bull-side reversal (13).

Do realize, though, that such a powerbar is never solely a marker of contrarian prowess; bears, too, will have contributed to the nature of it, as they toppled over one another in their hurried flight for safety (double pressure). Particularly in the lows or high of a range, this flight potential of fellow participants is always a serious concern and thus a good reason to practice caution rather than bravery.

If all of the above still raises some questions as to the validity of the skip below bar 12, in Chapter 7 we will dig into the matter of unfavorable conditions more deeply; and there will be countless more examples of pullback situations, both tradable and non-tradable, in the chapters ahead. For now, as a rule of thumb, if the pullback itself is already not of the most exemplary kind, and the conditions for follow-through at least questionable to some extent, by all means just skip the trade. For all your time and effort in the markets, *reward* yourself with high-odds wagers only, rather than throwing yourself too eagerly at the mercy of the market's fickle whims.

An event that shouldn't have raised any questions at all as to the proper cause of action is the pullback reversal offer above bar 16. You don't even have to assess whether the market is trending or ranging to decline a trade like this. Whenever these extraordinary tall bars show up (13-14 and 14-15), things are indeed out of the ordinary and for this reason alone, it is no longer safe to venture out with a tiny stop. Don't even consider trading this. Just skip.

Note: If you regularly find yourself caught in ventures that look okay at the onset yet rather questionable in hindsight, chances are your perception of the odds is affected by your desire to trade. It is therefore crucial to analyze all your past trades, both winners and losers, to find out how much the element of overtrading plays a part in your game. If it does so to an uncomfortable degree, and this turns out to be a habit hard to kick, a possible solution could be to start trading multiple markets simultaneously. Thus, rather than trying to squeeze the life out of one favorite instrument, set up a few more markets on your screens and trade their *nondebatable* offers only.

In any case, always keep in mind that a savvy trader has no need for a trade, which is why you will not easily catch him searching for one either. Although we may freely use the verb as a figure of speech, the best opportunities in the market are not *found,* they are *spotted.* The sooner a student trader understands this subtle distinction, the better his odds to emerge from the learning stages with funds left to trade and morale still intact.

Let's check out a couple more pullback reversal examples.

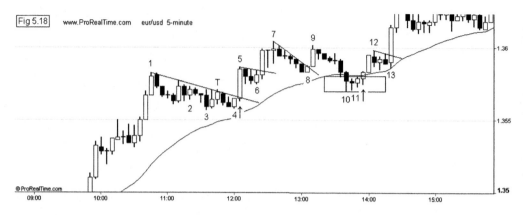

Figure 5.18 In almost all trading literature, the trend is passionately glorified as if it were a treasure trove full of high-odds opportunities. Whether or not this reputation is rightfully earned, it is a fact of trading life that on our 5-minute frame the beloved trend is more a rarity than a common sight; and even if it shows up in full-fledged fashion, it may offer very few pullbacks that retrace deep or lengthy enough to play a reversal with acceptable risk. One benefit of the trend is beyond question, though, and that is that it clearly tells us which side of the market to shun.

Although printed as a continuous curve, the 25ema has a closing price just like any regular bar. Since its slope is a reflection of the average closing price of the last 25 bars, it cannot help but lag behind if suddenly a frantic wave of buying or selling takes the current price bars away from the mean. In order for the average to catch up, so to speak, prices either need to pull back towards it or they need to go sideways for more than a bit and put in the so-called correction in time. A good example of such a sideways correction is illustrated by the bull-flag formation 1-4, hanging from the high of the UK morning bull rally.

In a more rangebound market, it usually doesn't take very long for a decent pullback to hit upon the 25ema. In a strong trend this may not be the case for many hours on end. Although our core strategy is designed to trade off the 25ema "base", there is no rule that says we cannot deviate from standard procedure. But for this to be granted, we best make sure to have the chart conditions strongly on our side.

I believe the entry above bar 4 provides a good example of a valid exception. By accepting this offer, we basically imply that it is not our entry that is premature, it is the average that is too late. Of course, trading is never a game of semantics. The only reason to accept a trade at all is simply because the odds favor a positive outcome.

As we know from earlier discussions, to qualify for a breakout it is essential for the flag to express a certain ripeness in harmony with the pole from which it hangs. We also took up that it's hard to determine the ideal presence of this concept. But maybe we can obtain a better understanding by imagining its absence first. For example, should we picture this flag to already have been broken above, say, bar 2, this would have made for an uncomfortably small flag in relation to the might of the bull rally. (Apart from the fact that such an entry would have been way too far removed from the average to accept.)

It is important to understand, though, that the idea of harmony is never a matter of bars per se, it is a function of the number of sideways bars relative to the strength of the flagpole. Flag progression 5-6, for example, was a nice flag in relation to its pole 4-5, even though it showed only a three-bar body before breaking out.

As already mentioned, popular perception has it that when a flag gets broken, this could induce a new swing more or less equal to the length of the flagpole. There may be some debate on the exact points from which to calculate this, but this doesn't take away from the pole-flag-swing potential itself. Therefore, whenever we see a flag take on "sufficient" body, this could portend the coming of a very interesting breakout.

To determine whether progression 1-4 could boast of such pleasurable characteristics, let's examine the available hints and clues up to that point. First off, the overall pressure was indisputably up. Second, the flag was the first decent pullback since the start of the bull rally. Third, a premature break at T had been fended off by the bears, but the subsequent correction had not surpassed the earlier low of 3 (the higher low after the tease break indicated bullish resilience). Fourth, progression 3-4 showed the blocky features of buildup. Fifth, bar 4 had put in a false low with its neighbor before spinning around and setting up as a bullish signal bar.

An element of concern may have been the 50-level adverse magnet which had been broken on the way up but not yet tested back. And then there was a slight issue with the flag line which *may* not have been broken yet on the break of bar 4 itself (depending on how sharply that line was drawn by our fellow participants). Nevertheless, considering all the elements that favored continuation, and with the flag itself more and more a token of 50-level defiance, I believe we should just bite the bullet here and accept.

If not in position on this flag break trade, or possibly already on target, could we deviate again from standard procedure so as to pick up the flag break entry above bar 6? And what about an entry above bar 8?

Conservatively regarded, both are easy skips. In a strong trend it is certainly not unthinkable to see some follow-through on these smaller flag breakouts—and if already in position, it is always a pleasure to see them break—but by themselves both entries would have demanded a serious violation of standard operating tactics. Just look at the distance away from the 25ema base. On the break above bar 4, we deliberately strayed from the regular path on account of the excellent prospects (big flag, first pullback); to do the same on subsequent wagers, of lesser quality also, could be asking for trouble.

In the 9-10 correction, the intermediate lows of 6 and 8 were taken out, but in the light of the bullish dominance these were minor breaks that weren't likely to harm the prevalent pressure. More interesting, therefore, was the fact the bar 10 had put in a technical test with the 3-4 cluster, thereby taking care of the only adverse magnet of significance in the area. Once this test was put in, it took only a couple of bars for the market to set up another pullback reversal (enter long above combi 11).

Prior to taking any position there are always two type of dangers to assess: adverse magnets on the way to the stop and obstructive elements on the way to the target. While adverse magnets deserve caution by default, if only as a consequence of a tight stop strategy, obstructive elements on the way to target are best judged in relation to the market's current strength. For example, in a more rangebound market, the 7-9 double top in the round number area may have called for more caution on the bull side. Yet it is the very nature of a trend to sooner take out such resistance than be obstructed by it.

Note: Since our entry bar (above the arrow) did not shoot off right away but instead closed bullishly a few pip above the average, this basically set up another pullback reversal (for those not yet in position). But here we touch upon a provocative issue: if the second break with the higher entry was also playable for 20 pip, should we then not adjust the target level of the first trade, if in position on it, to meet the higher objective of the second? That's a valid question for sure, but I leave it up to the reader to answer it. Personally, I am not a fan of meddling with an open trade in an attempt to gun for more profits than originally intended. But it's hard to argue with anyone taking a different view on this matter. By the same token, if position was taken on the first entry, the stop could then be lifted to the level of the stop on the higher entry. Yet all this is very much dependent on personal style and management technique. (Do recall that our 20/10 bracket, though highly effective, is merely a suggestion, too.)

Amazingly, just a few bars later, this bull trend came up with yet another flag pattern (12-13low) hanging sideways from the pole 11-12. Although the break of this flag did not set up in tradable fashion, the powerful pop in bar 13 shows us once again that when the market is in trending mode, contrarians have little business defying the obvious.

More than learning about specific entry techniques, probably the biggest lesson to take away from this chart is to always acknowledge the presence of a trend. When it comes to playing it for continuation, it may very well be that no valid entries are provided or that they feel too uncomfortable or too borderline to accept. If that is the case, just let these sessions be. It is always better to remain empty-handed on the sidelines than to chase the market up or down out of fear of missing out.

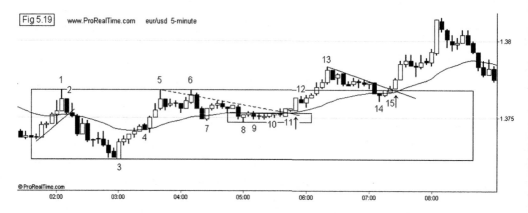

Figure 5.19 While it is impossible to predict the exact level for a trend to shift into a ranging phase, the shift from a sideways market into a trending phase can often be anticipated with the utmost precision. If only for this reason, every trader owes it to himself to get up to speed with range break tactics. But the barrier fights are not the sole determinants of participation. When showing sizable width, it is not unthinkable to trade within the range itself. In many an instance, the outer barriers may even work as magnets, pleasantly sucking an inside-range trade in the plus, or even to target.

A good indication of a ranging market is a rather flat 25ema with prices meandering above and below it without making much headway on either side. Always handy is to wrap a box around such action and extend it to the right for future purposes. The moment prices edged down from the high of bar 5, the box could already have been deployed as depicted. When it comes to the degree of its extension, just plot whatever looks harmonious in terms of width and length; a ratio of about 1:3 will usually do fine. You can always extend the box some more if necessary.

This range eventually got broken not from a buildup situation directly underneath the top barrier, but from a level well below it. This implies that we couldn't have traded the breakout in regular pattern break fashion. It is interesting to see, though, that the range barrier still played a role in both trades of the session: first it showed its magnetic powers on the break above combi 11, and later on it provided the base for a bull-flag reversal (13-15). Before we take up the details of these ventures, let us quickly run through some of the earlier action first.

On the far left there appeared a bearish combi at the end of a diagonal pullback to the 25ema (2), but from what is shown we cannot tell whether this set up a reversal that called for action.

A pullback reversal to have skipped for sure was the short below bar 4. Not only was there zero buildup in this turn, there was also a strong risk of the 50-level adverse magnet.

Bulls bravely marched on beyond the round number and soon hit upon the high of bar 1 at 5. As is quite common, the former high offered resistance and although it took some pulling and pushing in the area, ultimately prices were forced to retreat, leaving a triple top in their wake (1-5-6). Not long after, the 6-7 correction hit upon a supportive triple of the 25ema, the round number and what looked to be a 40 percent retracement of the 3-5 bull swing. As bears laid low in this tricky area, bulls were given ample chance to regroup and plan another charge on the top barrier defense.

The break of bar 7, however, was not a good place from where to launch this new attack. Prices may have pulled back to the average, and bar 7 may have been a turnaround bar in it, and even a false low with its direct neighbor, there was neither trend nor buildup to back up this charge. Instead, there was the 5-6 bear block directly overhead (M-pattern middle-part).

About an hour later, the 50-level defense was much more established. Despite the overall thinness of the "correction in time", both bar 9 and combi 10 had managed to put in a higher low, and bar 8 a false low with 7. Furthermore, if we zoom out a little, we can see that the 7-11 action was actually part of a much bigger pattern, the bull-flag 5-11 hanging from the pole 3-5.

Although the current development favored a bull break more than a bear break, the offer above combi 10 can be qualified as premature still. Considering the subdued action of the moment, and with the bigger flag line yet to be broken (dotted line), it just wasn't very likely that prices would shoot off like a rocket here. So why not grant the market a little extra time to set up the break in a stronger fashion.

In all fairness, the span of combi 11, too, was terribly nondescript, but with the dotted line now cleared, at least the issue of immediate resistance was solved. Looking closely, this pullback reversal harbored all the makings of a pattern break combi setup as well.

If we compare the break of combi 11 with the break of bar 7, both at the same price level, this nicely demonstrates that skipping or accepting an offer never comes down to price, it is always a function of pressure, buildup and conditions. And another thing: whereas the top barrier of the range was likely to act as resistance to a break above bar 7, on the break above combi 11 it stood to work as a favorable magnet. Simply as a consequence of the better buildup.

This example suggests also that, given certain conditions, a barrier breakout can indeed be anticipated from a level well within the range. Even though prices may still have to surpass the outer barrier to get to target, at least the position will be pleasantly in the plus on impact. Furthermore, there is usually less need also for a *substantial* break to reach destination. And not uninteresting either, should the barrier level prove too hard to crack, the current profits on the trade provide reasonable cushioning for the position to be scratched with minimal damage, or even for a profit still. (Intervention tactics will be taken up in Chapter 6.)

In earlier discussions we came to regard the pullback to a broken barrier as a continuation setup (13-14). But we also addressed the fact that, particularly in a tease break scenario, the pullback is not necessarily halted by the barrier level itself; prices are often seen to break back into the pattern to put in a ceiling test of sorts.

Regardless of whether a tease break correction remains outside of a broken pattern or travels back in, things usually do not differ much when it comes to assessing a pullback reversal or pattern break pullback setup. In all cases we have to monitor the behavior of the pullback, the amount of retracement, the harmony aspect and the potential level for a ceiling test bounce. And in all cases we have to locate a crucial bar from which break to play the reversal.

This leaves us to examine the options on the 13-14 correction. How about bar 14 itself? Although this bar had found support in bar 12 on the left, and also touched upon the 50 percent retracement of the 11-13 breakout swing, it didn't really set up as a very dependable signal bar. At that moment in time, the features of the pullback were still quite blocky and thus offered too much resistance for this breakout to qualify as a *high-odds* wager. Best to relax and see if the market once again would be kind enough to set up a better offer.

Depending on preference, there were several ways to have taken position on the bull-side breakout with reasonable odds attached. The first was to fire long in bar 15 the moment it took out its predecessor, which nicely coincided with the re-break of the range barrier. However, with the pullback still quite blocky overhead, and its angular barrier yet to be broken, this option, too, can be deemed quite aggressive. An immediate alternative here was to wait for bar 15 to take out the pullback line first, a few pip higher up, and then fire long. Evidently, this is a deviation from standard routine because the entry is not taken directly upon the break of a signal bar. Depending on the "ripeness" of the buildup, this *can* be a defensible tactic at times, but it should be taken into account that the bracket stop will be lifted along with a higher entry. Not necessarily a problem, but it may pay to check if this doesn't offer a very awkward stop in the situation at hand.

Standard procedure, although at the inevitable risk of missing the break, is to simply wait for a signal bar to set up either against the barrier of interest or slightly through, and then enter upon its break. Bar 15 set up perfectly in this respect, with its high just peeking through the flag line. With both barriers now cleared, the only obstruction of technical relevance on the way to the round number magnet was the high of the flag itself (13). Seldom a major concern.

Chapter 6

Manual Exits

When discussing our series of setups—the pattern break, the pattern break pullback, the pattern break combi and the pullback reversal—we mainly looked at the market from a trade entry perspective. If we are to use the bracket as the sole source of trade management there is indeed little point in elaborating on the matter of exits because it is all taken care of automatically from the moment of entry. With our personal bracket in place there are only two possible outcomes to consider: either the target is reached for a profit of 20 pip, or the stop is taken out for a loss of 10.

Although no claim is made as to the superiority of this approach over any other style of management, it does solve a problem that is known to wreak havoc on many a trader, even on the experienced: the loss of mental stability when exposed in the market. Unequivocally, this is an occupational hazard that sooner or later is bound to rear its ugly head and no trader is ever fully safe from the groping claws of this treacherous little demon. Throughout the years, a long range of clever psychologists has gone to great pains to investigate what lies at the root of this self-destructive phenomenon, yet very little so far has been offered in terms of curing the disease. In that light, praise should go out to those who have earned it the most: the inventors of the bracket.

Religiously abiding by the bracket order settings indeed knows many benefits, but it may not always be the most sensible approach for the situation at hand. For example, what if we can imagine resistance to kick in just a few pip shy of target. And what if a sideways cluster of bars gets broken against an open position; should we just stay in and hope for the best, or would it be more wise to intervene and close out the trade before more damage is done?

In this chapter we will try to shed some light on these matters, but it should be noted that if we venture out on this more discretionary path, there is no escaping the occasional gray area of arbitrary contemplations that may raise more questions after the fact than provide answers before it. On the good side, if any of the following for some reason seems too impractical to be put to good use, it can always be discarded. By simply applying a nonnegotiable bracket on all your *carefully selected* wagers in the market, the results should already be very promising.

But let this not stop us from reviewing some highly effective intervention techniques that at some point may come in very handy in the field, possibly even on a daily basis. They are: (1) exiting a trade with a news report coming up, (2) exiting a trade in resistance close to target, and (3) exiting a trade on account of a reversal development.

News Report Exit

Since the market's response to a major release can be dangerously fickly and is often seen to fully defy the earlier dominant pressures (spikes of more than 50 pip are not uncommon), the general recommendation is to avoid exposure when such news comes out. Whether this means not trading an hour, a half hour or just a few bars prior to the release is not so easy to point out. Among other things, it could depend on one's appetite for risk, the technical picture and the overall activity of the pre-news market, as well as the perceived significance of the report itself.

Very often the significance of an upcoming report can already be gauged by watching the way the market trades up towards the release. If the price action goes flat for several hours on end, this could be an indication that big parties are laying low in anticipation of the event; in such cases, we often see a vicious response the very second the news comes out.

Prior to the release, it is not uncommon for prices to break away from what appears to be acceptable buildup, but these can be highly poisonous breakouts to play, for obvious reasons, and so caution is definitely warranted.

When already *in* position, with a news report slowly drawing near, we basically have three options at our disposal: (a) stay in and take our chances on the news, (b) reduce exposure by taking off part of the position, or (c) get out of the way altogether.

To establish a course of action, let us ignore the option of reducing exposure (too arbitrary to discuss) and just look at the situation from an in-or-out perspective. First there is the weight of the report. Since not all releases tend to cause a hefty response, not all of them need to be feared. Reports and events to always watch out for are: nonfarm payroll (NFP), housing and production, job and unemployment, interest rate decisions, and of course the non-number incidents like central bank speeches and the like. The exact time of these releases are often scheduled well in advance and can be found on any thorough *Economic Calendar* freely available on the web. Not seldom their significance (possible impact) is rated on these sites as well. Cross-checking two calendars could never hurt.

Understandably, not all instruments are equally affected by whatever news is released. Since most reports recur on a monthly basis, establishing their significance beforehand will be time well spent. While nasty surprises can never be fully prevented, a rather dependable way to assess a market's sensitivity is to scroll back through a year of intraday price action, take note of all sudden blasts that are obviously out of the ordinary—probably no more than two or three per week in your time zone—and compare them with the tables of the economic calendar of that year (take heed also of daylight savings time). Should a certain report have little impact on your particular instrument, there is no real reason to shun the event when already in the market, or when aiming to take position.

When it comes to the eur/usd, and most other US dollar crosses, the biggest impact on prices can be expected at 14:30 CET—an hour before the US stock markets open—and to a lesser extent at 16:00. European reports are generally released at 08:00 and 11:00. But do take into account that not all of these releases need to be feared, otherwise no trading ever gets done.

It is easy to avoid the news when still on the sidelines, but what if we are already positioned in the market—should we just get out no matter what, or will the current status of the open position have a say in things? Let's delve into this more deeply by comparing two hypothetical open positions: prior to the release one trade is running, say, 15 pip in the plus and the other currently 5 pip in the red. Assuming further (wrongly) that a very fat news spike would either take out the target or the stop based on the original bracket order settings (20/10), we can quickly establish that the prospects on both ventures are not exactly equal. The profitable trade could make an additional 5 pip in a favorable spike, but could lose 25 pip the other way around (measured from its current profitable position). On the non-profitable trade, the situation is reversed. Now the venture could lose an extra 5 pip at the most, whereas it stands to rake in 25 pip should prices spike favorably.

The above is just one example of comparison. Should we tweak these numbers a little, it isn't hard to find the theoretical tipping point between bailing out and staying in, which would reside at a current profit of 5 pip: either win an extra 15 pip in a favorable spike, or lose 15 pip when shaken out.

Unfortunately, in practice none of this holds up. The main reason is that we can trust neither the market nor the platform to honor our stop should prices spike adversely. Remember, the stop side of the bracket is a market order, meaning it will be triggered as soon as prices hit upon it, but the platform will not necessarily fill the order at the requested price. If not, this is referred to as slippage.

In relatively normal conditions, slippage on a stop will seldom exceed a few pipettes (tenths of a pip). Yet on a news spike exit, slippage can be huge. Of course, the true extent of the damage will be a function of the actual spike and the liquidity in it, but the speed with which the trading platform can fill the order may have an effect on the outcome as well. Another element of concern is that the bid/ask spread may be raised artificially during the release, further crippling a trader's odds to come out unscathed. Incurring slippage of more than 10 pip (on top of the stop) is certainly not unheard of. To measure to possibility of truly unsavory slippage, here's a handy rule of thumb: if you repeatedly find your platform responding rather sluggishly in a calm environment, you are going to get smacked for sure when caught disadvantageously in a news spike event. And even more so with the spread cranked up.

Fortunately, throughout the years things have improved considerably and many brokers now can handle spikes without causing their customers excessive slippage, but there is still no guarantee not to be hurt even on the best of trading platforms.

In all fairness it should be noted that instead of fearing the news, plenty of traders have come up with strategies solely designed to *exploit* the spike potential, but little is known as to their rate of success. My definite advice would be to shun the news rather than try to trade it, and to get out of the way, rather than stay in. But since there are quite a few variables at work, all news report situations stand by themselves and are best judged accordingly.

A final warning: at the end of the US session (basically at the close of the US stock markets), prices very often trail sideways in a hibernating mode until the Asian markets open up for the day several hours later. If still in position on an otherwise valid trade, it is up to personal discretion whether to stay in or close up shop. The same basically holds up for any trade that lies dead in the water for many bars on end (like in the notorious lunch-hour doldrums). But under no circumstances should an intraday position be left open when the markets close up for the weekend. That can make for a rude awakening on the next Monday session.

Resistance Exit

Since the 20 pip target is essentially a nontechnical objective, it isn't hard to imagine an open position to run into serious resistance before the full target is met. If so, rather than religiously abiding by the bracket at the risk of the trade turning sour, an option could be to scratch the trade right in the level of anticipated obstruction and be done. This seems a fair approach, but it harbors an aspect of possible concern: if manual intervention is allowed, this could open the door to on-the-fly decision making and all sorts of fear-based exits that may ultimately do more harm than good. Therefore, when adopting discretionary management techniques as part of the plan, it is absolutely vital to learn to suppress the instinct of flight and to solely exit on chart technical grounds.

A great way to mitigate the likelihood of an unintended scratch is to always determine the resistance exit level *prior* to taking position. In other words, a reduced target objective should be part of the plan from the *outset* and not stem from a sudden urge to bail out.

Should we have put on a trade with the standard exit in mind, of course at some point the position may run into a wall of resistance not present at the time of entry; when such a sideways cluster gets broken adversely, this may call for intervention, too, but it is a different situation altogether. We will have a look at this in the following section on the reversal exit.

Before delving into the technical specifics of the resistance exit, let us first agree on a reasonable threshold beyond which this technique becomes applicable. It makes sense to employ a minimum objective in order to at least make the wager worth our while. When the 20 pip target is standard, how about, say, 14 pip. Of course, any trader can lower this threshold at his own discretion, but I would advice not to go below 10 pip, so as to at least maintain an acceptable risk/reward ratio of 1:1 (when trading with a 10 pip stop).

Thus for now, if the perceived level of obstruction resides at a distance that would yield a profit of less than 14 pip—but let's not split hairs—we simply skip the trade.

At all costs, do avoid entering into the habit of *spontaneously* lowering the bar on the target side of the bracket. Once this practice is granted permission, chances are that premature scratching will soon become the new standard, possibly depriving countless trades of their full potential.

Notwithstanding the psychological challenges involved, judging the validity of a resistance exit is a pretty straightforward practice. Prior to taking position, typical levels to examine are a well-defined range barrier, a nasty round number, a double top or bottom, a pattern line extension, a technical test, or even a former high or low a little to the left.

Before bailing out too quickly, though, it is important to assess the nature of the market first: is it ranging or trending. An idea could be *not* to apply this technique in a very trending market, based on the premise that a trend will sooner take out resistance than be obstructed by it. Conversely, it does make sense to be more cautious in a ranging market, especially near the highs and lows. Not only will there be more contrarians on the prowl, bulls are likely to exit in the highs of a range, and bears may do so in the lows. And these exits are likely to obstruct the open trade as well.

All good intentions aside, the line between a valid resistance exit and a fear-based scratch is still easily crossed in a live-market environment with ego and emotions always ready to cloud one's vision and thoughts. In the end, the only way to find out whether this technique pays off in your game at all is not through the theoretical drawing board, but to simply compare the assembled result of all your actual scratches with the market's verdict had the trades been left untouched.

Following are some examples to give an impression of when a resistance exit could become applicable from a technical perspective.

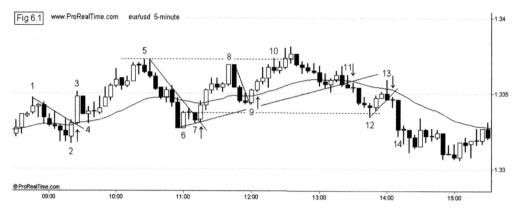

Figure 6.1 A great benefit of having the resistance exit in the toolbox of operating tactics is the possibility to engage in wagers that do not set up for a full 20 pip target. This is never an excuse to enter all over the place, but it may allow for a little more aggression into the plan. Some of the entries in the session above could strike the reader as somewhat unconventional, but they are quite doable when not too greedy on the target part. For now, just ignore whatever entry seems too opportunistic, but do try to grasp the rationale behind the various resistance exit calls.

In strict technical terms, there are only two levels in which to deploy a resistance exit: on a bull-side trade, the position is either exited in the low of a former high (or lows of a cluster), or in the high of a former high—whatever level comes first or is preferred in the situation at hand. Vice versa on the bear side. But let us be mindful not to embrace the resistance exit option *too* eagerly. Even in a ranging market our first priority should be to check if we can still trade for a full target.

On the first trade above bar 2, the breakout bar was sucked straight into the vacuum of the 50-level magnet (3). Despite the fact that we lack a bit of information on the left, it looks like an early exit may have been uncalled for. All we have in the way of possible obstruction is the former high of 1 and the round number a few pip higher up. In a very slow moving chart, it could at times be an option to just cash in the profits in such meager resistance, but there is usually little call for intervention when we still have pressure, conditions and volume on our side (UK opening hour here).

Note: The decision to stay in initially stood corrected, only to work out favorably in the end; although merely an outcome by itself, this provides a fine example of why the break-even exit on a *first* pullback reaction is such poor practice on balance (low of 4 hit upon a triple, a strong bounce candidate). Why do traders indulge in such destructive behavior? Could it be that their egos are forcing them to do so. For egos do not think in probabilities, they have an agenda fully of their own: to protect the mind from the pain and shame of seeing a once profitable trade turn red. So they bang the exit button. Before caving in, though, perhaps these traders should reflect on the following: missing out on 20 pip profit by scratching a valid trade at break-even is essentially synonymous to being shaken out twice on a 10 pip stop. Surely the ego should not like that one either. The point here: when considering intervention tactics, the aim should be to exit in *strength* rather than weakness. Hence the *resistance* exit.

The second long of this session, taken from the break of a three-bar combi (6-7), is a range variant of a pullback reversal. On this trade, the first resistance in sight was the ceiling test with the *low* of bar 5. If not yet fully on target there, closing out the trade in bar 8 is a valid call (avoids also the pull of the adverse 50-level magnet).

The pullback reversal trade above bar 9 (pretty aggressive entry considering the 5-8 double top to the left) is a classic intervention candidate. Bulls may have shown themselves a little more dominant in this session, the market was far from trending yet (note the rather flat 25ema), and that always makes it a fair call to anticipate resistance in the highs.

As to the exit, the ceiling test with the low of bar 5 was no longer a "usable" option because the touch of bar 8 in that level had already mitigated its earlier significance. That basically left either the high of bar 8 or the high of bar 5 to serve as an exit trigger. Since the former may not yet have yielded the minimum profit of about 14 pip, the dotted line was the level to gun for (scratch the trade in bar 10).

The trade below bar 11 (pattern break combi short) is another resistance exit candidate. The market had only just begun to defy the earlier bullish pressure, and so it could be rightfully questioned whether this short set up bearishly enough to shoot for a full 20 pip target. Since the low of bar 9 resided too close to entry, the ceiling test with the high of bar 7 was the first level to meet the requirements of a reduced target (scratch the trade in bar 12 on the dotted line for perhaps a little under 14 pip).

Not much later, bar 13 set up a pattern break pullback short in a bearish triple. This bar's message clearly defied the intentions of the higher low at 12, but the chart itself still wasn't overly bearish. Should we decide to take another shot on the sell side here, best to do so with a resistance exit in mind.

When in position on the break below bar 13, there is little point in fretting over the low of bar 12 as potential obstruction; if that level was already reason for concern, about 10 pip out, then we shouldn't have risked capital on this offer in first place. Therefore, the first level to qualify as a valid resistance exit was the former low of bar 6 (exit in bar 14). Considering the mean features of bar 14, the low of bar 2 may have been an exit level to shoot for as well (low of the range).

Figure 6.2 Before we address the exit on the long above bar 9, let us consider the price action up to that point. Clearly, this market was in ranging mode. Should we have wrapped a box around it, the top barrier may have been plotted across the high of bar 1 (ignoring the false high at 3), and the bottom barrier beneath the low of bar 2. Take specific note of the failed bull break above bar 5. Not only was this a continuation attempt in the highs of a range, progression 3-5 was an awfully small flag compared to the pole from which it hung (2-3); and the trade suffered

strong risk of the adverse magnet to boot. A poor break indeed.

More interesting was the 6-9 buildup in the middle of the range. Bulls again had been working their way up from the lows, but this time faced more opposition. These type of cluster progressions always call for attention. In fact, they harbor within them the very principle that lies at the base of our operating policy: to see *solid buildup*—attack and defense—prior to taking position.

An interesting variant of the flag formation is the *ascending* or *descending triangle*. In the ascending version, the pattern is capped by a horizontal line across the highs, with ascending lows at the other end. Progression 7-8-9, hanging from the pole 6-7, is a good example.

With prices thus capped on one side while pushing up at the other, the pressure can only build up. This implies that the ascending triangle might pop on the bull side, as with a regular bull-flag pattern. Should we aim to participate along this line of thought, the first task is to find a valid signal bar to trade off (9).

Always preferable is to see a signal bar close strongly *against* a barrier of interest, or perhaps a little through, but this is not a mandatory element of setup validity: at times, we could act on the break of a bar *before* the pattern barrier itself is broken. In such cases, very important is to assess whether the situation is truly ripe for a break, meaning the buildup has to be substantial. Of course, conservative traders can always skip; should they miss the initial breakout, there is still a reasonable chance to be offered an entry in second instance (pattern break pullback long above bar 10).

Note: An optional technique here, but best applied sparingly, is not to trade the break of bar 9 straightaway, but to fire long on the break of the pattern line itself, a few pip higher up. A decent marker with which to measure this alternative is to check whether a standard stop would still survive a quick retest of the 25ema. If not, ad hoc adjustments at the stop side are always an option, too.

Let us examine the exit options on the trades above bar 9 and 10. The first obstructive element to have taken into account was a ceiling test with the low of bar 4, about 13 pip out when measured from the break of bar 9. In regard to the break of bar 10, however, this level resided too close to meet the minimum target; this left the high of bar 3 as the first exit candidate in line. (An alternative tactic here, savvy but not without risk, is to deploy a resistance exit a little *above* bar 3, in anticipation of a false high turnaround.)

As stated, even in a ranging market it may not always be necessary to exit a trade in resistance. When the buildup prior to entry is of very fine quality, prices may very well pop beyond whatever obstruction lies on the way. As to the buildup within the ascending triangle, this was quite fat indeed, and so it may have been decided to simply let the bracket handle the trade above bar 9. On the higher entry above bar 10, however, there was a greater risk for opposition because the high of bar 3 now needed to be cleared quite a bit to get to target.

With multiple options to consider, some supposedly better than others, how is a trader to decide on the *best* course of action? Alas, there can be no easy answer to this question, but always a suitable tactic, in any time of doubt, is to embrace the power of common sense. It may not provide you with the best statistical alternative in the situation at hand, but at least your calls will be *defensible*, which is all that is required to come out ahead in this field.

How about the short below combi 13. A little before, the bullish dominance had taken a severe hit in the 11-12 bear attack, but there was still a lot of work for the bears to be done to clean out the resistance (chart support) within the earlier triangle (7-8-9); that was indeed a pretty thick block to eat through and probably the reason also why the 12-13 progression got formed in the first place. If we throw in some pattern lines here, we can see that the latter was a bear-flag hanging from the pole 11-12, and situated outside a broken pattern line extension (running up from the lows of 6).

Bulls had put up a decent fight within this flag, but the triple of the average, the round number and the pattern line extension proved too strong to crack. This is important info to obtain, because a failure to break free from the bearish grip could portend demoralization on the part of the bulls, and possibly their capitulation a little further down the line. In compliance with standard operating policy, there were two ways to have traded the flag breakout: either fire short below combi 13, or perhaps one bar earlier, on the break of the combi's "powerbar".

Note: It is important to realize that none of the examples shown in this book will ever show up in the market again. Even if by some freak miracle the present price action would mirror the exact same features of some earlier event, then still there will be other players and other volume behind it. By this I mean to say that all situations are truly unique and the best they can do is *resemble* one another. In other words, all we can do is form ourselves a reasonable idea on the market's *most likely* answer. When it comes to manual intervention, two options come to mind: action or reaction. The resistance exit is clearly a function of the first. By grabbing profits in a designated level of perceived resistance, we deliberately take action without waiting for the market's response. A good example would be to deploy an exit on the short in the dotted line at 14. If we are to defend the reason behind this scratch, we could start by saying that the market was back at the lower region of a range, which is a danger zone to any short. Furthermore, observation has it that when a double bottom is firmly in place (2-6), prices tend to sooner hammer in a higher bottom than a triple bottom. With this in mind, it made sense to pick the ceiling test exit (dotted line) rather than the level of the low of bar 6. Looking closely, the low of bar 14 was not only the "ceiling" (floor) of the 3-6-7 arch, it was also a double bottom with the low of bar 8, which further increased the bounce potential in the area.

The second popular management technique is to exit not in proactive but in reactive fashion. Instead of aiming to bail out before the market has a chance to turn adversely, this technique awaits the market's response first and then determines the course of action, based on whatever shows up. As an example: bears still in position could have exited above bar 16, *in response* to the faltering follow-through on the break below the dotted line at 15. We can refer to this as a *reversal exit*. In the following section will examine this technique in more detail.

Reversal Exit

Before we delve in, allow me to start out with a few words of caution. Since the reversal exit is based on a technical assessment that can only be formed while *in* position, there is always a certain risk of bias within its application. No trader takes pleasure in seeing a profitable trade turn bad, and strong can be the urge to protect whatever gains are still in place. But the trader be warned. Where improper usage of a resistance exit may pocket some decent profits still, faulty implementation of a reversal exit can come with serious regret; not only will there be little profit left, if at all, not seldom the towel is thrown in at the worst possible moment: right when prices stand good chance to turn favorably again. Enter the reversal exit *trap*.

That being said, when properly applied, the reversal exit is a fantastic weapon to wield and can indeed save many a faltering trade from full annihilation. How many times have we not seen a *sideways* development build up against our position in a way that the chances of ever reaching target appeared minimal at best.

What are the classic characteristics of such adverse development? As is the case with all patterns, reversal formations come in many shapes and sizes, but they do tend to share some very recognizable features that portray the adverse pressures within. The easiest way to visualize these patterns is to see them as either an M or W-variant. The M-shape, for example, starts out with an upswing (left leg), followed by a middle-part (often containing a double-top element) and is then completed by a downswing (right leg). In such a pattern, it is the break of the middle-part section that could trigger a reversal exit.

Whenever a number of bars start to cluster in a relatively tight span, ultimately prices can do only one of two things: they either break away from this buildup to continue the former dominant pressure (think flag), or they break out at the other end in an attempt to initiate an M or W-pattern reversal. In case of the latter, very important is to assess the reversal pressure in its proper light. While it can never be fully prevented to get tricked out of a trade, not all adverse pressure is created equal.

Let us visualize a valid exit from the viewpoint of a sell-side wager. Comfortably positioned in a profitable short (left leg of the W), with prices well on their way to target, a small cluster of bars starts to rebel against our trade; the bull attacks within this cluster may not pose an immediate threat, and all of it may still take place below a falling 25ema, but the action is worthy of attention if only for the fact that prices fail to set new lows. The longer this standoff continues, the fatter the cluster builds up and the bigger the potential impact of a break either way. Therefore, if at some point prices fail to break out at the bottom and instead a bullish powerbar pops up, this is a development not likely to go unnoticed. When this powerbar then gets broken on top by another bar, the market is sending out an even stronger message that prices have no intention to drop further anytime soon. This situation could call for a valid exit on the short.

When there is no adverse powerbar involved (or a combi version of it), exit tactics are not necessarily off, but there is a stronger chance that the cluster formation is still looked upon as a bear-flag variant, meaning that bear parties may now be less tempted to let go of their shorts, not even on a break of the current middle-part's high. And bulls may be less eager to enter on it. Considering the stronger potential for a false break, deploying a reversal exit may not be the smartest choice.

As the name suggests, the reversal exit is mostly a function of a profitable trade turning sour (otherwise there is little to *reverse*). This implies that in many an instance we may be able to deploy the exit with only minimal damage, or even for a tiny profit still. Or to put it in another way, if the adverse pressure already starts to build up shortly after entry, we are not just dealing with a faltering trade but with a faltering *breakout*, and in most such cases it is probably best to let the bracket stop take care of protection. Let's explore some practical examples to get an impression of the tactics involved.

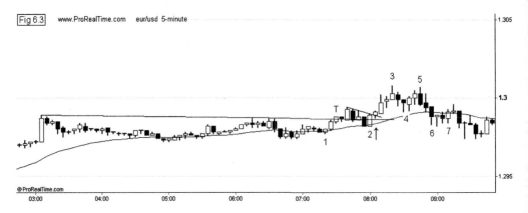

Figure 6.3 Progression 2-3-4-5-6 shows the classic contours of an M-pattern reversal. Since the aim of intervention is to protect a trade from "unnecessary" damage, a vital ingredient within these tactics is to be able to recognize the adverse pressures *before* the right leg of the reversal pattern is completed. Special attention, therefore, should go out to the forming of the *middle-part section.*

In an M-pattern, the low of the middle-part (4) is usually situated higher than the start of the left leg (2), quite like a flag hanging from a pole. Signs of trouble may arise when this correction fails to reverse in line with dominance, or does so but then fails to follow through (as was the case above).

Before we discuss the specifics of the reversal exit, let us first take up the entry on the pattern break pullback trade. The position could have been initiated above bar 2, which was a re-break of the dominant pattern line after a tease breakout had been forced to retreat (T-2). Note that prior to closing strongly outside the pattern line, our signal bar 2 had put in a textbook ceiling test with the high of bar 1. If for some reason not in on the break above bar 2, there was an opportunity to take position on the break of the breakout bar, just one bar later (pattern break combi variant).

At times, the magnet effect of a round number can harbor an ironic twist. Initially it may pull a trade pleasantly in the plus, but then the area may start to hinder further progression. In this instance, prices had come to a halt just a few pip shy of our target, from which a pullback emerged (3-4).

As already repeatedly addressed, the first pullback after a fresh breakout is seldom reason to bail out of a trade. More likely, it forms an opportunity for latecomers to take position in line with the original break (the low at 4 was a technical test with the combi on the left and also a 50 percent correction of the breakout swing 2-3).

So, initially, pullback 3-4 can be regarded as a bull-flag, which is a continuation pattern; prices indeed managed to break out topside, but that's about as far as it went. Instead of clearing the former high of 3, bar 5 suddenly took a nosedive from which it could not recoup before its close. Was this a sign to prepare for a reversal exit?

Looking closely, we can see that bar 5 not only put in a double top with bar 3 (lower top to be exact), it was a mean false high with its neighbor and it single-handedly completed the right side of the M-pattern's middle-part. There were only six bars involved in this cluster (3-5), but in relation to its modest pole 2-3 this was quite a telling pattern. Since we aim to exit on a break, we can grant the market one last chance to shape up; but the very moment bar 5 is taken out, all hopes should be cast aside and our trade is best exited without further thought.

Note that when bar 5 was broken, the actual low of the middle-part was not (4). To some this may have been reason to stay in the trade still, but in most cases I would advice not to resort to such optimism and to simply accept the message of the broken powerbar.

Note: To determine the degree of danger within adverse buildup, the harmony principle may help out once again. Just like we should avoid to trade a continuation break of a non-harmonious flag (in relation to its pole), so should we avoid to exit on a reversal break of a rather feeble middle-part (in relation to the left leg before it). What may help to assess the "ripeness" of this middle-part section is to see if we can already visualize the full pattern's completion in *symmetrical* fashion. For example, with double-top progression 3-5 hanging rather harmoniously from the left leg 2-3, it wasn't very hard to imagine this pattern to be completed by a right leg that would more or less copy the swing of the left leg (5-6 mimics 2-3). Do recall, though, that the actual completion of the right leg is basically irrelevant, since the plan is to already deploy the exit on the break of the middle-part. When responding promptly to the signal of the broken powerbar, in many cases we stand a pretty good chance of bailing out with next to no damage (the exit below bar 5 was around break-even).

Let us briefly examine also the aftermath of the M-pattern incident. Hanging from the right leg, progression 6-7 appeared to have found support in a pattern line extension; if you picture the extension in your mind's eye, you can see that the four bottoming tails of 6-7 all dipped below this line, yet each bar closed above it. This showed bullish resilience and may have given rise to the impression that the market was about ready for another move up. And since the 6-7 cluster hung sideways from its pole 5-6, this harbored characteristics of a pending W-reversal. Granted, this middle-part lacked the harmonious features of the situation on the left, but at least the break of bar 7 was *in line* with the earlier dominant pressure (think pullback reversal). With this in mind, should we have re-entered on the bull side again, on the break of bar 7?

Before accepting any wager, it is important to assess what exactly prices have to do in order to reach target. Here they would have had to eat themselves a path through the double-top cluster overhead, and fight out this battle in a major round number level to boot. Had progression 6-7 shown up at the end of a first correction, the break of bar 7 may have had a lot more merit. But now that the market had corrected not once but twice (M-pattern double top), the prospects for a substantial breakout were far less promising.

Here is another way to look at it: for any trade to succeed, we need assistance from sideline companions; if there was already little enthusiasm to take prices beyond the round number when the path was relatively free earlier on, what are the odds that new bulls would want to help out with now an M-pattern block spoiling the view. (In Chapter 7 we will take up this principle of unfavorable conditions in more detail.)

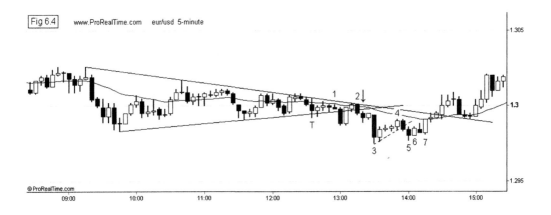

Figure 6.4 Whenever prices are confined in a triangle pattern, moving up and down between two converging barriers, at some point a break is unavoidable. Particularly in the small of the pattern, the so-called apex, the bars have no choice but to tighten up and this can really make the tension coil up like a spring.

Things can get tricky, though, when the fighting takes place with a major round number running right through the center of the triangle. This is a lot more common than one might think. In fact, more often than not these round number levels are the very cause of pattern for-mation.

As outlined in earlier discussions, when aiming to trade away from a strong magnet, it is vital to look for solid buildup and to shun all break-outs of the weaker kind. Particularly in a round number zone, things can get unpleasant very quickly when picking sides too eagerly. Always keep in mind that this is the favorite playground of contrarians; and if these parties already see little problem in defying a proper break, surely they will love to get their hands dirty on a poor one. The tease break at T is a classic example of a premature break, and equally common is the contrarian response.

Although of better standing (more buildup), the break below bar 1 was a tad bit premature as well. Even though this tiny bar was situated in a nice squeeze below the 25ema and the round number, it wasn't a signal bar to write home about. At times, in highly favorable surround-ings, front-running the break of a pattern line can be a defensible call, but this is generally not the best approach in the midst of a round number fight. The conservative route is to lay off and wait for more information. Should this cause us to miss the initial break, there is always a chance for a pattern break pullback setup.

If we assume to have taken position by means of the latter, on the break of bar 2, it looks like the low of bar 3 just missed our 20 pip target by a hairsbreadth before a correction set in.

The correction soon evolved into a bear-flag (3-4) hanging from the pole 2-3. Since a flag is a continuation pattern at heart, we need not be immediately alarmed by this type of adverse development (no W-features yet in place). Although the progression harbored a three-bar combi within, which was broken topside in bar 4, the counter activity was still relatively benign when measured against the strength of the bearish flagpole. Furthermore, the break in bar 4 ran into resistance of a little hiccup on the left (prior to bar 3). To make us give up on our short, bulls would have to do a little better than that.

Soon after the false high incident at 4, the short was pleasantly back on track, but it didn't take long for its momentum to peter out again, and this formed a little double bottom (3-5). The bullish close of bar 6 certainly called for attention, but to have deployed a reversal exit above this bar can be regarded as premature still. Technically, bar 6 was an adverse powerbar (opening low, closing high), but when compared to the neighboring activity, the bar did not really stand out, nor did it finish off a W-pattern middle-part in very harmonious fashion. All this is not to suggest that we need to see some sort of technical perfection first, but if we are to give up on a position, it makes sense that there should be as little ambiguity as possible as to the nature of the adverse implications. Logic dictates that weak signals are traps more often than those of a stronger kind. If this holds up for our *entries*, then so it should for our *exits*.

It was only when the bulls had managed to hammer in powerbar 7 that the bottoming features of the 3-7 progression took on the quality of a nondebatable reversal formation. Of course, the break above bar 7 could still turn out to be a reversal exit trap, why not, but to have stayed in the short merely on account of such possibility would have been in defiance of the technical message sent out.

Take note also of the subtle false low in bar 7. Before making its bull-ish turnaround, this bar had taken out the low of its bearish neighbor first, no doubt sucking a number of unfortunate bears into fresh shorts. That put these bears first on the list to help the subsequent bull break along (by buying back their shorts).

Was this truly a cleverly designed false low trap, or just a consequence of demand toppling supply in the lows? It is irrelevant. Our focus should be on the implications only.

When compared to its M-pattern counterpart in Figure 6.3, W-progression 2-3-4-5-7 was a little more elongated, yet the reversal implications were exactly the same, if not stronger. Why stronger? Argu-ably more telling than a double bottom is a double bottom with a higher bottom next to it; and that is exactly what the bulls had created in the 3-5-7 progression.

Once again, if our entries are a function of technical pressure, the same should apply to our manual exits. Perhaps an optimistic bear may have had his hopes still set on the resistance of the overhanging pattern line extension, a little above bar 7, if only with the intention to exit more economically on a bearish bounce away from that line; all very understandable, but these are tactics of the hope-and-pray variety and not likely to prove beneficial in the long run. Why not keep it simple and deploy a reversal exit on the break of bar 7. And without any damage done (practically a break-even exit).

Figure 6.5 Telling by the frantic activity within bar 1, the market had been hit by a news report in the European morning. If we follow the up/down motion within this bar, and its equally powerful neighbor, we can clearly see the impact a news release can have on the price action, and how dangerous such an environment can be for both bull and bear. After the dust settles down, not seldom the market simply re-establishes the direction it was heading in prior to the release, as if nothing happened. At other times the chart can be shaken up pretty bad and it may take many hours for anything tradable to show up again.

Figure 6.5 shows a picture of the latter variety. There are some interesting things worth noting, though. The first regards the bear-flag formation 2-3, hanging from the news swing 1-2. This situation presents us with a memorable example of how even the break of a classic chart pattern runs high risk of failure when unfavorably located within the bigger picture.

In terms of conditions, the break below bar 3 bore at least three elements of a valid skip: (a) the entry was far removed from the 25ema, (b) the flag hung from a news spike (always tricky) and (c) after the violent perforation, the 50-level hadn't been properly tested back. Not a great environment to aim for bearish *continuation*.

In the marketplace, contrarians possess a keen eye for traders in trouble and it is their favorite game to shake these "weak hands" out of the market. There are many ways to inflict demoralization on the opponent, but a tactic that seldom fails to deliver is to instigate the dreaded false break in powerbar fashion (4). Of course, not all bears will have been equally intimidated, but those working with tight stops will surely have taken note of the false low at 4, not to mention the reversal potential within the 2-4 progression. Indeed, in many an instance, a failed flag breakout almost automatically transforms into an M or W-pattern middle-part.

For argument's sake, if we imagine ourselves to have been trapped in the break below bar 3, our bracket stop will have been hit soon after; if not in bar 4 already, then surely on the topside break of it. That basically rules out the reversal exit option. Should we have been in short position from an earlier level (I don't see how), the break of powerbar 4 is one such adverse development worthy to exit on. The absolute point of no return would have concerned the break of bar 5, which was a pattern break combi variant in favor of the bulls. Both breaks may not yet have signaled a valid entry on the long side, they certainly warranted intervention when positioned short.

After the failed flag incident, prices more or less clung around the 50-level for several hours and nothing much was to make of it. Having fended off the bear-flag breakout, bulls had obtained a moral advantage over the bears, but they hadn't really been able to capitalize on the event. Nonetheless, by cleverly using the failed flag cluster as support (2-5), it had not cost them much effort to block all bearish charges in the round number area; even the more serious break at 6 was quickly undone (basically a failed M-pattern reversal).

When a session lacks a clear dominant party, this tends to have a limiting effect on breakout participation. Rather than hopping along on a break on first go, plenty of traders prefer to watch the market's response first. Understandably, this wait-and-see tactic is even more popular when the barrier in question is not broken distinctively yet. It may have been the core reason also for the poor follow-through on the tease breakout at T.

Technically seen, bar 7 was an interesting bar (false low with bullish close) and in a more favorable setting perhaps it may have earned more credit as a signal bar. Opinions may differ, but I would advise against trading long straightaway in this tricky 50 level area. But in the little skirmish that followed, bulls stood their ground well (T-8), and this now provided a stronger base for a bull-side wager (pattern break pullback entry above bar 8).

More interesting than the entry on this trade (if accepted at all) is the way the position could have been managed once open. In fact, the reason this chart is selected is to point out a reversal exit that seemingly defies standard operating policy, yet is defensible nonetheless. It concerns the exit below bar 10.

To understand this call, we have to examine closely what exactly took place after entry on the break of bar 8. First off, the breakout bar was a huge powerbar that provided the trade with an excellent start. But then the bears struck back. Their first feat was to put in a decent looking powerbar of their own (9), but since it failed to match the strength of its bullish neighbor, there was no reason yet to question the breakout, not even if another bar was to extend the pullback all the way to the breakout level. As we know very well, the *first* pullback that comes to test a broken barrier is a likely candidate to get picked up.

Things are different, though, when there are strong signs of contrarian aggression within the correction. This is more likely to instill suspicion, if not fear, in the minds of those positioned in line with the break. And their potential companions on the sidelines may now view the correction with less appetite as well. When in position and faced with such predicament, always an option is to embrace the principle of "better-safe-than-sorry".

Were such ominous signs present in the 9-10 progression? Let's take a moment to examine how things played out exactly. Right after bar 9 had come to a bearish close, new bulls arrived on the scene to counter the bear attack with equal prowess. To visualize their initial success, take careful note of the shape of bar 10. It started out at the low of bar 9 and then ran all the way up to the high of it; at the high, try to picture that at that point in time this bar will have shown a strong white body, no doubt a pleasurable sight to all bulls in position. But then things took a nasty turn. Within its 5-minute span, bar 10 went from highly bullish to super bearish, a collapse that will have alarmed even the most optimistic bull. Not only did the bar close at its low and even lower than its bearish neighbor, it also formed a strong bearish combi with that same bar (9-10).

This leaves us to answer whether the bearish implications were indeed disturbing enough for the break of bar 10 to have signaled a valid reversal exit on the long. To determine this with neutral eyes, we have to fully ignore the bearish panic move that followed, for this may have been a reaction to a US news report that favored the dollar (16:00 CET). The technical question of relevance here is whether the adverse combi 9-10 was to be regarded as part of a relatively harmless pullback, or a harbinger of more trouble ahead and thus a legitimate reason to exit below.

Apart from the fact that the upcoming news report may already have been reason to exit the long, or not to have entered on it in the first place (see News Report Exit earlier in this chapter), there is another way to address this issue and that is to find out if we can detect within the post-breakout action any signs of an M-pattern reversal formation.

There are only three bars outside the broken pattern line but if we track them closely, bar by bar, we can see that they indeed make up an M-formation variant. The bullish breakout bar is the right leg up; bar 9 is the middle-part down, and bar 10 is the middle-part up, as well as the right leg powerbar down. This is an M-pattern variant and it harbors within it the same breakout potential that we have come to appreciate when trading off a combi setup. This is not to suggest that we should make it a habit to immediately exit on *any* adverse combi; but the stronger they present themselves, particularly in conditions that weren't too favorable to begin with (but acceptable enough to trade), the more their message should be taken to heart. In our next example, Figure 6.6, we will explore some more variants of this most potent three-bar reversal pattern: a powerbar followed by an adverse combi.

Figure 6.6 Before closing up bullishly, bar 2 had put in a ceiling test with the high of bar 1, plus a touch on the 25ema and the round number; this triple provided a solid base for the pattern break combi setup as depicted, just outside the flag line. It is always nice to see a break immediately take off, but alas, that is no guarantee for reaching target. On the good side, when a trade starts to falter well away from entry, the chances to exit with minimal damage, or even with profit, are usually quite good. Of course, this is beneficial only if the reversal exit is part of operating tactics.

It may not be so obvious at first sight, but the three-bar progression 3-4 is an M-pattern variant, not unlike the one discussed in the previous example, Figure 6.5 (concerning the 9-10 situation). In this case, it is a *reversed* combi that followed the bullish powerbar, but such order does not alter the implications of the pattern itself. Readers familiar with Japanese candlestick analysis may have recognized this three-bar progression as the *evening-star*, a pattern renowned for its tendency to trigger a bearish reversal from the top of a bull swing. Progression 3-4 represents a most classic version: a bullish powerbar on the left, a small doji in the middle (false high) and a bearish powerbar on the right. The 6-7 progression is a variant of it.

Equally notorious is the evening-star's bullish mirror image, the *morning-star*, particularly when situated in the bottom of a bear swing. Progression 8-9 depicts a rather aggressive version, but if we track the bars individually, the W-characteristics are easily found: bar 8 forms the right leg down as well as the middle-part up; the bar in the middle, although not the classic doji, is the middle-part down and a false low with bar 8; powerbar 9 is the right leg up. Take note of the bullish response when the high of bar 9 was taken out (a bit over the top, though).

It doesn't require much imagination to find variations of evening and morning-star patterns in almost every notable turn; but before looking upon them as holy grail setups, do keep in mind that these patterns are best judged in the light of the bigger picture. For example, an evening-star break in a bull trend could trigger an exit on a long, but does not necessarily make for a "safe" entry short.

In accordance with reversal exit policy, we could have used the break of bar 4 to exit the long position for a minimal loss of 1 or 2 pip. One could argue that this is against standard procedure, because it involves the much-refuted break-even exit on a first pullback reaction. All true, but if we compare progression 3-4 with the overall price action up to that point, we can clearly see that we are not dealing here with a "harmless" pullback in which the bars calmly retrace against the initial breakout. In fact, bar 4 was the most bearish bar of the session so far. Another issue of concern was that the entry on the long was taken about 7 or 8 pip *above* the 50-level, which had the stop uncomfortably positioned a little below the adverse magnet. While not necessarily a reason to have skipped the trade altogether (although I am never a big fan of trading for continuation in the highs of a rally, especially during lunch hours), this is certainly something to take into account when a position starts to struggle and turn.

Furthermore, the 3-4 evening-star was not only of concern to bulls who had bought themselves in from above the 50-level; those sitting on profit from the UK morning bull rally will have taken note of the implications as well (extra sell-side potential). All in all, with adverse pressure clearly visible, and possibly more of it on the lurk, a reversal exit on the break of bar 4 is a defensible call.

Not much later the chart sent out another strong warning that bears meant business above this round number. Following a brief bounce at 5, the market had printed a *second* evening-star pattern (6-7). Interestingly, if we link both of them together, they make up the unmistakable contours of an even bigger M-pattern (3-7). If this does still not fit the description of a reversal exit candidate, then what does. On top of that, bar 7 had already pierced a trendline on the way down; although a line perforation by itself is usually not the most reliable harbinger of *immediate* follow-through, with an M-pattern preceding the break, the event certainly gains relevance.

Note: Whenever a significant trendline, or even a mediocre pattern line, gets broken against a position, the implications *can* be equally strong as those of the broken right leg powerbar in an M or W-formation. This implies that these perforations can also be used for exiting purposes, or at least they should be taken into account on the scale of pros and cons. In the end, when it comes to staying in or bailing out, it is always a matter of weighing the technical odds. Should the prospects of reaching target have gone down considerably, for whatever reason, then, by all means, bailing out is *always* an option, regardless of what exactly triggers the exit. The trick, of course, is to overrule the instinct of flight and to judge each situation purely on technical grounds.

Later in the session, the chart came up with another evening-star pattern, and this one, too, clearly lived up to its reputation: progression 10-11 (quite a rough variant). And at the end of the ensuing pullback, yet another morning-star popped up (12-13).

Slightly off topic: if we are to judge pullback 11-12 purely on its relation with the foregoing rally 9-10, it was an orderly, diagonal progression and although it had retraced only about 40 percent, the correction was substantial enough to reach the trending 25ema. That usually sits well with a pullback reversal. However, if we consider the *origin* of the trending move before it, there is a good reason here to be very cautious about trading for continuation. Rallies that apparently take off "out of nowhere", like the 9-10 progression, crossing from bearish to bullish territory without so much as a fight, are often regarded with a healthy dose of suspicion. And that tends to have a limiting effect on pullback reversal participation (and thus on follow-through). This is not to say, however, that we should label these situations as untradable per se; but should we decide to give it a shot, some specific entry conditions need to be taken into account.

First off, zooming in on the action in the turn, we can see that morning-star 12-13 (pullback reversal setup) was followed by an inside bar doji outside the pullback line. So this set up a very nice pattern break combi as well. But more important here were the entry *conditions*. Note that the setup bars were all positioned right underneath the round number level; although prices still needed to trade away from it, the immediate danger of the adverse magnet was now reduced most considerably. To understand the benefit, imagine for a moment that not long after a successful breakout, prices would have come back to test the round number, say, at point 14. If so, they stood to bounce favorably in a triple of the 25ema, the round number and a ceiling test with the highs of the morning-star pattern. And without the trade turning red (no immediate danger for the stop). Although hardly a guarantee for a successful outcome, such bounce potential is always a welcome asset in the total concept of a trade (a bounce could also facilitate a reversal exit later on).

If we compare this entry setting with the break above bar 2, we can see that on our earlier trade the round number was not nearly as favorably positioned, as a consequence of our entry being a number of pip *above* it. Insignificant as these differences may appear on the price axis, they can make all the difference when working with tight stops. Put in another way: in questionable situations as shown above (regarding continuation), entry conditions of excellent standing may at times tip the balance in favor of participation. But do be mindful not to resort to these tactics when the session's overall pressure speaks unfavorably of the event. And needless to mention also, conservative traders can always skip *any* offer that does not meet their standard of indisputable validity.

In our next chapter, we will have a closer look at the often subtle yet crucial differences between favorable and unfavorable conditions. But before going there, let us take up one last example of reversal exit technique.

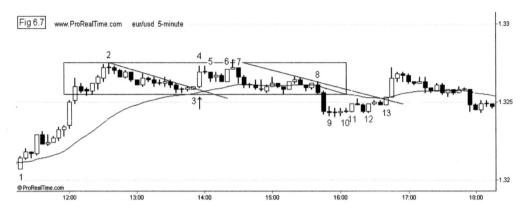

Figure 6.7 It's not hard to detect the features of an M-pattern reversal in progression 4-5-6-7. But how about 4-5? Although less outspoken, these three bars make up an evening-star variant, not unlike the first pattern discussed in our previous chart (Figure 6.6, progression 3-4). However, in this version, the bear leg at 5 is rather small in comparison to the bull leg at 4. When it comes to a signal bar for exiting purposes, a powerbar (in relation to the neighboring activity) definitely earns preference over a mediocre bar. The break of the latter tends to have less of a bite, and is thus more prone to result in a shake (reversal exit trap).

Even though bar 5 wasn't taken out in this chart, an exit below it may have been premature for another reason also: the market was in very bullish mode and had just broken away from a fine bull-flag (2-3 hanging from 1-2). In such an environment, it is fair to anticipate that not too many bulls would immediately chicken out of their longs when presented with a relatively minor reversal bar break.

Fair enough. But what if there are two evening-stars in a row. As we can see, just a few bars later progression 6-7 finished off a textbook M-pattern formation (4-7); and this time the right leg of it was more prominently displayed (7).

An M-pattern like 4-7 may not have the power to fully turn a trending session around, it is certainly an element of concern, specifically to the parties, like ourselves, who entered on the flag break with a tight stop for protection. If we then look at where the 50-level magnet was located in relation to our stop, I believe we have little explaining to do to justify a reversal exit on the break of bar 7. A pretty easy scratch, at next to no damage.

This leaves us to evaluate the break of the rectangle pattern. The reader is prompted to take note of a rather common mistake, quite resilient among traders, but essentially not too hard to avoid. It regards the distinction between a reversal pattern for exiting purposes and one on which break to take position.

Neutrally regarded, the four-hour range within the box had all the makings of a reversal formation. If we track the bars from left to right, we could look upon the total progression as an elongated M-pattern, or maybe a flattened version of the head-and-shoulders formation. Thus, we cannot blame a bull for exiting his long on the break of bar 8. But a bear would have done well here to at least think twice about shorting the event.

How could the break of such a fine barrier get a bear in trouble? If we solely concentrate on the box progression, shorting below bar 8 does not look so bad. But if we take into account the bull rally from which the box was hanging, it is not hard to grasp why the sell-side potential was limited. For several hours the bullish pressure may have lain dormant, but that doesn't take away from the fact that the chart was still in bullish mode. In such a session, basically any lower level could trigger a new round of buying, even below a broken range. This is not to say that a nimble scalper would not be able to steal some pip in the initial breakout, but those who aim for more are well advised to at least monitor their positions with a sharp eye on the post-breakout action.

Not serving the bearish cause either was the 50-level running directly underfoot. And not much below it there waited another level of potential support: a 50 percent retracement of the UK morning bull rally. All told, the overall conditions were unsupportive of a *serious* break, which is why the short below bar 8 was of dubious quality at best. But now that we're at it, let us look at the options on how to have handled a situation like this if caught in it anyway.

Initially, the break met with nice follow-through. Surely a number of bulls will have exited their longs below the box barrier, and eager bears will have been happy to play short; that is double pressure in favor of the break. However, as is often seen in breakout situations that go against the tide, participation tends to dry up quickly at the first signs of stalling momentum. And with reason: if taking position a little too far away from a breakout level is already dangerous when going *with* the trend, then even more so when going *against* it.

When compared to some of the reversal clusters discussed earlier on, the 9-11 buildup below the box barrier may appear quite nondescript, but this hardly mitigates the message within. Perhaps a bear in position may have argued that prices stood good chance to bounce back from the box barrier extension, as in many a post-breakout situation (think pattern break pullback setup). But before such reasoning is applied, it would be wise not to lose track of *the way* the correction to the broken barrier is built up.

Note: To distinguish between a "harmless" pullback and its more poisonous counterpart, chart conditions may already put in their bit, but very often the nature of the correction itself provides all the information needed. On balance, an orderly, diagonal pullback to a broken barrier is much less likely to scare breakout traders out of position than anything that rebelliously travels sideways for a number of consecutive bars. Such an ominous cluster may still break in favor of the original breakout, but should it be broken at the other end, particularly with a powerbar involved, the adverse implications are best not taken lightly.

Given the poor prospects for the bear break to begin with, perhaps a reversal exit on the break of bar 10 was already a defensible call, but most certainly on the break of bar 11.

If not fully convinced of the bullish implications yet, three bars later the break of bar 12 offered bears another major clue that prices weren't likely to travel south anytime soon. And if that too was still no reason to throw in the towel on the short, the absolute point of no return lay above bar 13. And still at zero damage. Best to accept!

For future purposes, it is elementary to absorb and remember the way the bearish break below bar 8 was defied, for it is very common practice. Take specific note of the W-features already in the making, 8-11, 8-12 and 8-13. But do realize also that this type of response is not just a consequence of the unfavorable conditions regarding the bearish breakout, it is often seen following a "proper" break in line with dominance as well. Therefore, when the reversal exit is part of operating procedure, any sideways development following a breakout always deserves the utmost attention.

The two main things to take away from the chart above is that (a) trend players in position will not easily exit, and (b) trend players on the sidelines will be happy to accept almost *any* favorable level to join in, even in defiance of a countertrend break. In other words, the more a trade is set against the prevailing trend, the better the climate for the contrarian trap.

This concludes our discussion on the reversal exit, but we will see many more examples in the pages and chapters to come. On a final note, as much as we can train our eyes to detect the typical warning signs of an upcoming reversal, not always will we be so fortunate as to receive them in time. In this respect, the best thing any trader can do for himself is to at least shun the ventures that stand poor chance of success from the *outset*. Our next chapter is specifically designed to shed more light on this most crucial concept.

Chapter 7

Skipping Trades and Trading Breaks for Failure

Now that we have established a practical framework for entry and exit techniques, it is essential to dig a bit deeper into the subtleties of trade selection. For even with a decent methodology in place, nothing is more common than to slip into the habit of accepting wagers of the unsavory kind. Sure enough, psychological issues may play their fair part in these matters, but all too often the root of this behavior simply lies within a technical misconception of sorts. And chances are, we need not look hard to pinpoint the most likely culprit: spending too much attention on the limited sphere of a setup and too little on the conditions and pressures in which it shows up.

Saving yourself just one or two unnecessary losses per week could already mean the difference between success and failure in this field. It is therefore of crucial importance to embrace the virtues of trade selection from the very start. And this will keep you pleasantly ahead of all those who take a less diligent approach.

Learning to be more selective not only serves to minimize our own misfortunes, it will give us a better view on the trials and tribulations of our fellow traders in the field. This harbors a strategic benefit not to be taken lightly. After all, if we perceive the conditions highly unsupportive of a certain break, yet we see traders act on the offer, this could entail that at least some of these parties may soon find themselves forced to bail out. And as we know, their flights to safety could help to swing the market the other way around.

There is one such setting that, in a certain climate of conditions, could set up so well that it deserves a special spot in our toolbox of favorite trade setups. This is when a particular breakout shows all the characteristics of a tradable event (boundary, buildup, signal bar, etc), if not for the fact that it clearly goes up *against* the dominant pressure. Should the trap indeed fall shut on those who accept, this could set up a counterbreak *in line with* dominance.

Understandably, not all false breakouts automatically qualify to be traded in the opposite direction, which is why we need to establish a good view on the requirements involved. But those that do pass the test may very well be among the most potent of trade setups when it comes to generating immediate follow-through. Should we take position on such a counterbreak event, we can refer to this as *trading a break for failure.*

How is this different from our other ventures? The main difference lies within the contrarian touch. On a regular pattern break trade, for example, the pre-breakout tension at the pattern boundary builds up towards a breakout in line with the dominant pressure; on these type of wagers there is no contrarian element involved. When we trade a break for failure, on the other hand, the *initial* buildup is directed towards what we perceive to be the nonfavorable side of the market. Now the idea is not to trade the break from this buildup progression, but to anticipate and trade the failure of it. (At times, this setup can bear strong resemblance with a pullback reversal, or even a pattern break variant.)

In the coming pages, several chart examples will demonstrate the tactics involved, but do keep in mind that before even considering to exploit the follies of others, our first priority, always, is to avoid getting caught in the notorious traps ourselves. Below is a list of common trading errors, all of which we have already taken up one way or another in earlier discussions. Yet as easy as these mistakes can be pointed out on the drawing board, with similar ease they can be overlooked in a live-market environment where all sorts of devious emotions are known to take their toll on a trader's better judgment.

Typical trading errors are:

1: Trading against a strong trend or an otherwise dominant pressure.

2: Trading with the pressure but into resistance overhead or underfoot.

3: Perceiving a trend to be in place when the market is actually ranging.

4: Choosing entries too far removed from the 25ema, or with little regard for the adverse round number magnet.

5: Picking entries in a frantic environment in which the majority of bars exceed their average span.

6: Aiming to trade a reversal of a pullback that shows aggressive powerbars or clusters within.

7: Front-running a break or turn of the market with too little buildup to warrant such action.

Ultimately, knowing when to skip or trade a break is a matter of trading experience, no doubt, but there are quite a few pointers to pick up that even the novice should have little trouble putting into practice straightaway. As stated, most of these essentials have already been addressed, but with our focus mainly on the timing aspect for trade *acceptance*. Let us now take a slightly different approach by discussing some classic tricks and traps that should give us fair warning as to when to *stay out*; and while we're at it, why not explore also if there are ways to take advantage of some of these treacherous breakouts, by trading them for failure in the opposite direction.

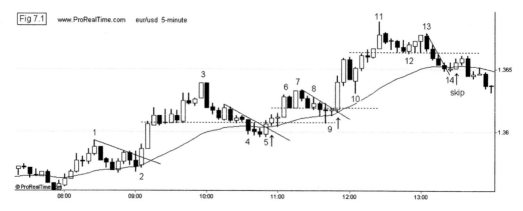

Figure 7.1 Trending sessions are easy to spot. Unless we are dealing with a lengthy flag we need only to follow the direction of the 25ema to understand who is currently in charge. And nine times out of ten, that is the line also to follow for our trades. This information is so easy to obtain, so unambiguous in nature, and such an excellent filter that it's hard to believe that anyone would willingly discard it. But many do by mistake.

Beyond question, one of the main causes for traders to get tricked into rebellion is the appearance of a so-called "reversal pattern". The bull trend in Figure 7.1 shows three such patterns (above the dotted lines), each with reversal features of its own. What these patterns share in common, though, is the typical horizontal barrier below them and the fact that all three were broken *towards* the 25ema. In contrast, bull-flag 1-2, was broken *away* from the average (hence it being referred to as a "continuation pattern").

More often than not, trading a break of a reversal pattern straight into a trending 25ema is a gamble more than a trade, and a poor one at that. But here's the interesting part: when such a break indeed harbors all the makings of a trap, we may soon have an excellent shot at trading the event for failure.

In a way, the tactics involved are not far removed from pullback reversal technique, but we do have to consider a specific signal bar requirement. This is best explained with some practical examples.

Let's start out with the break at bar 4. First off, there's no need for close scrutiny to see why this event was a trade-for-failure candidate:

bears had shorted straight into a bullish triple of the 25ema, the round number and the 50 percent retracement of the 2-3 bull swing.

When aiming to trade for failure, it is vital not to run ahead of things but to calmly monitor the way the market handles the break first. In a bear break situation, special attention should go out to a bullish turn-around bar; the first to come along could already set up the re-break entry (5).

Of critical importance, though, is the high of this turnaround bar. Since we are looking to trade the break *below* the dotted barrier for failure, we have to make sure that our entry is back *above* it (failure confirmation). This implies that the high of our signal bar should reside either at the exact level of the broken barrier or slightly above it. Under no circumstances should we enter on a break of this bar below the barrier.

As long as we keep this requirement in mind, the situation can indeed be traded like a regular pullback reversal. A bullish bonus here was to see the 4-5 cluster take on the features of a mini W-pattern middle-part, or, if you wish, a thicker version of the morning-star pattern. Another favorable element was to see bar 5 set up a flag break entry as well. All told, this represented a trade-for-failure setup of the high-odds category (enter long above bar 5).

It may not be so obvious at first sight, but the break below the 6-7-8 block is almost an exact copy of the situation on the left. Once again bears had shown little regard for the bullish conditions. And again they had shorted straight into a trending average and into a 50/60 percent retracement of a foregoing swing (5-7); and while doing so, they had totally neglected the technical support of a ceiling test with our former signal bar (low of 9 tests high of 5).

What may have inspired this bearish bravery? Maybe these players had perceived the lower top at 7 to be a sign of bullish weakness. Maybe they were only gunning for the round number magnet about 15 pip below; who is to say what these bears were thinking. But we can form ourselves a pretty good idea of what they failed to consider: the hazards of defying the tide.

Of course, all this is not to suggest that you cannot trade against dominance with decent odds attached, but if you insist on going the obstinate route, seldom a smart idea is to pull the rebellious trigger straight into a trending 25ema.

Note: An interesting element within of the trade-for-failure concept is that due to the faltering breakout, we often see the blocky features of the perceived *reversal* pattern take on the more angular characteristics of a flag formation, which is a *continuation* pattern. In the 6-7-8 situation, it had taken just two extra bars to produce this transformation (combi 9 added). By the way, the entry here was offered above the inside bar of the combi, as in a regular combi breakout.

This was already the third pattern breakout of the session, but the bullish enthusiasm was no less powerful. Granted, bull parties did have a very nice 50-level magnet to shoot for. But what about the second leg of this breakout, the near vertical swing 10-11. Were bulls overdoing it?

It is a common observation that when prices accelerate in an already mature rally, say, in the third or fourth leg of it, this often indicates the final burst of the trending environment; while this principle by itself is rather fickle and not easy to exploit, it can serve as an excellent reminder not to be too eager in regard to the next continuation offer.

Aside from the acceleration issue, the break of bar 12 was an easy skip for several reasons. For starters, trading for continuation in the highs of a bull rally on such a shallow correction cannot be regarded as a high-odds play. And the entry was offered far away from the 25ema. Plus there was the issue of the broken 50-level magnet.

This brings us to the third reversal block of the session, the 11-13 situation. With prices run up well over 100 pip since the start of the UK Open at 09:00, the market had now entered what is often referred to as the "lunch-hour doldrums" (12:00-14:00). Indeed, in the majority of sessions there isn't much firework going on in this low-volume environment; but with an uncontested rally on the board, and plenty of profits yet to be pocketed by the bulls, it is certainly not unthinkable for the lunch hours to put in their fair bit of action, too.

Recalling our discussions on the reversal exit in Chapter 6, the 10-13 progression is a perfect example of an M-pattern reversal in the making. Notice also how the right side of the middle-part had tried to break out on the bull side before spinning around bearishly in powerbar fashion (13). A bull in position could not have wished for a better hint to get the bearish message (reversal exit option below bar 13).

Was the break below bar 13 a shortable event as well? Frankly, when compared to the earlier reversal attempts, this offer definitely had more merit; but let us not forget that the session itself was still in bullish mode (higher lows throughout, trending 25ema). Thus, conservatively seen, the break is a skip. But it is hard to argue with a nimble scalper for taking his chances on a quick short into the double magnet of the round number and the 25ema.

With the average still trending up nicely, why not trade long again above bar 14? Apart from the fact that the M-pattern block already hindered the bullish outlook most considerably, the chart offers an *indisputable* clue that the time was not right for a buy-side wager: the bear break below the dotted line had not yet been proven false. Even if bar 14 had set up more powerfully as a turnaround bar (or perhaps was seen as part of a morning-star variant with its neighbors left and right), still the entry was offered *below* the barrier of the overhanging resistance. And that's a definite skip.

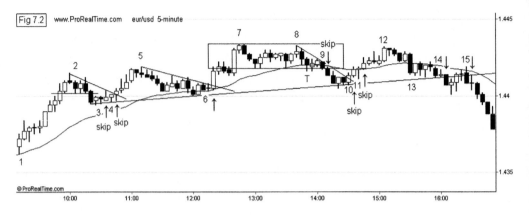

Figure 7.2 Now here is a reversal pattern truly worthy of acknowledge-
ment (big head-and-shoulders variant 3-14). But do note that it had
taken no less than three hours since the high at 7 was put in for the
bullish dominance to fully drain out.

Within the total pattern there were several smaller patterns of interest to be detected. The first notable development was bull-flag 2-4,
hanging from the pole 1-2. This correction had started out as a tiny
M-pattern reversal (above the little horizontal line), but with four doji
bars added (3-4), the pattern had taken on the shape of a flag, thereby
turning itself into a continuation candidate.

The break above combi 3 is an easy skip: prices still resided below
the mini barrier of the bearish breakout. But the break above bar 4 does
not qualify as a high-odds wager either. At that point the flag was still
rather small in relation to its pole and there was the adverse magnet of
the average to consider. Unpleasant also was the total absence of support beneath this flag in case of a faltering start.

Next up was another flag formation (5-6), decent in shape but hanging a bit awkwardly from the rather short pole 4-5. Perhaps we could
say that it related to a larger pole, the two-legged swing 1-5. More interesting, this flag had found solid footing in the 25ema, the round
number and a technical test with the flag on the left (favorable triple).

Notice also that the last three bars had formed a three-bar combi (6).
With no room for another bar in the squeeze to get printed, something
had to give. We can look upon this as a flag break setup, but since a
bull break would confirm the failure of the bear break in the low of the

184

flag, this was a trade-for-failure setup as well. (Not that it matters how we label our breaks.)

As we know, accelerations in the highs or lows of a mature rally can be a gift as well as a curse (6-7). Surely there was no denying the bullish supremacy here, but it remained to be seen how this dominance would hold up in the often tricky lunch-hour doldrums (12:00-14:00).

In the first hour of consolidation (box), bulls stood their ground well, with prices calmly drifting sideways a little above the 25ema. No trouble on the bullish horizon yet. Things took an interesting turn, though, when new bulls came to attack the session high with a break in bar 8, but then were forced to retreat from it.

Just like a failed reversal can swing things around in favor of continuation, so too can a failed continuation trigger a reaction in favor of a reversal (think double top or bottom). Such failure may not have immediate consequences upon occurrence, but it will not go unnoticed, and could trigger demoralization further down the line. Or put differently, if you were a bull in position and you saw that M-pattern block take shape on your screen (box), would you not be at least a little concerned?

The box break at T was a bit thinly built up, hence the tease annotation, but the incident did give fair warning of weakening support. If not yet on target in the 6-7 breakout, this may have called for a reversal exit.

A few bars later, the box barrier skirmish (T-9) got "resolved" in favor of the bears with a break below bar 9. With now more buildup showing, was this a signal to play short?

Shorting below bar 9 does make sense in some respects; for starters, this second break confirmed the failure of the bulls to undo the first break at T. Taking into account also that the M-pattern was already the third corrective block to show up, and the most prominent one at that, it makes sense to at least *consider* our sell-side options—if only with the intention to exploit the pull of the round number magnet about 15 pip below.

But before we put our precious capital at risk, let us not forget to examine the obstructive elements that may have kept our short from reaching target. How about the earlier lows of 3 and 6 (pattern line extension); how about the cluster progression in the flag on the left; how about the fact that the chart had been very bullish from the UK Open on, which may have left quite a few bulls lurking for lower prices still. As we can see, as much as there was pressure to be detected that favored the sell side, the situation wasn't exactly hopeless for the bulls. And all the while the 25ema was still trending *up*.

As it turned out, bears indeed were unable to push through the pattern line defense. This printed yet another higher low in the chart, but definitely not something to pursue. After all, the break above bar 10 was offered *below* the broken box, and that simply rules out the trade-for-failure option.

But how about the break above combi 11; if we visualize the box to be extended a little to the right, we can see that prices were now pushing up against the bottom barrier of it, meaning a break *above* combi 11 would now technically confirm, if somewhat belatedly, the failure of the reversal break below bar 9. All true, but not every such re-break calls for action.

Note: Without putting a strict rule on it, trading for failure is best done in response to the *first* reversal attempt in a fresh dominant swing. That is when the market is most likely to reject the reversal breakout in favor of continuation. The later in the trend a reversal pattern shows up, and the blockier its features, the harder it will be for the dominant parties to dismantle the reversal implications.

In this particular instance, brave bulls did manage to eat themselves back through the contents of the 7-8 block, but this left them extremely vulnerable upon reaching the highs (12). When the selling then started, they had no ammo left to fight back.

On their subsequent retreat, bulls not only left a triple top in their wake (7-8-12), they inadvertently helped to complete the final arch of the big head-and-shoulders formation. As is often seen, though, they took it upon themselves not to give up on their cause without a good fight first. This resulted in yet another element of interest: a squeeze in pattern line support that ended with a bearish combi (13-14).

When measured against the total span of the big head-and-shoulders pattern, this pre-breakout tension wasn't very extensive—a few more bars of buildup would have been nice; on the other hand, the odds for follow-through certainly weren't poor. In most such "border-line" cases it is probably best to just bite the bullet and fire along (enter short on the break of combi 14).

Note: A round number not far from entry—or any other magnet, for that matter—could provide a trade with an excellent start. Upon arrival, however, the bounce effect could instantly reclaim all of the current gains. In fact, this type of response is so notoriously commonplace that it has led many traders to adopt a routine of raking in some, if not all of the profits in a danger zone with the intention to reposition after a "fa-vorable" bounce (basically a variant of the resistance exit). In theory this makes perfect sense, but in reality, this practice harbors some dangers of its own: it is easy to miss out on a lot of follow-through in all cases where the market simply refuses to bounce (sufficiently).

Alas, sticking to the bracket, although largely recommended, is no guarantee for a successful wager either. In the session above, the bounce up from the round number may very well have shaken out our short in the high of bar 15. If so, it is crucial to accept such mishap with grace and above all, not to lose track of the action! Recalling our discussions on the pattern break pullback setup in Chapter 5, when a post-breakout correction puts in a ceiling test back inside the broken pattern, this could easily set up a second break in line with the first. Thus, rather than walking away from a shake in an act of disgust, it may pay to stay alert for another try (re-enter short below bar 15).

Figure 7.3 Around the EU Open at 08:00, a small but gracious flag hung harmoniously from its pole. The last three bars in it were jammed tight in a squeeze between the 25ema and the flag line (1); looking closely, we can detect within the latter element the up/down motions of an evening-star, which is a mini three-bar M-pattern with reversal implications of its own. A nice flag. On the downside, if we consider the hours prior to 08:00, this set up as a continuation trade in the lows of the Asian session. As we know, the first volume of the EU/UK session is never so keen on immediately following up on the Asian pressure, particularly in the lows or highs of it—but that is no reason to skip a trade per se. We could even say that this flag harbored a *failed* attempt of the bulls to counter the Asian pressure, which basically turned it into a trade-for-failure setup. But let us not overanalyze the situation: this was a decent short setup with decent odds attached.

Shortly after the UK Open, bulls had tried to hammer in a double-bottom with combi 2, but their efforts were quickly undone. Bears, however, despite the backup of powerbar 3, proved wholly unable to capitalize on their advantage. Another fine example of how tricky this opening hour can be (09:00-10:00).

Whenever a sideways cluster of bars halts an advance or decline, there are basically two options of interest. Either this cluster builds up towards another leg in line with the dominant pressure (continuation), or it is getting ready to defy it (reversal). While the market's verdict will only be known after the fact, in plenty of cases the attentive observer may already pick up some cues that favor one outcome more than the other. Plotting a box around the clustering action will certainly help to keep good track of the pressures in play (pullback 4-5 provided the box boundaries).

As already stated, when a sideways progression shows up as part of a *first* pullback to the 25ema, its reversal implications are usually not that potent. The bear-flag at 08:00 is a good example: a failed reversal that played out in favor of bearish continuation. In the later stages of a rally, the contrarian prospects naturally improve. Especially when a sideways cluster shows up at quite some distance from the trending 25ema (as was the case with the box), and then gets broken towards it, contrarian parties stand to benefit from a very powerful ally: the magnet of the 25ema.

When not in position, all this is just information; we would neither use such a box for shorting purposes, nor go long above it. Of course, when already *in* position, the adverse break of a box could have serious consequences.

So let us examine this situation as if still in short position. To begin, the 4-6 double bottom showed signs of contrarian effort, but not of major concern yet. More indicative was the break of the box in powerbar 7. Perhaps we could already exit our short at this point, but in strict technical terms, the bar had only just stuck its head through the top of the box without being broken itself (no *technical* confirmation yet).

In this instance, the break was quickly confirmed when bar 8 took out the high of bar 7 (reversal exit). If still not convinced of the bullish implications, bears would have done well not to ignore the subsequent break of bar 8 also, which was now a combi breakout.

As prices were reeled in by the 25ema magnet, but then started to struggle in it, this may have prompted some eager bears to consider their sell-side options. But before doing so ourselves, let us not forget to check the conditions first. As discussed in Chapter 5, an important aspect in pullback reversal technique is to see a correction of interest travel diagonally and orderly against the dominant swing, with little signs of aggression within. With this in mind, hopefully it isn't hard to see why the short below bar 9 is annotated as a skip: although diagonally shaped and guided along by a decent pullback line, the 6-9

correction was part of a *box* pattern and contained some powerful bullish bars as well. In fact, we could look upon this bull swing as the
right leg of a W-pattern reversal; and that puts a short against it in the
low-odds corner. After all, to get to target, prices would now have to
plow themselves a way through the contents of the middle-part section
below; not only will this keep many bears from hopping along, there will
be plenty of contrarians on the lurk to buy themselves in from the base
of that very same cluster. (All this in terms of probability.)

W and M-patterns in the lows or highs of a rally are a very common
occurrence. By themselves they may not possess the power to fully flip a
trending session around, but it will certainly pay to at least respect the
implications attached to their presence.

As it turned out, the supportive powers of the box progression were
not even tested on first go; but if we extend the level to the right (dotted
line), it is plain to see that the market had not forgotten about its technical significance (sharp bounce in the low of bar 10).

Figure 7.4 If we compare this chart with the previous one, Figure 7.3,
the price action may send out a totally different feel, if only for the difference in volatility. But when viewed price technically, the similarities
are actually quite striking. Both charts feature a bear rally from a flag
breakout in a round number area and then later on a bullish turnaround on the break of a W-middle-part box. But where the bear-flag
in the previous chart met all the requirements of a valid short setup,
the frantic motion within the flag above basically rendered the situation
untradable (1-4).

Whenever the majority of bars visibly exceed their average span, standard protection may no longer suffice. In such an environment, a standard stop may already get taken out in an otherwise relatively harmless pullback. Of course, there is always the option of adjusting the 20/10 bracket to a wider span, if only on the stop side, but my advice would be to do so only if the volatile conditions persist for many sessions on end. Within a single session, more often than not, things will "turn back to normal" soon enough.

The short below bar 3 is an easy skip; it went straight up against the double-bottom element to the left (1-2); the offer below bar 4 was of better standing (more buildup), but in the light of the fickle conditions, this did not meet the requirements of a conservative wager either.

The high of bar 5 shows an interesting test with the flag line extension, but the bar itself was way too tall to set up a valid pattern break pullback short. Nonetheless, the market did continue its bearish path and not much later even fell through the 00-level with hardly a contrarian bull in sight.

Inevitably, at some point in a bear rally bulls will come in more strongly; their first notable feat here was to test back the round number in the 6-7 correction. Three reasons immediately come to mind why this did not set up a valid short below combi 7: there was no harmony between the shallow flag and the tall pole from which it hung (5-6); the short entry was offered at quite some distance away from the 25ema (adverse magnet); the unbroken pullback line offered potential obstruction that coincided with a level of technical support (highs of the three-bar block starting at 6).

Notwithstanding our reservations, prices slid down once again, which added another leg to the bear rally. But do take note of the accelerated fashion in which this took place. Was this the dying breath of the bearish market? Telling by the way the low of bar 8 was bought up (long bottoming tail) plenty of bulls indeed thought it was time for some contrarian fun. Or else there were plenty of bears cashing in on their windfall profits in the face of the US lunch-hour "doldrums" (18:00-20:00).

In price technical terms, progression 7-8-9-10-11 is almost an exact copy of the W-reversal discussed in the foregoing chart. The middle-part section (box) was arguably even more "predictive" here, almost trumpeting the pending completion of the right leg (note the bullish combi starting at 10).

But let us recall also the point of our previous discussion on the topic: when a box is broken against the dominant pressure and prices follow through towards a trending 25ema, this generally renders the correction unsuited for pullback reversal tactics. Hence the skips below bar 12 and 13; both signal bars were of poor quality anyway.

But even without the box attached, the near-vertical correction of the 10-11 swing was way too aggressive in appearance to even consider shorting against it.

While there is usually little need for the power of foresight to anticipate a modest box reversal in the lows or highs of a session, it is absolutely impossible to foretell these full-fledged turnarounds as depicted in the chart above (10-15). When they show up, though, it is crucial not to look upon them as irrational or overextended and thus ripe for punishment. Whenever the bars start to position themselves *firmly* at the other side of the average, we are technically no longer dealing with a regular pullback or a flag-shaped correction of sorts; for the action clearly tells us that the current consensus on the 5-minute has changed in favor of the turnaround. This means that all conservative bets in line with the earlier trend are now off.

But in most such cases, similar caution is warranted on the new dominant side as well. Remember, when a trend is followed by a trend in the other direction, the market is essentially traveling in a range and this is generally not the best climate to play for substantial continuation. (For an initial discussion on this concept, check Chapter 5, Figure 5.17.)

The bullish acceleration in the 14-15 swing—stemming from a failed bearish reversal below the little horizontal line—shows another telling example of the final burst principle. The fact that prices had run into fat resistance of the earlier flag on the left made the situation even more precarious for the bulls, particularly for those late to the party.

Pullback 15-16 indeed came down pretty hard, but upon arrival in the 25ema, the bearish counterpressure almost instantly subsided. Still, this was not a safe place to think long again. Aside from the fact that the market was in ranging mode, pullback 15-16 had retraced much too aggressively to justify a pullback reversal wager (skip the buy offer above combi 17).

As it turned out, most of the skipped entries in this session would have worked out well for 20 pip. Are we being too conservative? It really is up to the individual to answer this. Sometimes the environment may allow for a little more aggression, but it is no easy chore to *define* the requirements that determine these special conditions.

If only for the sake of testing your personal method, reviewing indisputable high-odds wagers only (say, on a year's worth of intraday price action) is by far the best way to establish a reliable take on the extent of opportunities, and their possible outcomes, in the actual market. By contrast, it remains to be seen how well such a test would reflect reality if you include in your analysis a mix of borderline ventures that may or may not have been accepted in a live-market session.

Anyway, for what it is worth, try not to fall into the classic trap of accepting mediocre wagers for the mere sake of wanting to trade. If it is more action you crave, rather than forcing your will upon a single instrument, add some more markets to your screens and play their high-odds offers only.

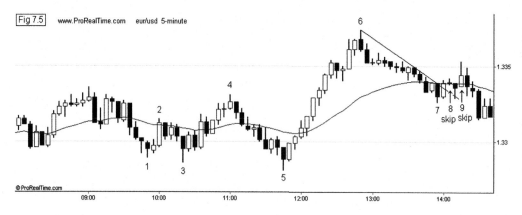

Figure 7.5 Neutrally regarded, the 5-6 maneuver shows unmistakable supremacy on the part of the bulls. Unfortunately, there was no build-up involved in its starting point and that leaves us to ponder on its technical justification. This is a textbook example of what we can refer to as a *bull rally starting from a false bear low*. How is this information useful? Brisk and sharp these counter rallies can be, they make poor *continuation* candidates on balance.

Before we delve into the specifics of the pullback reversal skips, let's have a look at the foregoing action first. A quick glance tells us the UK morning session had ranged aimlessly around the 1.33 round number. Above it, bears had had little trouble keeping the bullish charges in check; below the number, bulls had shown tenacity of their own. On no less than three consecutive occasions, they had successfully taken their shots at the new lows of 1, 3 and 5, proving all of them false. The latter event then led up to the wild bullish upswing 5-6, which appeared totally uncontested.

More often than not, the general consensus on these "moves-out-of-nowhere" is one of suspicion rather than trust and this tends to have a restraining impact on the continuation potential, even after a substantial correction has been put in (6-7).

This pullback had retraced about 50 percent of the bull rally, and while doing so had found support in the highs of the morning session range (level of 4). How does this differ from a valid pullback reversal candidate?

When aiming for a bull-side reversal, it is always a plus to see a former level of resistance act as support in favor of the turn. However, the reliability of technical backup is generally the highest when this supportive element resides *directly to the left of the pullback*. For a bearish example of such "directness", check how the high of bar 2 had run into resistance of a fat cluster of bars not far to the left; at least theoretically, that bear block provided *dependable* resistance (technical test).

As is plain to see, things were different in the situation on the far right. With the 5-6 maneuver being so straight and not showing any bearish hiccups on the way up, the first support for the pullback to touch upon was the high of the earlier range at the level of 4, "way out" to the left. Perhaps for want of a better alternative, prices did manage to find some footing in this level, but this did not mitigate the issue of the poor conditions on the whole. Technically seen, the first dependable support in sight—and thus an adverse magnet—resided all the way down at the 00-level: a "ceiling" test with the floor in the 4-5-6 arch.

In summary, the conservative take on a situation like this would be to decline both the pullback reversal offer in bar 8 and the pattern break pullback entry in bar 9. The latter was of better quality (second break showed bullish persistence), but still not solid enough to alleviate the concerns regarding the shady conditions.

Note: This is not to suggest that a lack of direct support should make us skip all pullback reversals by default. But for any such wager to earn passage, at least the entry conditions should be optimal. To understand this distinction, let us briefly recall our discussion concerning Figure 6.6 in Chapter 6. Similar reservations were uttered in regard to the continuation prospects of a foregoing rally, but when we took a closer look at the reversal setup itself (the 12-13 situation), we did come to appreciate the conditions regarding the entry. Were such circumstances present in our current chart?

Considering the feeble support underneath both entries, and the potential for obstruction above them (round number contrarians lying in wait), the prospects for continuation here were not nearly as promising. Perhaps an optimistic bull could argue that the round number now stood to work as a magnet, if only to get the trade going; fair enough, but let us not underestimate the danger for obstruction within that very same magnet (bounce effect), particularly in the light of the nontechnical bull run.

Regardless of the actual outcome, the point here is that *if* you do decide to take your chances on a borderline trade, it will pay to at least have the entry conditions unmistakably on your side. This may not necessarily get your trade to target, but it *might* give you a better shot at exiting with minimal damage should the trade at some point need to be scratched (possible reversal exit versus a quick shake after entry). Just something to take into account.

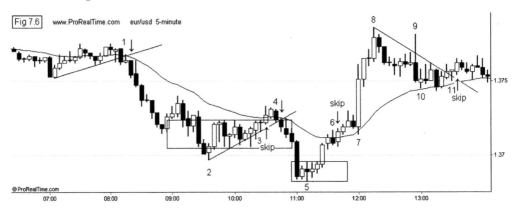

Figure 7.6 In our discussions on the pattern break combi setup in Chapter 5, we already took up the entry specifics on the first trade, the short below combi 1 (Figure 5.11). This chart shows the follow-up action during the UK morning session.

After a stale Asian market, it is not uncommon for the action to immediately pick up pace in the EU Open at 08:00. It is the more powerful UK Open at 09:00, however, that tends to have the biggest say in the nature of the coming session. How many times have we not seen a powerful breakout in the first few bars of this hour. But when there is already a trend in place, either still standing from the Asian hours or freshly started in the EU Open, as was the case above, the first UK traders are usually *not* so keen on immediately following up on the current pressure. Sooner we will see a sideways correction of sorts, if not a rebellious counterattack. Of course, these are just general observations to keep a trader sharp; they should never compete with what the price action itself is saying.

In this session, the UK Open didn't put up much of a fight; after a brief bout of bullish opposition, the dominant bears were allowed to march on to their 00-level magnet (2). But as soon as prices hit upon that number, the climate definitely changed.

From around 09:30 to 10:30 there appeared an interesting sequence of bars that can be regarded as a W-middle-part variant. (To better illustrate its blocky features, the low of 2 was excluded from the box.) Even though this pattern showed up bearishly below a downtrending 25ema, within it there were quite a few bars that had managed to close well away from their lows. Was the market bracing itself for a bullish reversal?

In all fairness, when such a reversal block shows up as part of a first decent correction in a newly established trend, the chances for a substantial break against the dominant pressure are usually not that good. But this may not stop parties from trying, though.

Before things turned sour on them, bulls will have liked the way their box break came about. It wasn't hard to find a valid top barrier to play long above, and the combi setup, too, looked playable in all respects (3). In a *bullish* environment, a box break like this may very well have called for an entry on the buy side. In this bearish chart, however, the situation harbored all the ingredients of a trap.

For future purposes, examine closely the way this bull break failed and how it was followed by a bear break in the opposite direction (trade-for-failure setup). Variations on this theme are practically endless but they usually share some common characteristics. Arguably the most noticeable feature is that the breakout often takes place on a *first* touch with the average since the start of the dominant swing. Another element of interest is the "otherwise attractive" reversal pattern, which basically adds to the trap. And should prices indeed fail to follow through on the breakout, very common also is to see a strong reversal bar set up a trade-for-failure break in the other direction (4).

Do notice that the short entry here was presented *below* the top of the box, meaning this bear break provided a technical confirmation of the bull break failure. (Check Figure 7.1 for the initial discussions on this topic.) Very pleasant also was to have this break coincide with the perforation of an *angular* pullback line. As previously argued, blocky clusters that can still be framed by an angular line on the right are generally easier to cut through than are the square blocks that lack this favorable element. We could say that the angular versions look more like flag variants and therefore may sooner be regarded as continuation patterns. Taking all these bearish elements into account, we can safely state that the offer below bar 4 was a trade-for-failure wager of the high-odds category.

Not much later, pullback 5-6 had retraced about 60 percent of the foregoing swing 4-5. In the highs of this correction, prices had hit upon the trending 25ema and even pierced it a little before a turnaround bar showed up (6). With the market still in bearish mode, why is the pullback reversal below bar 6 annotated as a skip?

Several reasons come to mind. First off, the pullback, though decent in height, showed only one reversal bar in its top (6). While it is not uncommon for prices break away from a single turnaround bar in the average, the most reliable reversals tend to stem from a bit more pulling and pushing in the turn, especially when the pullback in question is not the first to defy the trend.

But there were more warning signs to consider. For example, had we run a pattern line beneath the lows of this pullback, it would not have been broken yet at the break of bar 6. Also, there was an adverse magnet on the lurk: the ceiling test with the low of bar 4 from where the earlier trade-for-failure break had taken off (not a major drawback, but potent enough to take into account). And lastly, in creating the 5-6 correction, bulls had broken back through the 00-level with a *powerbar* that had sprung from a little *box* progression; all very good reasons to be highly cautious on the sell side.

As it turned out, the market never even bothered to put in a test with that box; instead, bulls set out to establish a massive bull run that would completely destroy the earlier bearish dominance (5-8).

As taken up in previous discussions, a counterrally that fully defies the earlier dominant pressure is best not seen as a new trend. This is not to say that we shouldn't acknowledge the authority displayed, but these brutal surges seldom set up for *continuation*. And even more caution is warranted when such a move starts out from a false break event with little buildup (5). With no technical justification to back up the market's sudden change of heart, consensus on future direction stands to be highly divided. This may not stop the rally itself from marching on (initial shock-effect can be very strong), but as soon as the first signs of exhaustion come forth, countercharges can be equally brutal. Bar 9 is a telling example of what can happen when a market "comes back to its senses".

Despite the ominous features of bar 9, which had turned the 7-8-9 sequence in an M-pattern reversal candidate, prices held up very well in the 50-level and the average, the latter now trending nicely up. In fact, the blocky features of the 10-11 buildup show us that bull parties had responded with a middle-part of their own (of a W-pattern). Moreover, with the pullback line drawn as depicted (ignoring the topping tail of bar 9), the 8-11 price action now harbored all the ingredients of a bull-flag ready to pop.

It is therefore important to grasp the rationale behind declining the pattern break pullback offer above bar 11. In other circumstances—or should we say, in a bull *trend*—perhaps this breakout may have been worth a shot. But here the event set up in the higher region of a *range*, and after a nontechnical turnaround to boot (5-8).

Interesting also is to compare the entry conditions on the break above bar 11 with those of the earlier shorts, below combi 1 and bar 4. On the shorts, the round number magnets worked in favor of the breakout and lay pleasantly in line with the dominant pressure. On the long entry above bar 11, offered at about 7 pip *above* the round number, the magnet effect stood to work the other way around, to the possible detriment of the stop. To top it off, the break above 11 was presented in the lunch-hour doldrums (12:00-14:00) following a mega bull run in the morning session. That generally doesn't sit well with continuation either. Conditions, conditions, conditions.

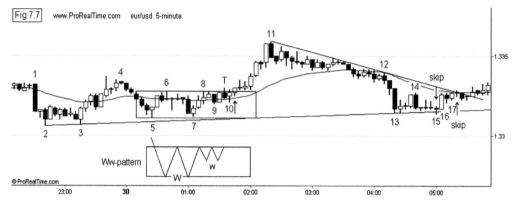

Figure 7.7 Asian sessions (00:00-08:00) can be awfully stale on the eur/usd pair, but they do tend to behave quite orderly and if they are kind enough to offer a valid setup, if only just one in the early hours, not seldom it is relatively easy to spot.

In the very thin volume prior to the Asian Open, prices were already on their way to the 00-level magnet (1-2), but then bulls had responded with a classic middle-part block (2-3). Note the tricky false low in bar 3 before the pressure spun around in powerbar fashion (bear-flag failure). Had we been in bearish position, the break above bar 3 may have called for a reversal exit. Pretty standard stuff.

This chart is selected to explore a very potent chart pattern of which there are many variations, both in length and width. It concerns progression 4 through 10; the box part in particular is worthy of remembrance. We can refer to this type of price action as a *Ww-pattern*, in which the bigger *W* represents a double-bottom base, and the smaller *w* a squeeze that sets up the future breakout. Like all patterns, this one has a bearish counterpart, the *Mm-pattern*.

In favorable conditions, Ww and Mm-pattern breakouts are among the most potent of follow-through generators, arguably even more powerful than their popular close cousins, the cup-and-handle formations (Vv and Nn). Breakout traders are well advised to get themselves acquainted with the way these progressions come about.

In a textbook Ww-pattern box, the top side is formed by the high of the big *W*'s middle-part (6), a level that is then repeatedly matched as the pattern progresses over time. Naturally, the less debatable this top barrier can be drawn, the more consensus on its break later on. At the other side of the pattern, a double bottom is likely to show (5-7), but the exact features here are not so relevant since we do not anticipate a break at this end. While the big W-element already hints at the market's bullish intentions, a mere break of the middle-part section may not be the place to hop on board with a tight stop. As always, for participation to be granted, we need to see some buildup first. This is where the smaller *w* comes in.

If we track the up/down motion of the 8-9-T-10 progression, we can see some bullish and bearish bars switching position, as in a regular squeeze. Very common also in this kind of buildup is a *failed first breakout*, generally referred to as a tease (T).

In any pattern break situation there are essentially two ways for a tease break scenario to set up. Either the breakout originates from a level "too deep" within the pattern, or the event does take place from a squeeze situation at the barrier, but the buildup appears too thin to meet the requirements of proper tension. The former situation is addressed in Chapter 2 in the section on "False Breaks, Tease Breaks and Proper Breaks"; along the way, we have already seen a number of such examples, the majority of which not too hard to dodge. Thin buildup, on the other hand, may cause a little more confusion, because the price action does show tension prior to the breakout but too little of it. But what is enough and what is too little?

To answer this in regard to a Ww-pattern, let us briefly recall the concept of harmony within the flag and flagpole relation. In some examples on the topic, we came to appreciate the guiding hand of proportion, whether it was to warrant action on a break, or to postpone it. Similar forces are often at work within the Ww-pattern (as in its Mm-counterpart). In a simplified way, we could say that the small *w* is essentially a flag hanging from big *W*'s right leg. Therefore, the Ww-breakout is best acted on when both elements (W and w) relate proportionally to one another. For example, if the vertical span of a big *W* is relatively wide, the smaller *w* should not be too compressed either. That would look rather "non-harmonious" and may not provide sufficient tension for prices to pop. Should the big *W* be rather stretched out, horizontally, then the small *w* should show itself more elongated also.

A subtle example of a premature break can be spotted at point T. Casually regarded, this breakout appeared acceptable since it took off from a bullish signal bar with its close right up against the box barrier; but on close inspection we can see that at that point there was only one black bar present in the squeeze, indicating that the alternating motion of bullish and bearish bars had not fully completed W-characteristics; or to put it more simply, the small *w* was underdeveloped when measured against its bigger *W* neighbor.

Please understand that assessing buildup is never a matter of counting bars per se, nor about striving for technical perfection. While we may entertain some preference for one situation more than another (for example to see at least four bars in a squeeze), we better not limit ourselves with strict rules on these matters.

If the break at T was premature, then how about the break above bar 10? With now two bars added (T-10), the small *w* had definitely fattened up. Furthermore, before turning bullishly around, bar 10 had briefly broken *below* bar T, which had left a false low on the chart (showing bullish persistence). And it was a higher low within the Ww-box. Considering also the ideal magnet of the 50-level above, just begging to be targeted, it really would have been a waste not to take our chances on the break of bar 10.

Granted, it is not always easy to tell a valid break from a tease break trap. At times the line between them can be very thin indeed. Nonetheless, I am absolutely positive that you can train your eye to at least recognize the breakouts of poor quality; from that pleasant base, your feel for harmony and proportion can only progress over time.

Not long after reaching the 50-level magnet, the Asian market slid into a slow but steady decline. The bottom barrier here may initially have been drawn to connect the lows of 5 and 7 with the lows of 2 and 3, but after the 13-15 element showed up, it makes sense to have plotted the line as depicted.

Just like the Ww-box had set up the bull break earlier on, so did progression 13-15 attempt to build up to a bear break. However, there are some major differences in both the setup and the conditions. For example, the lows of the Ww-box were technically and very favorably supported by the 2-3 cluster on the left. This formed higher lows along the way and ultimately provided a base for higher prices away from support. The pre-breakout tension of 13-15, on the other hand, showed up unfavorably in the lows of a range. As we know, when buildup is absent or lacking in substance, this seldom sets up favorably for continuation.

There may have been some stalling on the pattern line from 13 to 15, but in terms of buildup it all looked a bit feeble; and the 25ema wasn't exactly helping out either (no squeeze whatsoever). In other words, the bear break in bar 15 enjoyed little technical backup, yet it had to overcome strong support of multiple lows on the left (2, 3, 5 and 7, take your pick). Not surprisingly, few parties were prepared to commit themselves on the sell side here; and it didn't take long for contrarian bulls to pick up on this reluctance.

A failed breakout on one side of buildup often sets the stage for a counterbreak at the other end; and not seldom this one comes with better credentials attached. In fact, with combi 16 added, the 12-13-14-15-16 progression now bore all the features of a W-pattern ready to be completed.

Considering the bullish implications, we cannot blame a bear for bailing out on his short on the break of combi 16 (reversal exit). An even stronger warning was sent out when bar 17 was broken on top, for this was now a *three*-bar combi breakout, and it coincided with a pattern line perforation to boot.

So why not trade long on the break of bar 17? Technically regarded, this was not an offer of the most unsavory kind; but we cannot say the conditions were of such favorable nature to look upon this wager as a *high-odds* proposition. Here's another way to look at it: earlier on, we saw little problem in declining the break in bar T, although the environment already spoke in favor of the bull side; why then risk capital on a trade with arguably less buildup beneath it and facing more overhead resistance as well (the 11-12 cluster).

Figure 7.8 If totally new to price action trading, the reader may have gotten the impression that it takes a very detailed weighing of the pros and cons to determine whether or not action is warranted. Quite the opposite is true, really, and most certainly so on the skipping part. Why evaluate the market's every little move under a microscope when a quick glance would already suffice to determine that there are no trades anywhere near. Remember, if we have to look hard for a trade, it is probably not there. And even when the action builds up to a point of interest, nine times out of ten we should be able to assess the situation in the blink of an eye still.

Let's put this to the test. If we imagine to have switched on our trading platform at, say, 10:00, what could we have derived, in just a few seconds of evaluation, from the hints and clues presented? 1: A decent bear swing from 08:00 to 09:00 had put the market in bearish mode. 2: From 09:00 to 10:00, bulls had found footing in the round number level, which had stalled the bearish momentum in a sideways pattern that now came to attack the trending 25ema. 3: It will have taken us no more than a few seconds also to wrap a box around this action and to recognize the setup as a bull break trap.

It is safe to suggest that these observations could have been made with minimal effort in the opening seconds of the bar that followed the combi at 4, so even before the bull break had fully materialized. And it will have taken no longer than the forming of bar 5 itself to have understood the bearish implications should this bar be broken at the bottom. In fact, bar 5 was a textbook trade-for-failure setup (enter short below it).

Notice that in the evaluation of the box progression there was no need to discuss the false low at 1, the higher low at 3 and the fact that the first bull attack on the 25ema had failed at 2 with a false high to show for it. These were elements that all bore technical meaning, but since they represented the smaller parts of a bigger total (box), a quick assessment of their sum more than sufficed.

Very helpful also in the analysis process is to simply tap into your mental database of price technical patterns and see if you can match the current action with a variant of a pattern that you have seen fail or succeed many times before. For example, compare the bull trap above combi 4 with the one discussed in Figure 7.6 (above 3), or with the one in the next chart, Figure 7.9 (above 3). Indeed, these poisonous break-outs are far from unique and they show us most evidently that lessons can be learned from the past. To see a bullish version, check Figure 7.1 again and the way we handled the bear break below the first dotted line (longing it for failure above bar 5).

Soon after the bull break had fallen through, the bearish pressure picked up its earlier pace. An interesting feature here is to see the 5-6 swing mimic the bear move that had preceded the box progression; a fine example of the pole-flag-swing principle.

Bulls had tried to hammer in a double bottom even before the 50-level was reached (6-8); but this was not the time or place for bullish bravery to pay off. However, pullbacks 6-7 and 8-9 did not set up well for bearish purposes, either. The former was too shallow to short, the latter lacked a proper signal bar; and there was powerbar 8 to consider as well, which had created the double-bottom element with the low of bar 6.

It usually doesn't take much technical savvy to question the prospects of a break against a newly established trend. But how exactly do we rate the failure potential when the trend is already well on its way? Surely, at some point, the market will attempt to turn with better odds attached, and maybe this could set up a reversal trade worthy of acceptance.

Here's a little rule of thumb that may prove a very handy filter in the vast majority of trending sessions: for as long as the 25ema is still trending, even when slowly flattening out, all wagers against its slope are essentially off. If we translate this to the buildup situation between 12:00 and 13:40, there should have been no discomfort in declining the bull-side breaks offered, simply because the 25ema was still sloping down. (**Note:** In a breakout situation that stems from a lengthy pull-back, like an angular flag progression, it is not unthinkable to take position against the *current* slope of the 25ema, because the extent of the correction may have tilted the average the other way; but this is quite different from trading breaks against a *trending* average.)

With bulls and bears keeping each other in check throughout the lunch-hour doldrums (12:00-14:00), the activity within the second box slowly took on the shape of a W-pattern middle-part. The top barrier is drawn across the highs of the lowest block, but it could also have been plotted a few pip higher up, across the series of highs at the level of 10. This was another good reason to be cautious regarding the buy side, for a debatable pattern barrier is likely to keep consensus on its break divided, and that never sits too well with follow-through.

Although rather compressed vertically, the price action within the second box did show signs of bullish determination; in it there were false lows, higher lows and even a three-bar combi right underneath the top barrier (11-12). Nonetheless, both the box break entry above combi 12 and the pattern break pullback offer above bar 14 were easy skips, if only for the 25ema "rule". A point of concern also was the 7-9 double top not far to the left (potential obstruction).

When it comes to trading for failure, it is crucial to realize that a poor break against dominance does not *automatically* set up a high-odds break in the dominant direction. For example, the break below bar 13, the first bearish bar to challenge the box breakout, failed to meet the re-quirements of a valid short. Not only was the bull break not yet proven false (prices still resided above the box barrier), bar 13 set up too tiny to be considered a reliable signal bar for shorting purposes within the circumstances present.

But how about bar 15? Apart from displaying persistence on the part of the bears, this bar definitely showed more substance as a signal bar; and a break below it would now technically confirm the failure of the box breakout. Should we not accept?

If we compare the break below bar 15 with the break below bar 5, similarities cannot be denied; in both cases a bull break from a reversal progression was proven false in the 25ema region. And on both breaks an angular pullback line was taken out in the process. But there are differences also. Personally, I am not a big fan of trading for failure when it doesn't regard a *first* contrarian break against a *trending* 25ema. From this perspective, the break below bar 5 met all the requirements of a valid play. Subsequent wagers of this kind are not necessarily unsavory, but they seldom match the quality of the preferable situation. In the end, though, it is always a personal call, and one very much dependent on the situation at hand. Hence the break below bar 15 annotated as optional.

Figure 7.9 Contrary to popular notion, catching a ride on the high-and-mighty supertrend can be far more challenging than, say, trading a breakout from a well-defined range. So prominently displayed is the dominance in the chart that it stands to attract a wide array of strategies that all aim to trade the same thing (a pullback reversal), but with highly divided consensus on the actual levels of entry. This could produce a tricky environment with traders entering all over the place and getting trapped while at it.

A situation that certainly doesn't help to promote unanimity among the majority is when a rally shows no hiccups on its march that could serve as focus points for a later correction to gun for and possibly reverse in; this may leave a pullback no choice but to roll over in "midair". And as we can see also from the picture above, when the market is in supertrend mode, the 25ema may have a hard time keeping up. As a consequence of these exceptional conditions, plenty of strategies designed for the "ordinary" and generally slower market may now fail to produce dependable entry signals, leaving countless traders to ponder on when and where to catch their ride on the bandwagon.

These worries are essentially irrelevant to a conservative breakout trader, because he has no need for a trade. He doesn't care either whether the market is trending or ranging, or lying dead in the water; his sole aim is to participate in breakouts of the high-odds category and he will lay low on all offers of the weaker kind.

Such a relaxed disposition is not exactly commonplace among aspiring traders, particularly when confronted with a very lively market. And even among the more experienced there are many that become so blinded by the might of the trend that all they want for themselves is a piece of the pie. But how should they go about it? Should they aim for continuation in a round number level; should they pick the first turnaround bar to come along; should they wait for a miniature hiccup in the trend to be tested; should they trade the break of a pullback boundary line?

Depending on the situation, any of these techniques could get a trader in position; but since consensus on the "most sensible" course of action is likely to be divided, trend traders and contrarians may have to battle it out somewhat further still, and this can make for pretty bumpy rides.

In other words, as much as we can almost be certain that a supertrend will find some form of continuation, it remains to be seen how well a 10 pip stop—or any tight stop, for that matter—would hold up if the chosen entry is only a wee bit premature. It is up to the individual, of course, whether he is comfortable trading this sort of environment. Plenty of traders do love it, particularly those with a soft target in mind. If not shaken out in the early stages of the trade, these players may be so fortunate as to see their winners run for many, many pip on end.

Even when aiming for "just" 20 pip, entry may have been accepted on the pattern break pullback offer below bar 1, or perhaps on the second break offer below bar 2, which now confirmed the bearish pressure and set up from a better signal bar as well. However, the trouble with both entries was the "poor" technical base from which they had to be deployed and the fact that there were strong adverse magnets running above (00-level and 25ema).

Regardless of personal style and trading technique, there is no escaping the fact that any wager in the market—be it a bounce, break, scalp, swing, range or trend trade—is always a function of weighing the pros against the cons; in essence, of whether the prospect for profit makes up for the danger of an unpleasant shake. That is trading in a nutshell.

But no matter how savvy one's view on the market, and how carefully chosen one's trading ventures in it, shakeouts do come with the territory, for the losses in the field are an inevitable byproduct of *profitable* trading.

That being said, there is never any need to get caught in a very conspicuous trap. When it comes to the occasional supertrend, hopefully it needs little explaining that at all times a trader should not be so foolish as to go out and *defy* it on account of a perception that its decline or rise is way overextended. That can be a very dangerous practice.

In the session above, some unfortunate bulls had to learn this lesson the hard way when they bought themselves in on the box break above bar 3. Beyond doubt, this was a breakout of the poisonous variety. Yet what is poisonous to one, can taste very sweet to another (short for failure below bar 4).

Chapter 8

Recap Part 1

Before we go on to evaluate our studying efforts on six consecutive months of intraday price action in Part 2, it might be a good idea to recap all that we have taken up so far, so as to have everything fresh on the mind.

For this purpose, a new series of charts will be introduced, but they will not be taken apart as extensively as before. Not unlike gauging the current environment in an actual session, we will approach these charts with an overview perspective first, and then dig in a little deeper on the points of interest offered. To ease this process further, it is chosen to use a two-page layout for each example, starting at the left page, which will keep the charts in view at all times when reading through the text.

Upon reviewing this recap series, try not to focus too much on the setups alone; instead, really work on reading the full picture. For each wager is always a consequence of pressure, conditions and setup. Do take into account as well that the suggested entry and exit techniques are meant to reflect the conservative mode of operation as discussed in the foregoing chapters; in any given session, there are always more ways to take advantage of double pressure, for instance by incorporating contrarian tactics and quick in-and-out scalps.

Note: As one's understanding of price action is likely to grow over time, so may the urge to expand the range of conservative routines with all sorts of outings of the more aggressive variety. This is a very natural process and can only be encouraged. However, it is strongly recommended not to implement any of these additional tactics into the plan of attack until fully comfortable, and consistently profitable, trading *conservatively* and *methodically* first.

As in all foregoing examples, the trade suggestions can be evaluated by imagining the application of a rigid 20/10 bracket, but please recall that these settings do not claim to represent the *ideal* target and stop on the 5-minute eur/usd chart. In a "normally" active environment, however, this bracket will prove very effective, on both sides of the fence, but more important than the exact type of management is to understand why position is suggested in the first place. In this recap series, too, all entry techniques are based on the five trade setups as discussed in Chapter 5 and 7: the pattern break, the pattern break pullback, the pattern break combi, the pullback reversal and the trade-for-failure setup.

Of course, the bracket can be overruled at any time as one sees fit, and additional wagers and alternative techniques can always be considered—but try not to let this be a function of hindsight reflection. Studying price action—or trading itself, for that matter—is never about how to have reaped the *maximum* amount of profit from a certain situation; that is a pointless goal and quite undoable in practice. The only task of relevance, for any student trader, is to first develop an *edge* in the plan of attack, so as to come out ahead in the game; once this is accomplished, the sharpening of tactics and the honing of skills are just a matter of experience, as is the case with any other endeavor and profession in life.

As taken up in Chapter 6 on Manual Exits, valid bailout options are the news report exit, the exit in resistance and the exit on a reversal development, like the break of an M or W-pattern middle-part. The first two should already be on the radar *prior* to taking position; the latter is always a function of a price technical development adverse to the open position (reversal exit).

Before we dig in, allow me to again call up the list of common trading mistakes that we came to address at an earlier stage. With now more practice behind us, some of these errors may hardly need mentioning, but it's good to realize that no folly is ever the sole prerogative of the less savvy in the field. When capital and ego are at stake, even the most experienced and stoic of traders are never fully safe from the powers of delusion. We would do well not to think ourselves above these players. So once again, classic trading errors are:

1: Trading against a strong trend or an otherwise dominant pressure.
2: Trading with the pressure but into resistance overhead or underfoot.
3: Perceiving a trend to be in place when the market is actually ranging.
4: Choosing entries too far removed from the 25ema, or with little regard for the adverse round number magnet.
5: Picking entries in a frantic environment in which the majority of bars exceed their average span.
6: Aiming to trade a reversal of a pullback that shows aggressive powerbars or clusters within.
7: Front-running a break or turn of the market with too little buildup to warrant such action.

And lastly, let us one more time summarize the seven most essential price action principles in any chart. They concern:

Double pressure.
Support and resistance.
False breaks, tease breaks and proper breaks.
False highs and lows.
Pullback reversals.
Ceiling test.
Round number effect.

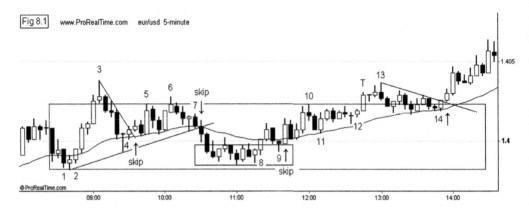

Fig 8.1 www.ProRealTime.com eur/usd 5-minute

Figure 8.1 Session overview: Before trending up, prices were caught in a choppy round number range all throughout the UK morning session. Bears had been successful in keeping the bullish charges in check above 1.40, but they had shown little power below it. From the footing of the smaller box, bulls had managed to slowly reclaim the initiative and this had set them on their way to the next round number in line (50-level).

  Points of interest: The break above combi 4 failed to qualify as a pullback reversal offer of the conservative kind; prices had corrected rather aggressively within the 3-4 retracement and there was a danger of the adverse round number magnet kicking in (1.40). If position was accepted, a reversal exit below bar 7 will have kept the damage to a minimum.

  While a bull may have justifiably exited below bar 7, a bear would have done well to lay low on the offer. This is not to say that the bearish pressure was weak, but the conditions did not allow for a substantial break on the sell side yet; the chart still showed higher lows on the whole and there was the potential obstruction of the big round number to consider as well.

  Prices did sink through the number a bit, and they even fell below the low of the nearest turnaround (combi at 4); but the more prominent low of the morning-star on the left held up well (1-2), which will surely have helped to keep the prospects of re-conquering the round number alive for the bulls.

  In bar 8, prices broke out of what can be regarded as a W-pattern middle-part (box), but nothing for us to pursue. A few bars later, a pattern break pullback entry was offered above bar 9, but this break, too, could not yet boast of a top-quality label. Just look at that wall of resistance within the 5-6-7 cluster, still very much in view.

Bulls did emerge victoriously from the round number skirmish, but they had no easy time plowing through the bearish opposition.

In the absence of matching highs, it was only when bar 10 had bounced away from the high of bar 5 that the range barrier could have been drawn as depicted. It wasn't a very distinctive boundary by any means, but good enough to plot and extend for futures purposes. It could always be adjusted later on.

With prices caught between the box barrier and the 25ema, progression 11-12 bore elements of a squeeze, but it wasn't very tight. For this reason, we can look upon the initial perforation of the barrier as a tease break candidate, in essence a premature break (T).

Prices indeed were forced to retreat from the tease, but it was a slow-going affair with no signs of aggression on the part of the bears. This ultimately formed the 13-14 bull-flag, which was well supported by the 10-12 cluster on the left (technical test). Note that throughout this correction, the trending average hadn't even flinched. Quite the contrary, it helpfully guided the bars back out of the box.

The flag break setup at 14 was a reversed combi variant in which the bullish powerbar came second to the inside bar; it was also a textbook morning-star pattern, if we include the bearish bar before it (compare with progression 1-2).

With the bulk of obstruction now out of the way, the 50-level magnet, about 25 pip out, stood to reel prices in from the moment of entry. Beyond question, this was a pattern breakout (range and flag) of the *high-odds* category, and well worth the wait.

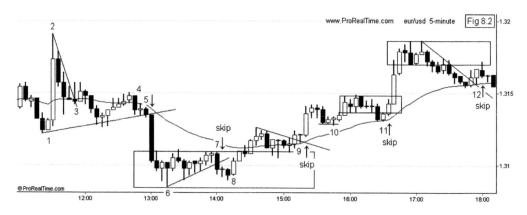

Figure 8.2 Session overview: Whatever it was that caused the violent bull spike in the UK morning (1-2), it didn't take long for the situation to correct to levels prior to the pop. Ironically, the bull spike not much later provided the pole for a bear-flag formation whose break below bar 5 sent the market flying the other way around (pole-flag-swing). In the 00-level below, another bear-flag set up (6-7), but the break of it failed to follow through. As is often seen, the flag formation then took on the blocky features of a W-pattern middle-part (6-8), which soon served as a stepping stone for a rather impressive bullish comeback.

Points of interest: Although no setup was provided, there were good reasons for declining any long in the area of bar 3: the bull spike had started from a bear low at 1 (no buildup), had penetrated the round number on the way up, and was most likely a news driven event (questionable dominance); and not unimportant either, the 2-3 correction had shown too much aggression to set up a valid turn.

Conservative traders can ignore the bear-flag setup at 5 also (flag barrier somewhat arbitrarily drawn), but this situation does offer an interesting example of how one extra bar of buildup can sometimes swing the pendulum from skipping to accepting a break. Initially, bears had judged combi 4 as too weak a setup for shorting purposes (no follow-through on its break); but when bar 5 was added, this now set up a three-bar combi with better odds attached (showing bearish persistence).

As prices violently broke down, it was only when the collapse had equaled the span of the bull spike (5-6 mirrors 1-2) that the bearish momentum petered out. As the first brave bulls returned on the scene, and savvy bears quickly cashed in on their windfall profits (temporary double pressure on the buy side), another bear-flag formed (6-7), but it was a poisonous pattern to be traded for continuation. Of course, with the break below bar 7 far removed from the 25ema, and with the round number here working as an adverse magnet, this was a very easy skip from where we stand.

When powerbar 8 flipped the flag break around, setting up the W-middle-part as mentioned, the climate was still very bearish. Moreover, even if the bulls would manage to position themselves firmly on top of the 25ema again, then still the market would be ranging rather than trending. As we know, this always calls for caution.

The otherwise attractive long above combi 9 is best declined. Maybe a nimble scalper may have taken a shot at gathering a handful of pip on the way up to the technical test with the low of combi 5 (a likely magnet), but the overall environment clearly lacked a dominant party and that generally rules out 20 pip targets. Also, should prices have stalled on that upside break, we can imagine the bears to have had little trouble testing back the 1.31 round number.

As it turned out, bulls remained persistent and they even traded a bearish mini-break at 10 for failure. And within the hour, they pulled a similar trick by trading the box break for failure as well, above bar 11. In a *trending* market, the latter offer may have been a reasonable option to pursue, but with prices traveling in a range, and in the tricky 50-level area to boot, not to mention the technical resistance of the flag on the left (1-5), trading the break above bar 11 cannot be regarded as a high-odds play.

At the end of the UK session (which is the start of the US lunch-hour doldrums), the break of bar 12 was a definite skip for three reasons at least: (a) the bear break of the final box had not been proven false; (b) prices resided in the danger zone of the range's highs, and (c) the bull entry suffered high risk of the 50-level adverse magnet. A poisonous offer indeed.

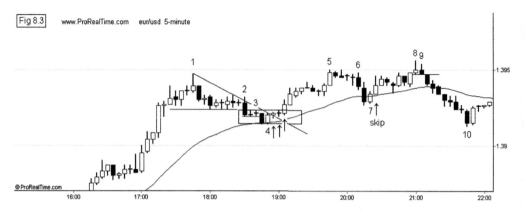

Figure 8.3 Session overview: Whenever we have a one-sided market on our hands, all bets against dominance are basically off. A better idea, on the whole, is to pick up a pullback reversal in the 25ema region. So patience is required.

Points of interest: Both the bear break in bar 2 and the one below bar 3 (three-bar combi) were reversal wagers in defiance of a very explicit trend—and arguably deployed at the worst possible moment as well, straight into a trending 25ema. It didn't take long for these eager bears to realize their mistake, nor for savvy bulls to start examining their trade-for-failure options.

Depending on one's appetite for aggression, there were three bull breaks offered (above the first three arrows), the latter of which was a textbook trade-for-failure entry. The "problem" with the first break, above bar 4, was the fact that the horizontal line below the reversal progression had not yet been broken back. On the other hand, a less conservative bull could argue that the mini break below combi 2-3 *was* broken back, and also that this situation bore all the makings of a regular bull-flag breakout (1-4).

The subsequent breakout (second arrow) showed persistence on the part of the bulls, but this break, too, was still offered *below* the horizontal barrier extension. So in strict technical terms, that did not qualify as a textbook trade-for-failure wager either.

Even without the benefit of hindsight, we can safely state that the third arrow depicts the superior break, for this offered an entry *above* the reversal barrier extension. A cute feature here was that the bearish three-bar combi 2-3 had been answered with a bullish three-bar combi, starting at 4, and this had set up a mini inverse head-and-shoulders variant (box). This situation serves well to highlight a most crucial concept: where the break of a reversal pattern *against* dominance is generally met with suspicion, the break of such a pattern *in line* with it (in the turn of a pullback) is very often acted on with little in the way of reservation, even when of lesser prowess.

Note: When there is a strong potential for *immediate* continuation, alternative entry tactics can be considered. For instance, a bull could have decided to overrule standard procedure by firing long not on the break of signal bar 4, but on the first re-break of the reversal barrier extension, should this be offered before a standard entry came to pass. Whether or not to go this route is always a personal call. When straying from the regular path, definitely preferable is to have one special condition on your side: a quick retest of the 25ema after entry (very common) should not shake out the trade.

The subsequent break above bar 7 was still very much in line with the trend, but the offer lacked the ideal features of a high-odds pullback reversal. The signal bar was a one-bar turnaround on a second pullback (not necessarily a major deal-breaker), and not far above it there resided some blocky resistance within the 5-6 progression. Considering the bullish climate, this offer was not entirely devoid of appeal, but probably an easy skip to the more conservatively inclined.

Prices found their way up again and not much later even built up towards another bull break (8). **Note:** A continuation breakout in the highs or lows of the market, particularly near the close of the US session (or in lunch-hour doldrums), can be a very tricky proposition, for such event often lacks the volume necessary to force a *substantial* break. And contrarians may counter more aggressively as well.

This is not to suggest that these breakouts are best traded for failure, as was boldly done below bar 9; but as soon as the first signs of trouble come forth, it is certainly no rarity to see a sharp bout of profit taking for the night (9-10).

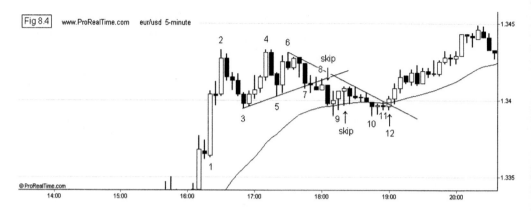

Figure 8.4 Session overview: Whenever a rally carries the supertrend label, even a fat triple-top reversal formation (M-pattern variant 1-7) may have a hard time swinging prices around. The thicker the pattern shows up, though, the more work there is to be done by trend trading parties to undo the reversal implications. This generally means that we cannot trade the break of such a pattern for failure on *any* first sign of faltering follow-through.

Points of interest: A nimble bear may have taken his chances on the double-bar break below 8 (basically a four-bar combi starting at powerbar 7), if only to scalp some pip on the way down to the double magnet of the 25ema and the round number. But this is one such wager that we should avoid at all cost. It is best not to forget that it takes other parties to get our trades to target. And quite a few of them are needed to force prices through a *trending* 25ema.

But there can be danger in trading with the trend as well. A very common mistake is to let directional bias get the best of prudence. Of course, the lessons of the market cannot be learned in a single session and many of them may have to be repeatedly taught before they finally sink in. But there is such a thing as an obvious trap; if only for this reason, the price action student is well advised to build himself a mental database not only of favorable conditions, but of those of the poisonous kind as well.

With such knowledge in mind, it should not have been too hard to dodge the bull trap above combi 9, straight into the overhanging resistance of the M-pattern block.

In several earlier discussions we took up the fact that reversal progressions of the blocky kind are harder to dig through than are their more angular counterparts. When aiming to trade for failure, this usually means that we should wait for the market to "edge off" most of the compactness of the obstruction first. Always welcome is to see the blocky features of a reversal pattern transform into the angular characteristics of a continuation pattern, as in a bull or bear-flag formation. This is essentially what happened when the 9-12 progression was added to the right of the reversal pattern.

Notice how the low of bar 10 matched the low of combi 9. This set up a double-bottom element in the trending average and was about to confirm a false break with the low of bar 3. (Imagine a horizontal barrier from the low of 3 extended to the right.)

In the meantime, the angular flag line could have been plotted as depicted and its slope lined up perfectly with the three-bar combi 10-11. The chart couldn't have offered a better view on the sweetspot at hand. Of course, above this flag line there was still the overhead resistance of the M-pattern to consider (it doesn't just evaporate), but with the right side of it now more angular shaped, the obstructive potential was no longer that extensive.

If the pattern break entry above bar 11 was deemed a little too aggressive still, bulls were offered a second instance entry just a few minutes later, on the break of bar 12. The entry on this break may have been a few pip higher up, but that hardly mitigated the attraction of the setup: the bullish close of signal bar 12 confirmed the flag breakout, and the entry above it could boast of triple support of the flag line, the 25ema and the round number (no adverse magnets). And with bar 12 added, the 9-12 progression harbored strong features of a W-pattern middle-part. Better not let this one escape also.

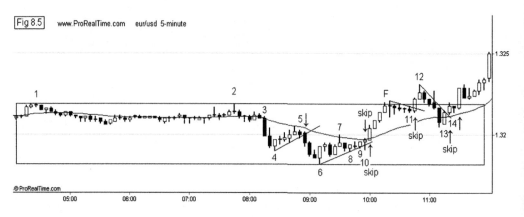

Fig 8.5   www.ProRealTime.com   eur/usd 5-minute

Figure 8.5 Session overview: In the event of a flat Asian session, the volume coming in on the EU Open at 08:00 is likely to break whatever thin range is in place. In most sessions, however, it is the activity between 09:00 and 10:00 (UK Open) that will set a more distinctive tone for the market's direction in the hours ahead.

Points of interest: Despite the UK Open drawing near there was little reason to skip the flag break entry below bar 5. The flag hung harmoniously from its pole 3-4 in a bearish looking market and the entry was guided along by a resistive triple of the 25ema, the round number and the 50 percent retracement of the 3-4 swing. But bears in position would have done well to monitor the UK Open closely for signs of adverse pressure; the blockier it showed up, the more telling its message.

As prices started to stall unpleasantly below the round number (6), there were several ways out of the short. The first was offered in bar 7 when it broke the high of its bullish neighbor (or else a few pip higher up, on the break of the middle-part's high). In the high of bar 7, prices bounced in a bearish triple (ceiling test, round number and 25ema) but we cannot say the bulls were very impressed. If still in the short, the second option was to bail out on the break of mini bar 8; if that break was deemed too meager, the short was a definite scratch on the break of bar 9. And still at zero damage.

Not a good idea would have been to immediately reposition on the bear side when bar 10 dipped below bar 9 (bear-flag break), so as to trade the bull break for failure. Not only was no valid entry provided (no bearish signal bar to short below), there was the adverse magnet of the round number to consider, plus the fact that the first hour of the UK session had shown the bulls quite persistent.

By the same token, it would have been quite aggressive also to have entered *long* on the break of bar 10, so as to trade the bear break for failure in turn. Perhaps the prospect of trapped bears running for cover may have allowed for a quick scalp, the overall conditions were not yet supportive enough to shoot for anything substantial.

If not done so already, a range box may have been plotted as depicted when the market came to attack the former highs of 1 and 2. Note the classic false break trap when prices peeked through this barrier by a mere one or two pip (F). But a bear, too, can get hurt in that very same break, should he have placed a protective stop just outside of the range.

As contrarians laid low for the moment, this formed a flag progression underneath the range barrier (F-11), but way too weak and poorly positioned to trade for continuation (skip the break of bar 11).

Bulls who took a shot at the flag break soon had to pay dearly for their efforts (12-13). But to their companions on the sidelines, this failure offered opportunity. While there are many ways to pick up a tease break pullback, the conservative route is to at least wait for prices to hit upon a technical test of sorts. Since no real support was offered, we can regard the break of bar 13 as too aggressive for our taste. But it is important not to lose track of the action here. Just two bars later combi 14 built up better tension below the barrier, thereby setting up a promising break into the pull of the 50-level above.

Although the range barrier itself wasn't broken yet, position may have been initiated on the break of the inside bar. Perhaps a very conservative bull could have decided to postpone entry until the barrier, or even the high the combi's powerbar was taken out, but such breakout "confirmation" is not *necessarily* beneficial, and in some unfortunate cases may even backfire (after all, if unadjusted, it carries with it a higher stop, and the target lies a bit further out as well).

Figure 8.6 Session overview: Shortly after the UK Open, bulls had broken away from a sideways congestion (pattern break entry above bar 1). Prices headed out nicely, but they never made it to the 00-level above. Always an interesting cue. Slowly but surely the bearish defense on the angular pattern line took on the shape of a head-and-shoulders variant (three arches). While this bore strong signs of an upcoming 50-level retest, few traders will have anticipated the extent of the collapse later on in the session.

   Points of interest: Progression 2-3 possessed double-top characteristics of the M-pattern variety; but not all adverse breaks need to be feared. Especially when going up against a pretty strong pop (1-2), the break of a relatively small middle-part is sooner known to trap traders out of profitable position than to ruin their trades at the stop side. Also, the further away the adverse break from entry, the more chance for prices to recoup before doing any damage. In the case above, consider the potential for triple support should prices have come down to hit the top of the box (25ema, barrier test and a 50/60 percent correction of 1-2).

   Bulls indeed managed to undo the adverse break (they traded it for failure), but still had a hard time forcing the bears out of the way higher up. This formed the series of arches on the pattern line. Note that the last one was a lovely evening-star pattern (4-5-6).

   In strict visual terms, accepting the short below bar 6 would violate the rule of not trading against a trending 25ema. But before we dismiss this offer as invalid too easily, let us assess the situation from a technical perspective first. If we compare the rather fat reversal formation on top of the angular line with the trending pole from which it hung (1-2), we can safely say that we were no longer dealing with a bull-flag situation, or some other type of correction in time. Much more likely, this was a reversal setup. Note also the false high in bar 5. And just look at that fine 50-level magnet. Putting all this together, it is fair to suggest that this was one such situation that called for a little more aggression (enter short below bar 6).

The flag break entry below bar 8 and the pattern break combi below 9 are annotated as skips simply because these breaks were (a) offered in the lows of a range, (b) in 50-level support, and (c) suffered the risk of the 25ema adverse magnet. This is not to imply that we cannot short the bottom of a range, but for this to be granted, we really need to see some solid buildup first (think squeeze). The 7-8 flag did offer some tension, but I believe it is fair to have anticipated some more fighting in the round number area first rather than an immediate break.

Despite these reservations, prices did collapse and with not a bull in sight to stem the decline before the next round number was touched upon. Upon arrival, the bearish momentum instantly subsided, but the buying was done in very modest fashion. This formed a sideways standoff of the bear-flag variety, but *extremely poisonous* to be traded for continuation (skip the break below combi 10).

In a trending market, a pullback reversal in the 25ema is always worthy of consideration. But let us not forget to take into account the requirements of validity. Most preferably, the pullback shows up as an orderly, angular retracement that travels almost reluctantly towards the 25ema. Not only was the near vertical correction 11-12 way too aggressive in appearance, it had broken free from an inverse head-and-shoulders reversal pattern (below the horizontal line). These conditions clearly failed to comply with a *conservative* bet on the turn. Hence the skip below bar 13.

Figure 8.7 Session overview: Halfway the UK morning, bulls had broken away from a box progression (1) but had suffered a hard time capitalizing on the event. Demoralization kicked in when their pattern line was broken below bar 5, which allowed the bears a smooth ride to the 50-level magnet. In the skirmishes that followed (lunch hours 12:00-14:00), bulls had found some footing in the 50-level, but their efforts to trade up were easily fended off in the 25ema. As the pressure remained down, they eventually threw in the towel. The ensuing collapse was a bit over the top, though.

    Points of interest: Take a moment to compare progression 1-6 with progression 1-7 in our previous chart, Figure 8.6. The similarities are quite striking. Upon close inspection, however, we can detect some major differences also. In our current chart, bulls had broken away in bar 1 from buildup that still resided *below* the 25ema. Technically, this stood to attract more contrarian attention than the break in the foregoing chart. Consider also that the 50-level here lay positioned *in line* with the descending average (adverse magnet).

    The break took off nicely regardless, but this hardly changed the conditions at hand. For this reason, the pattern break pullback offer above bar 2 is best left untouched.

    It took about an hour for the bulls to realize that their efforts to bring prices higher were futile. Note how once again a little evening-star pattern set up the break below the angular pattern line (3-4-5). This offered an attractive short into the 50-level magnet.

    There were basically two ways to exit this short manually: either rake in the profits for about 15 pip in the 50-level (resistance exit in the bottom of a range), or exit the position above bar 7 (reversal exit on the break of a small W-pattern middle-part). There is no escaping the fact that a reversal exit always harbors a certain potential for a trap; it is after all a break against the earlier dominant pressure. Depending on the situation, you may at times decide to sit it out in the hopes of a false break turnaround. But before going this route, do realize also that *declining* a reversal exit can backfire with equal prowess; so this is best applied only when the adverse break appears relatively benign, which is a personal call.

If out on the trade, not very prudent would have been to reposition the short below bar 8, so as to trade the little box break for failure. Apart from the fact that the market wasn't trending bearishly enough to warrant such aggression, the break of the box had not yet been proven false at that point.

The false low at 9 depicts a fine example of contrarian response to a *poor* bear break below a round number.

The break below bar 10 was an easy skip also. Not only was this signal bar quite tall in comparison with the surrounding activity (likely to provoke a counterstrike), the entry below it was offered right in the lows of the market, with both the 50-level and the 25ema pulling adversely.

The next break was a tricky one: now prices had broken away from a three-bar combi (10-11), but the situation in the 50-level still looked a bit fishy. True, bears had shown themselves the stronger party on the whole, but we cannot say the bullish defense in the lows was broken in a very distinctive fashion. Again a personal call, hence the optional mark.

Pullback 13-14 was calm and orderly, in relation to the bear rally, but had emerged from a blocky cluster (12-13). That technically invalidated the short below bar 14; the second break, below bar 15, showed prove of bearish persistence, but did not set up as a *conservative* wager either (danger of contrarian opposition in support of the 12-13 block). Tricky also was the pending US Open at 15:30.

Figure 8.8 Session overview: Bearish dominance throughout. All the
bulls could bring to the table in this session was to hammer in a couple
of pullbacks before taking yet another beating. In a newly established
trend, the first retracement to the 25ema is always worthy of attention
(pullback reversal candidate).

Points of interest: Whenever prices travel from one round number
to the next relatively uncontested (1-3), a pullback reversal setup halfway these two levels comes with an added bonus: a favorable magnet.
But before stepping in on the turn too eagerly, let us not forget to gauge
the features of the pullback first. Remember, we do not want to see too
much aggression displayed within the retracement, nor elements of the
blocky kind.

In regard to the latter, I wrapped a small box around the lows of the
first pullback to capture the clustering motion of a little round number
skirmish. As we can see, this pullback started out somewhat blocky,
which could pose a problem for prices on the way back from the turn
later on. But then again, if we follow the 3-5 correction up to its breaking point, it is hard to dismiss the many signs that spoke in favor of
bearish follow-through.

First off, a very decent pattern line had guided prices on the way
up (no debate on its perforation). Second, bar 5 had put in a welcome
technical test with the little hiccup in the earlier downtrend (high of 5
tests low of 2). Third, the correction was a 50 percent retracement of
the dominant bear swing and the first to defy it. Fourth, an evening-
star variant in the top set up the short (4-5-6). The entry below bar 6

was offered slightly above the 25ema, but with the average still trending
this can even be a plus (little risk for an even deeper perforation). And
lastly, there was the 50-level magnet waiting below. All in all, it is fair to
suggest that these bearish elements sufficiently offset the potential for
obstruction within the little box progression.

Bulls may have done their best to extend the correction for as long
as possible, but once the break below bar 6 was set, the bearish dominance quickly reemerged. As prices hit the 50-level, a resistance exit
may have been an option, but strictly seen, there was no reason to intervene since the market was in *trending* mode.

Subsequent pullbacks to the 25ema can reverse equally well as can
their primary counterparts, but on the whole, they are trickier to play.
For example, if we compare the offer below bar 6 with the one below
bar 7, it doesn't take much technical savvy to regard the latter of lesser
quality. Not only stood the 50-level to meddle with the trade, prices had
to dig through the cluster of the second box, whose earlier upside break
had not been proven false at that point (visualize the extension of the
box's top barrier).

Contrarian bulls chose the bear break in bar 8 to initiate a counter
play, which appeared successful at first, but soon faced the triple defense of the round number, the 25ema and the angular pattern line's
extension. One bar later, this set up a short below bar 9, but still quite
unpleasant to accept. If you place your thumb on the chart to block the
follow-up action from view, maybe you can imagine more easily that it
wouldn't have taken much of an adverse thrust to have shaken out the
short above signal bar 9, if only to put in another test with the 50-level
above.

Do keep in mind that the entry and exit suggestions in this guide are
deliberately meant to reflect the *conservative* approach. The reader can
always explore for himself a more aggressive style of trading that better suits his personality and appetite for risk. But all students are well
advised not to start these practices in the live market when not yet fully
confident trading conservatively first.

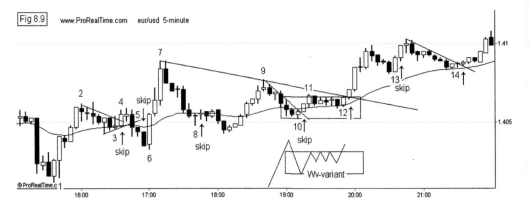

Figure 8.9 Session overview: A sudden burst of pressure that swings prices from one side of the average to the other is best met with a healthy dose of suspicion (1-2). Whatever causes such response, always anticipate that it takes time for a market to absorb and accept a "new" situation. This generally translates into a reduced potential for follow-through, even on the otherwise highly acceptable continuation setups, like a first pullback reversal or a flag break of sorts. And not unimportant either, plenty of contrarians will be happy to take the other side of such a breakout contract.

Points of interest: Flag progression 2-3 may have hung bullishly from its pole 1-2, the breakout in bar 4 (or above it) was a poisonous one, to be avoided at all cost. The main reason is found in the starting point of the flagpole. Swinging aggressively up from well below the 25ema, this bullish charge clearly was in disrespect of the foregoing pressure (bull swing starting from a bear low). This doesn't take away from the bullish feat itself, but it does tend to compromise the continuation prospects. Even if the 3-4 bull-flag had set up in a better technical fashion, that would hardly have improved the odds for follow-through on its break.

Poor odds on a break in one direction do not necessarily imply high odds on a break in the other. Trading breaks for failure is a practice best applied in trending conditions with the overall consensus visibly lined up in favor of the trade. For example, shorting below the double-bar lows of combi 5 would have been in complete disregard of the strong bull swing 1-2. As was the case with the bull break, this break on the bear side stood to invite contrarian aggression also, if not immediately, then possibly somewhere halfway that flagpole (6). In other words, even though we may not hold its *continuation prospect* in high esteem, we do have to pay our respects to the strength of the flagpole itself, and thus not trade against it.

The aggressive bull swing 6-7 was yet another poorly built up thrust through bearish defense, which basically rendered the pullback 7-8 un-suitable to be traded for continuation. On top of that, the entry above bar 8 was vulnerable to the pull of the 50-level magnet below it. Not much later, the 9-10 pullback invited similar concerns. Just skip these weak offers.

Although the market was essentially in ranging mode, bulls were in control throughout, buying every higher low in sight; but we cannot say they built up well towards their breaks. From where we stand, things finally got interesting when progression 10-12 showed up as part of a Ww-variant (Vw if you wish), which contained a textbook squeeze in the smaller w-part (11-12). Pleasant also was to see the breakout coincide with the perforation of the angular pattern line coming down from ear-lier highs. Finally a high-odds setup.

The flag break offer above bar 13 is of course an easy skip (entry way too far removed from the base of the 25ema); but how about the break above combi 14? Apart from the fact that it was rather late in the US session, which "closes" at 22:00 CET, and that the bars were already getting very thin and nondescript, this offer set up relatively well as a pullback reversal. The pullback did contain a little blocky element in the highs (sideways action just below the 00-level), but not too trouble-some to fully disqualify the setup in the trending average. In the light of the dwindling activity, however, an option could be to skip the offer anyway, or maybe accept it with the intention to cash in the profits in the 00-level and be done for the day.

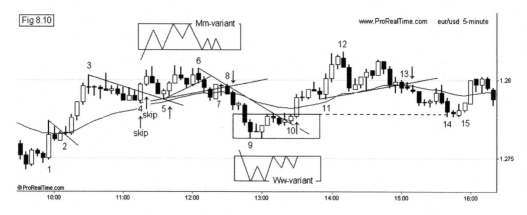

Figure 8.10 Session overview: Few charts better illustrate what is meant by round number resilience. The bulk of this session was all about the bull attacks on 1.28. It is always interesting to see how a major round number can be breached multiple times but hold up nonetheless. In sessions like this, patience truly is a virtue, but so is staying alert. At some point demoralization is bound to kick in and this could set the wheels in motion for a double-pressure event.

Points of interest: Telling by the slope of the 25ema on the far left, the UK Open had brought prices down to the 50-level, from where they were eagerly run up all the way to the round number above (1-3). But as we know, this kind of development does not sit well with immediate continuation. Both flag break entries, *in* bar 4 and above it, were of poor quality anyway (far removed from the 25ema magnet).

The pattern break pullback offer above bar 5 indicated bullish persistence, but this is one such wager best accepted only if manual intervention is part of operating tactics. Should prices start to falter in the round number again, this could induce a serious wave of selling. Thus, by intending to scratch the trade if necessary, a bull could possibly save himself a *full* stop-out. Put differently, when pondering on whether to accept an offer of somewhat lesser quality, flexibility in exit technique can have a say in things. If the trade was accepted, a reversal exit became applicable below bar 6 (M-pattern middle-part break in round number resistance).

Progression 4-8 represents an Mm-variant, a pattern known to harbor even stronger reversal implications than an M-pattern alone. Here it clearly bore evidence of the bulls' failure to crack the round number defense; how could this not have a demoralizing effect.

Bulls who still believed in a comeback from below the round number would have done well not to dismiss the way their combi 7 was countered in bar 8. With this skirmish taking place below a pattern line as well, things certainly didn't look *up*. Technically this set up a great short, but there is a little catch: to get to target, prices had to go up against the earlier bull swing 1-3. Since this rally was the most notable swing in the chart so far, plenty of bulls may still have been lying in wait for a 50 percent correction. For this reason, the short below bar 8 qualifies as a resistance exit candidate. An option here could be to cash in as soon as bar 9 hit upon the highs of the hiccup at 2, or thereabouts, a little shy of 20 pip.

It took bull parties about forty minutes to create a very interesting reversal pattern from which to launch another upside attack: the Ww-variant in the box around 13:00.

The break above bar 10 set up from below a falling 25ema, but this was more a consequence of the substantial pullback rather than bearish pressure on the whole. Certainly a pleasant bonus here was the favorable round number magnet about 25 pip out.

The 10-12 bull swing marched straight through former highs, but as soon as its momentum petered out, bears simply continued their favorite practice of the day: trapping bulls above the round number. And as was the case earlier on, this eventually led to another Mm-pattern (11-13). A short away from this pattern, however, would now oppose the 10-12 bull swing, with resistance lurking in the box top extension (dotted line). Therefore, the offer below combi 13 is best accepted with a resistance exit in mind (14).

Not much later, progression 14-15 sent out a pretty strong hint that bulls were planning yet another round number attack (small W-pattern middle-part following the US Open at 15:30). If still in position, a bear could deploy a reversal exit on the break of bar 15.

Figure 8.11 Session overview: Rallies that run for 100 pip or more within the space of a few hours are usually not a result of your typical intraday skirmishes. More likely, they are caused by an external catalyst and if they are not countered within the first 60 minutes or so, chances are they will just continue on their march, or else trail out the session more or less flatly. Understandably, when not in on these surges from the start, conservative players may have little alternative but to idly watch from the sidelines how others feast away on the event. Therefore, we can imagine plenty of bulls to have felt the sweet tingle of hope when finally a correction set in with still some hours to go in the US session.

Points of interest: Ironically, the more parties lying in wait to trade a pullback reversal, the less likely the actual turning point will set itself up in nondebatable fashion. Not uncommonly, culprit number one is the fear of missing out, which is known to trick traders into abandoning their natural caution and pick their entries all over the place. But this can come with quick regret should the anticipated turn fail to materialize. And as these early-bird traders watch in horror how their tight stops get triggered one after the other, this will make it all the more interesting to those still waiting on the sidelines. Should prices then start to stall second time around, this is much more likely to set up a turn in "dependable" fashion (second break principle).

Pullback 3-5 had retraced about 40 percent of the trending pole (counting from the flag breakout at 1), which was quite a substantial bounce considering the extent of bullish dominance. The length of a

234

pullback, however, is always inferior to its nature of appearance. The more aggressive the pullback (take note of powerbar 4), the less likely a mere one-bar reversal setup (bar 5) would do as a valid signal bar. Of course, not all traders will play their turns with a tiny 10 pip stop, but that doesn't release them from picking their entries with attention for detail. Those who traded long above bar 5 with a protective stop below that same bar may have miraculously survived the immediate contrarian charge, but that doesn't take away from the fact that they took great risk on entry. It certainly wasn't unlikely here for prices to test the high of bar 2 in the box on the left. Why not wait for a little more buildup to set up the trade properly.

Progression 5-6 (morning-star variant) set up a second break entry in the turn, but still not an offer to accept. At that point, even an otherwise relatively harmless touch on the 25ema would already have jeopardized our stop, let alone a test of the 50-level magnet a few pip further south.

Ultimately, it took the market seven bars in the base of the 25ema to set up a valid combi long at 7. Although we cannot tell with certainty, it seems likely that the low of bar 8 had put in the test with the average *first* (and thus a false low with its neighbor) before triggering the entry above combi 7. This is of course the preferable order, but with the buildup now solid and the market still very strong, the trade may have been accepted the other way around as well. (Granted, with perhaps a bit of slippage on entry, the touch on the average *afterwards* may very well have shaken us out—such mishap is all part and parcel of trading with tight stops.)

By the way, the inside bar of combi 7 showed a bearish body, which isn't preferable in a bullish combi setup, but it was still attractively positioned in the higher part of its bullish neighbor; pleasant also was to see both bars share equal highs, which set up a double-bar break.

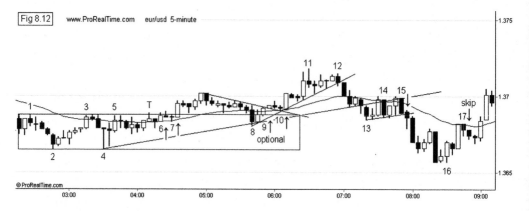

Figure 8.12 Session overview: Halfway a bearish Asian session, bulls had broken free from a Ww-box (1-6), but soon met with round number opposition. After being forced to retreat on first go, they built up towards another attack, from which they emerged with a little more to show for it (10-11). But by the time the EU Opening bell rang at 08:00, all their efforts had been fully undone and they even found themselves busy fighting off the implications of a bear-flag progression (13-15). Such can be the fickle nature of victory.

Points of interest: Just like the pullback to a trend needs to have a certain slope and span in order to build up consensus on the turn, so too does the smaller *w* need to relate harmoniously with the bigger *W* to increase the chances of a successful Ww-breakout. Since this is never a matter of absolutes, there is perhaps a certain "feel" involved, but nothing a little patience can't solve. For example, at the moment prices broke away in bar T (tease), the smaller *w* (5-T) still hung rather thinly next to its bigger *W* brother (1-5). But when bar 6 showed up, the two extra bars had built up the tension more harmoniously. If for some reason the break above bar 6 was declined, there was another chance to hop on, on the break of bar 7.

Even though the box breakout may have been tradable, we can tell by the slope of the average on the far left that the Ww-pattern had only just begun to defy the bearish dominance. This meant that the conditions were not optimal in regard to the bull-side potential. Also, in situations like this, it is very common for the round number to initially work as a favorable magnet, only to then turn upon the trade. In view of such potential obstruction, an idea could be to accept these type of wagers only if the reversal exit is part of operating tactics. Should prices start to falter, manual intervention *could* then save the trade from incurring more damage than necessary.

In this particular instance, it may have been an option to have scratched the trade as soon as bar 8 re-entered the box extension, but let us just assume to have been shaken out in the low of bar 8. The follow-up action illustrates how important it is for a trader to accept his mishaps as a cost of business and always remain on the alert for another try (without any need for vindication!). Possible re-entries may have been deployed either above bar 9, or on the pattern break pullback variant above bar 10.

If the 20 pip target hadn't been met in the high of bar 11, a sharp reversal exit below bar 12 would have been a valid call, in avoidance of the 00-level adverse magnet (M-pattern middle-part reversal, coinciding with an angular line perforation).

As bears took over, bulls were forced to retreat and this had prices falling below the round number and the 25ema again. And they even fell below a pattern line extension coming up from the earlier lows of 4 and 8. In anticipation of the EU Open, a bear-flag appeared, hanging ominously from the pole 12-13.

Bar 14 wasn't broken on the bear side, but it wasn't a great signal bar anyway; next to being relatively tall, there was no harmony yet in the flag and flagpole relation. Bar 15 may have shown a similar tall span, but with three more bars added to the flag, at least the issue of harmony was solved. Also, the progression now showed more bearish persistence in the squeeze and it is fair to suggest that the short below bar 15 was a valid call. Should this trade not yet have reached target on arrival in the former lows of 2 and 4 (extension of the *bottom* barrier of the box), a resistance exit in that level may have been an option (ranging market).

Pullback 16-17 showed too much aggression to have accepted the weak one-bar reversal entry below bar 17; and it is advised not to trade for immediate continuation in the lows of a range anyway.

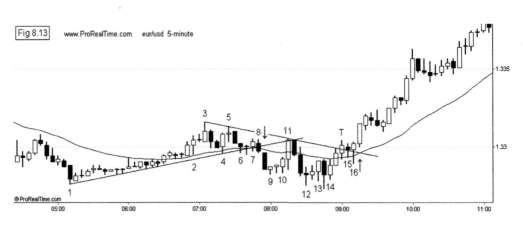

Fig 8.13   www.ProRealTime.com   eur/usd 5-minute

Figure 8.13 Session overview: This chart nicely demonstrates the difference in volatility between the often lackluster Asian hours and the more voluminous activity of the EU morning starting at 08:00, generally referred to as the UK session from 09:00 on. But as we can see also, increased volatility doesn't necessarily equal clarity on the market's next intentions. But nothing is ever lost on the attentive observer. Therefore, rather than labeling the activity between 08:00 and 09:00 here as a useless blob of price action, let's find out if we somehow could have seen the shift in pressure coming.

Points of interest: In the early hours of the Asian market, bears were in control but they were unable to keep the pressure going. This provoked a slow but steady pullback, which very typically set course to the broken round number (1-2). Bulls had even managed to bring prices above it, but then met with serious opposition.

In the skirmishes that followed, a bearish M-pattern took shape (2-6) in support of the round number and the ascending pattern line coming up from the Asian low. The 6-7 follow-up shows the bullish efforts to undo the implications, but alas, the conditions spoke in favor of the bears. By the time bar 8 closed bearishly below the pattern line, the M-pattern had turned into its more dangerous cousin, the Mm-pattern (2-8). Since the pressures clearly pointed south, bar 8 qualified as a signal bar for sell-side purposes.

The first few bars in the EU Open were printed bullishly (9-10) and featured signs of a mini W-pattern middle-part. This may have been reason to exit the short on the break of bar 10, but we cannot blame a bear for sticking it out in the hopes of a favorable triple coming to the rescue (25ema, round number and breakout test).

If still in position, it's hard to tell whether or not our stop was taken out in the high of bar 11. Indeed, the line between a winning and a losing wager can be extremely thin; and the difference in balance can be no less than 30 pip (minus 10 versus plus 20). When counting results by the session or even by the trade, as many traders tend to do, this can have a disturbing impact when currently on the losing side of the equation. Yet on a monthly basis, good and bad fortune will surely balance out more evenly; anxiously keeping track of the account status in midsession is a pointless practice.

If not shaken out, but not on target either in the low of bar 12, our short once again faced the troubling implications of a reversal block (12-13). Since this indicated bullish resilience second time around, a reversal exit could have been deployed on the break of bar 13. If still in on the short, the next two bars fattened up the adverse middle-part even more, and this definitely called for an exit above bar 14. All this isn't rocket science. It is just a matter of gauging pressure.

The first bar of the UK session (T) enthusiastically perforated the overhanging pattern line coming down from earlier highs, but this breakout clearly fell into the category of the tease break variety. But as prices moved back a little, they were quickly supported by the 12-14 block. This technically set up a combi pattern breakout (T-15), but still lacking substance in this tricky round number environment.

One bar later, patient bulls were offered a much better setup that met all the requirements of a high-odds play. Before posing as a signal bar, powerbar 16 had put in a false low with bar 15, and this was also a 50 percent retracement of the latest bull swing 14-T. Granted, the double-pressure response to the break of bar 16 may have been totally over the top, but the fat 08:00-09:00 buildup most certainly justified a 20 pip target in the generally voluminous environment of the early UK session.

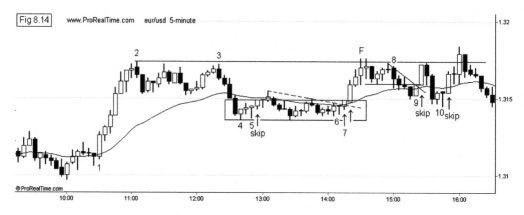

Figure 8.14 Session overview: Let's conclude our recap series with another fine example of what a little patience can do for your bottom line. It also shows the impact a brief bout of one-sided aggression can have on the rest of the session (1-2). Once this bull swing was put in, with not a bear in sight, all the market did, or could do, was range between the high and the halfway mark of it.

Points of interest: Even well before anything tradable shows up, we can usually form ourselves a pretty good idea on the themes of the upcoming battles. For example, we have witnessed time and time again that when a round number gets broken without any sign of protest, it will remain a strong magnet for as long as it hasn't been tested back. Another thing we can almost be sure of is that when a pullback comes to challenge a trending move, plenty of parties will aim to pick up position around the halfway mark. We also have seen many a double-pressure pop originate from a solidly built up pullback reversal. Of course, countless participants will have observed similar tendencies, and their focus, like ours, will be on anticipating these events as well. This is essentially what creates the climate for the abundant repetitive ways of the market.

All this "knowledge" is nice, of course, but it is crucial not to let any of it lead to feelings of bias or premature acting. Sure, a pullback will probably come to visit the magnet and chances are the subsequent turn will be bought; but we have no way of knowing how exactly these things will play out in the session at hand. One of the major traps of price technical repetition is that it may lead a trader to believe that all of it can be predicted. It can't. It can only be anticipated. On the good side, when

240

we have at our service the best possible guide we could ever wish for, the market itself, there is no need for a crystal ball to come out ahead.

In the lows of the first decent pullback, the three-bar combi 4-5 may have been strategically placed about halfway the 1-2 bull swing, but it was too weak a setup to oppose the rather prominent M-pattern residing overhead (2-3). With such solid obstruction blocking the path, the situation simply called for more buildup. This is basically a variation on the harmony theme, and I can only hope it makes sense.

In this respect, the 4-7 block, a W-pattern middle-part hanging below the 50-level, built up the tension in much better fashion. In fact, one could hardly wish for a better setup: (a) its horizontal span now had sufficient body to counter the bearish M-pattern overhead; (b) it was a Ww-variant; (c) the box resided in the 50 percent region of the foregoing bull swing; (d) the entry above it suffered no adverse magnets; (e) should prices at some point after the break have come back to test the breakout, they stood to bounce favorably right on the 50-level support, coinciding with the top of the box.

There were two ways to have taken position on the box breakout: either enter on the break of combi 6 (little aggressive still), or one bar later, above bar 7, when the box barrier was visibly broken.

A 20 pip target will have been reached before the highs of 2 and 3 were met; should this level have fallen shy, a resistance exit will have been a valid call. When the earlier highs indeed proved obstructive (note the classic false break trap at F), the market went about printing yet another M-pattern middle-part (F-8).

Should we have traded the bear break for failure, above bar 9? It is an easy skip, since it isn't wise to resort to these tactics when the market is no longer in trending mode (despite the bullish dominance, the market was ranging for over four hours). The break above combi 10 is an easy skip as well. There was just too much resistance to overcome for this to represent a high-odds play.

Part 2

Evaluation and
Management

Chapter 9

Consecutive Intraday Charts

In Part 1 of our studies we have covered the essentials of price action on a wide array of educational charts. Like cardiologists, we opened up the chest of the 5-minute frame, cut through the tissue, pushed aside the ribs and laid bare the mechanics of its wondrous beating heart. As we dug in further, we learned all about price action principles and the telling messages within. As our journey went on, we picked up valuable lessons on strategy and tactics, and slowly came to see how all these findings can be molded into a viable plan of attack. Nonetheless, as much as all this can make perfect sense from the safety of the drawing board, a vital question still remains: how does price action trading hold up in practice?

While no guide could ever begin to describe the true essence of what it means to trade live, let alone explain the many pitfalls and emotional challenges a trader will surely come to face in battle, this second part of the book is put in to at least give the student a fair view on the *continuity* aspect of price technical repetition. It can of course be argued whether six months of consecutive intraday sessions sufficiently mitigates the element of cherry-picked material, but there is a limit to what a trading book can do. If nothing else, this unique series of close to 400 charts will furnish the price action student with a massive database of annotated intraday activity.

Before we dig in, allow me to point out some basic details regarding this series. First of all, since the eur/usd instrument is traded most actively in the EU/UK session and the so-called UK/US overlap (the US morning session), it is chosen to have the charts reflect this more or less 10-hour window. This means that, in Central European time (CET), the trading opportunities are picked up from the EU Open at 08:00 to about the close of the London session at 18:00. However, the bulk of the preceding Asian session is incorporated also in order to make a technical assessment of the EU and UK Open possible.

While our studies are all done on the eur/usd 5-minute, do recall that we used this instrument solely as a platform for price action analysis; all is applicable to any market and time frame of choice. Of course, it will certainly pay to always study the instruments and time frames of your liking with appropriate attention for their personal characteristics, and particularly in regard to the time zones in which you wish to trade them. As to the latter, the eur/usd pair may very well offer decent opportunities outside the hours mentioned (think Asian Open), but in order to optimize the educational value within the available space, it is chosen to focus on the instrument's most active stretch. On a 24-hour time axis, the hours in CET can more or less be divided as follows:

00:00-08:00: Asian session.
08:00-09:00: EU Open.
09:00-10:00: UK Open.
12:00-14:00: EU/UK Lunch Hours.
15:30-18:00: UK/US overlap.
18:00-20:00: US Lunch Hours.
20:00-22:00: End of US session.

For the purpose of clarity, the daily sessions in the coming series are divided into three charts each (with sufficient overlap), starting at the top of a page, ending at the bottom. So each new page represents a new trading day. On six months, this will amount to 132 trading days in total.

Since we have already discussed the price action concepts and trading techniques most extensively in earlier chapters, chart explanations are kept to a minimum and are done in annotated format. To point out

entry and exit specifics and some patterns of interest, the following ab-
breviations are used:

pb: pattern break

pbp: pattern break pullback

pbc: pattern break combi

pr: pullback reversal

tff: trade-for-failure

@: entry somewhat aggressive

Res. exit: resistance exit

Rev. exit: reversal exit

F: false break

T: tease Break

W: W-pattern middle-part

M: M-pattern middle-part

Ww: Ww-pattern variant

Mm: Mm-pattern variant

SHS: head-and-shoulders variant

The series will run from March through August 2012 and basically follows up on the chart examples used in Part 1, which were all taken from
a handful of months prior to March.

How to view and study these charts is up to the reader, but my advice would be not to concentrate too much on the extent of profits to be
reaped from these historical sessions. It's all in the past. These charts
serve their best purpose when seen as a thick package of price technical
information with which to strengthen your grasp of pressure, buildup,
conditions and tactics. While the trade suggestions are offered from the
perspective of a 20/10 bracket, do not let this keep you from exploring
alternative settings that may better suit your personal trading style or
management ideas.

Furthermore, since the only horizontal markings in the charts are
the round number levels of 00 and 50, on occasion it may not be so
evident whether a specific trade reached its designated target or fell
a little shy. Or whether a stop was taken out in an adverse thrust or

miraculously survived. Do not let this disturb you in any way. As addressed earlier on, good and bad fortune on any individual wager may have quite an impact on a single session result, but will balance out more or less evenly in the long run.

Note: These six months of intraday charts should give a decent impression of average volatility per session in a "normally active" environment, but it still represents a small window of price technical conditions that may not match up with the nature of the present-day environment. Always a common theme in currency land is to see a session go relatively flat in anticipation of a news report and then go haywire the moment the numbers are released, only to go flat again soon after; rarely a week goes by without at least one such stale session printed. From time to time, however, these conditions can persist for weeks or even months on end. Whereas some strategies may thrive pleasantly in a slower climate (think contrarian), breakout traders generally fare less well when volatility and follow-through are minimal. This could call for periodic adjustments. Obviously, one way to adapt is to shoot for smaller targets. But quite popular also is to switch over to a faster intraday frame. In Chapter 11 we will have a close look at how this can be done in a most effective manner.

Another excellent remedy with which to counter the issue of a less compliant environment is not necessarily to adjust the plan of attack, but to simply trade more markets simultaneously, and to be very selective on each. Three or four markets will usually do. (Tip: an easy way to add an extra monitor to your home setup is to hook it up via a graphic adapter in the USB port, rather than replacing the standard dual-head card with an expensive triple or four-head card.)

To see the benefits of a multiple-market approach, here's a quick preview on some accounting principles to be discussed in Chapter 10. When adhering to a ratio between risk and reward of 1:2, a winning trade will add 2 "points" and a non-scratch loss will take off 1; should an intermediate trader score an average of, say, a full winner, a full loser and a half loser a day, this will amount to about 10 points profit per month (a 0.5 point per day times 20 trading days). If this prospect does not seem too unreasonable, consider also the following. When increasing unit size on a weekly basis, as will be explained in detail, any account will grow tenfold within the year on 10 points profit per month—provided this hypothetical consistency is maintained on an average of 2.5 points per week, and by risking 2 percent of capital per trade. But of course it is totally irrelevant from what market(s) these 10 points are gathered. On four markets it needs an average score of just 2.5 points per market per month to get the job done. Seen in this light, it's hard not to praise the virtues of trading three or four markets simultaneously, and especially so in a stale environment with fewer opportunities on the whole.

The reflection above is not meant to trap the price action student into silly fantasies of points per months and future riches, it mainly serves to stress the importance of always looking at trading from the viewpoint of the bigger picture, or at least from a monthly perspective. Obsessively focusing on raking in a certain profit per day or even per week can only lead to stress and anxiety and that seldom does a trader any good.

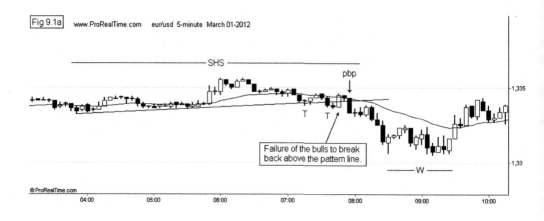

Fig 9.1a   www.ProRealTime.com   eur/usd 5-minute March 01-2012

SHS

pbp

Failure of the bulls to break back above the pattern line.

W

1,335
1,33

04:00   05:00   06:00   07:00   08:00   09:00   10:00

© ProRealTime.com

Fig 9.1b

tall signal bar

M

@
pb

Rev. exit

W

Res.exit in ceiling test missed by a few pip.

1,335
1,33

08:00   09:00   10:00   11:00   12:00   13:00   14:00

© ProRealTime.com

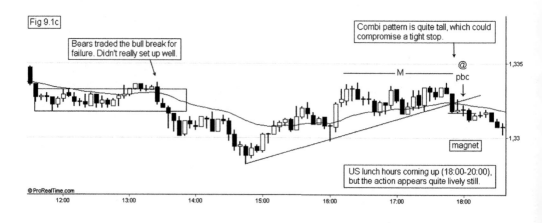

Fig 9.1c

Combi pattern is quite tall, which could compromise a tight stop.

Bears traded the bull break for failure. Didn't really set up well.

M

@
pbc

magnet

US lunch hours coming up (18:00-20:00), but the action appears quite lively still.

1,335
1,33

12:00   13:00   14:00   15:00   16:00   17:00   18:00

© ProRealTime.com

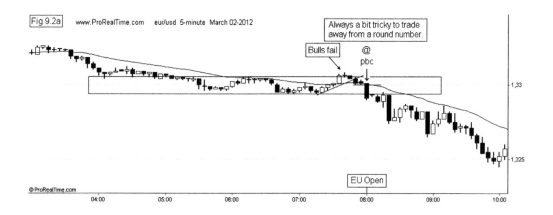

Fig 9.2a   www.ProRealTime.com   eur/usd 5-minute March 02-2012

Always a bit tricky to trade
away from a round number.

Bulls fail

@
pbc

1,33

EU Open

1,325

© ProRealTime.com

04:00   05:00   06:00   07:00   08:00   09:00   10:00

Fig 9.2b

1,33

Bear trend remains intact.

false highs   pr / tff

@
pr

1,325

© ProRealTime.com

08:00   09:00   10:00   11:00   12:00   13:00   14:00

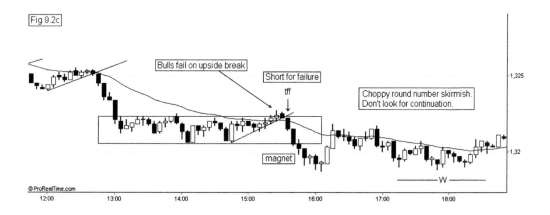

Fig 9.2c

1,325

Bulls fail on upside break

Short for failure

tff

Choppy round number skirmish.
Don't look for continuation.

magnet

1,32

——— W ———

© ProRealTime.com

12:00   13:00   14:00   15:00   16:00   17:00   18:00

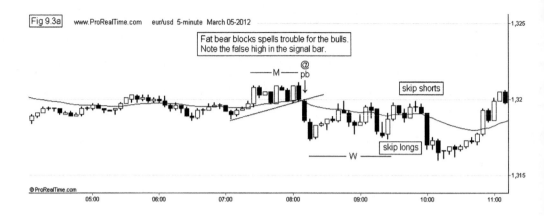

Fig 9.3a www.ProRealTime.com eur/usd 5-minute March 05-2012

Fat bear blocks spells trouble for the bulls.
Note the false high in the signal bar.

M — pb

skip shorts

skip longs

W

@ ProRealTime.com

Fig 9.3b

No entry provided
(bearish signal bar)

Ww

false low

Bulls hold up well, which could
portend another 00-level visit,

@ ProRealTime.com

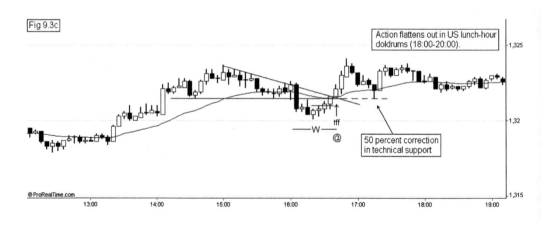

Fig 9.3c

Action flattens out in US lunch-hour
doldrums (18:00-20:00).

W

tff

@

50 percent correction
in technical support

@ ProRealTime.com

Fig 9.4a   www.ProRealTime.com   eur/usd 5-minute March 06-2012

If not already on target, this could serve as a reversal exit, but of the weaker kind. (W-middle-part not strongly established.

Second bear break confirms failure of the bulls to reach 00 level.

Multiple arches on pattern line

Fig 9.4b

Double evening-star M-pattern. Strong bearish implications.

Res. exit in low of range.

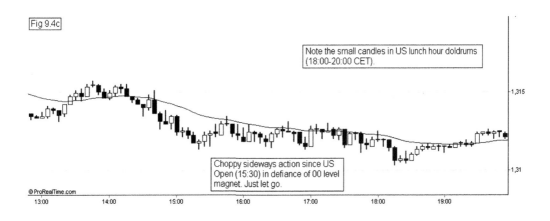

Fig 9.4c

Note the small candles in US lunch hour doldrums (18:00-20:00 CET).

Choppy sideways action since US Open (15:30) in defiance of 00 level magnet. Just let go.

253

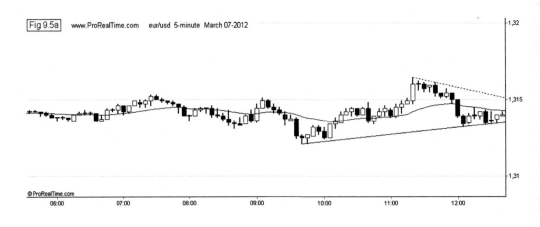

Fig 9.5a   www.ProRealTime.com   eur/usd 5-minute March 07-2012

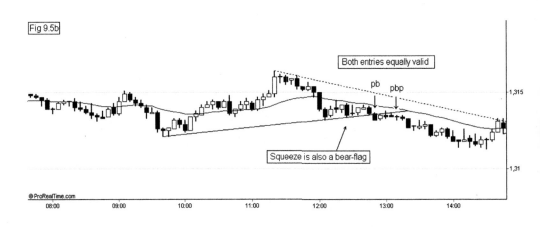

Fig 9.5b

Both entries equally valid

pb   pbp

Squeeze is also a bear-flag

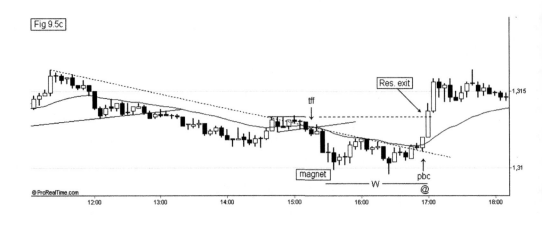

Fig 9.5c

Res. exit

tff

magnet

W

pbc

@

Fig 9.6a   www.ProRealTime.com   eur/usd 5-minute March 08-2012

Bulls manage to keep the pressure up.

SHS   pb

T

T

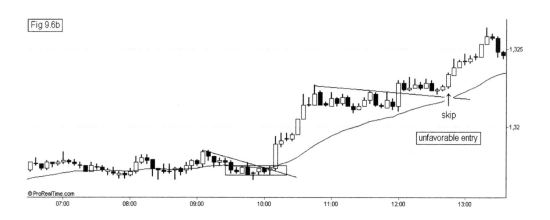

Fig 9.6b

skip

unfavorable entry

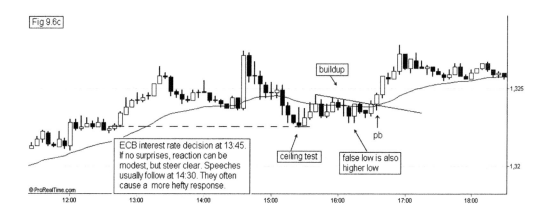

Fig 9.6c

buildup

ECB interest rate decision at 13:45.
If no surprises, reaction can be
modest, but steer clear. Speeches
usually follow at 14:30. They often
cause a more hefty response.

ceiling test

false low is also
higher low

pb

255

Fig 9.7a   www.ProRealTime.com   eur/usd 5-minute March 09-2012

Asian breaks

false high

pb / pr

bear-flag

W

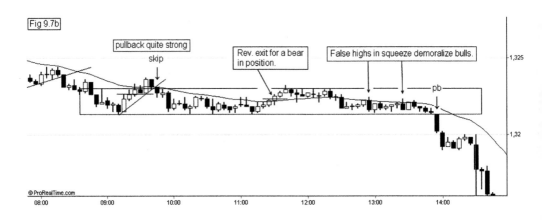

Fig 9.7b

pullback quite strong

skip

Rev. exit for a bear in position.

False highs in squeeze demoralize bulls.

pb

Fig 9.7c

Let go

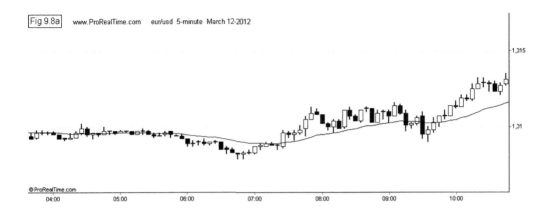

Fig 9.8a   www.ProRealTime.com   eur/usd 5-minute March 12-2012

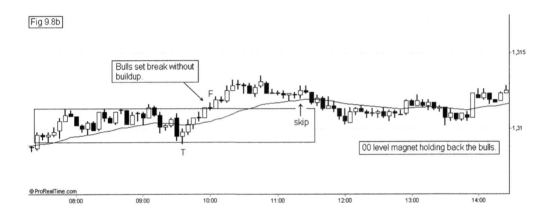

Fig 9.8b

Bulls set break without buildup.

F

skip

T

00 level magnet holding back the bulls.

Fig 9.8c

debatable barrier

magnet

F   T

squeeze   pb

T

Fig 9.9a   www.ProRealTime.com   eur/usd 5-minute March 13-2012

bear-flag

M   pb / tff

magnet

Fig 9.9b

this was not a signal bar

pbc

EU news at
11:00 CET

Fig 9.9c

Third bear-flag fails

Fig 9.10a   www.ProRealTime.com   eur/usd 5-minute March 14-2012

Tall signal bar perforates
debatable barrier.

skip

Adverse magnet plus
poor conditions.

skip

Bulls build up a block below 50 level

Fig 9.10b

Do not short for continuation.
Market is ranging and the 50
level is likely to obstruct passage.

skip

Fig 9.10c

skip

Pullback too strong

skip

W

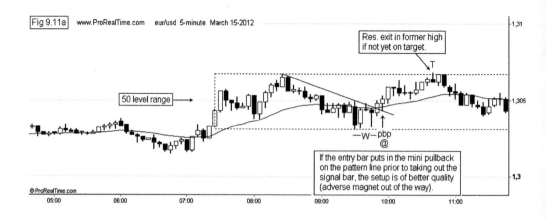

Fig 9.11a   www.ProRealTime.com   eur/usd 5-minute March 15-2012

Res. exit in former high
if not yet on target.

50 level range →

If the entry bar puts in the mini pullback
on the pattern line prior to taking out the
signal bar, the setup is of better quality
(adverse magnet out of the way).

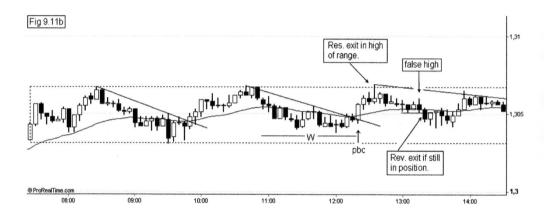

Fig 9.11b

Res. exit in high
of range.

false high

Rev. exit if still
in position.

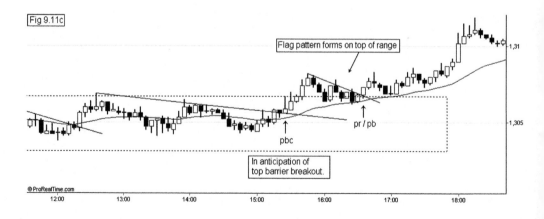

Fig 9.11c

Flag pattern forms on top of range

In anticipation of
top barrier breakout.

Fig 9.12a   www.ProRealTime.com   eur/usd 5-minute March 16-2012

Sometimes it's hard to tell the difference between a reversal block (middle-part) and a flag pattern. There is no escaping the occasional rev. exit trap.

pb / pr   pbp   rev. exits   skip

magnet

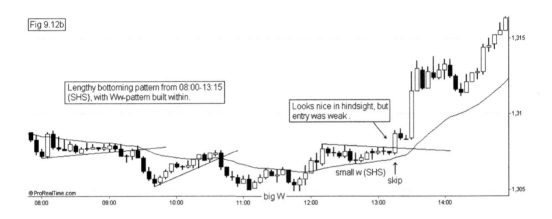

Fig 9.12b

Lengthy bottoming pattern from 08:00-13:15 (SHS), with Ww-pattern built within.

Looks nice in hindsight, but entry was weak.

small w (SHS)   skip

big W

Fig 9.12c

another SHS variant

skip

Strictly seen, this is a long setup, but it is very high up in the rally and the pullback correction is very shallow. Also, the bear block to the left needs to be cleared (traded for failure) and the US lunch hour doldrums are coming up (around 18:00). Good reasons to lay low on this long offer.

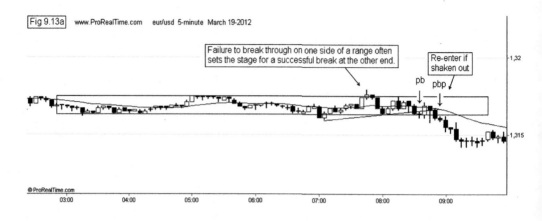

Fig 9.13a   www.ProRealTime.com   eur/usd 5-minute March 19-2012

Failure to break through on one side of a range often sets the stage for a successful break at the other end.

Re-enter if shaken out

pb pbp

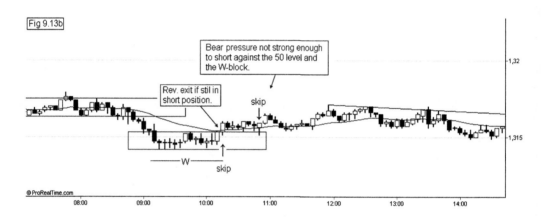

Fig 9.13b

Bear pressure not strong enough to short against the 50 level and the W-block.

Rev. exit if stil in short position.

skip

W

skip

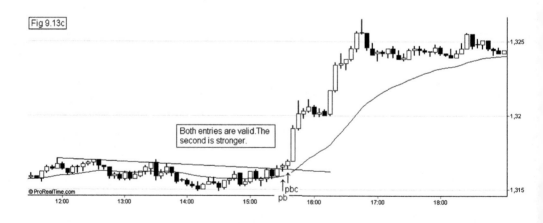

Fig 9.13c

Both entries are valid.The second is stronger.

pbc

pb

Fig 9.14a   www.ProRealTime.com   eur/usd 5-minute March 20-2012

ceiling test level

skip

F

Weak pullback. Adverse magnet of 25ema and possible ceiling test

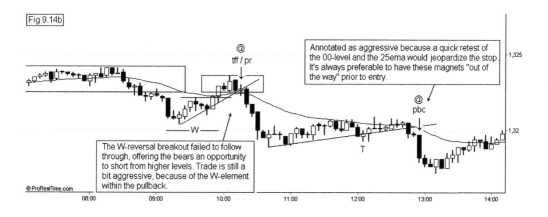

Fig 9.14b

@ tff / pr

Annotated as aggressive because a quick retest of the 00-level and the 25ema would jeopardize the stop. It's always preferable to have these magnets "out of the way" prior to entry.

@ pbc

W

T

The W-reversal breakout failed to follow through, offering the bears an opportunity to short from higher levels. Trade is still a bit aggressive, because of the W-element within the pullback.

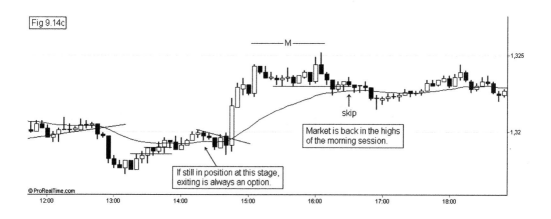

Fig 9.14c

M

skip

Market is back in the highs of the morning session.

If still in position at this stage, exiting is always an option.

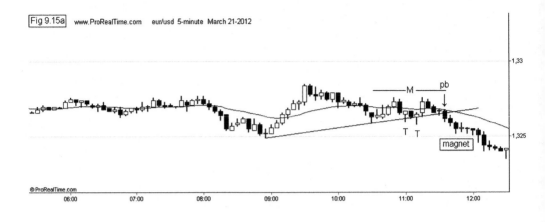

Fig 9.15a   www.ProRealTime.com   eur/usd 5-minute March 21-2012

Fig 9.15b

Very aggressive short because the entry is nearing the lows of the bear-flag and the 25ema is not really helping out. The ceiling test level (little horizontal line) could start to pull adversely as well. The 1.32 level is a favorable magnet, though.

Fig 9.15c

Do not short for failure.

Bull swing too strong

264

Fig 9.16a   www.ProRealTime.com   eur/usd   5-minute   March 22-2012

Bull break failed

Re-break failed also

@ pbp

T T

Entry quite far removed from pattern line.

Fig 9.16b

Annotated as aggressive because it counters the tall bullish powerbar. However, with the trend un-mistakably bearish, a little aggression may be called for.

@ tff

powerbar

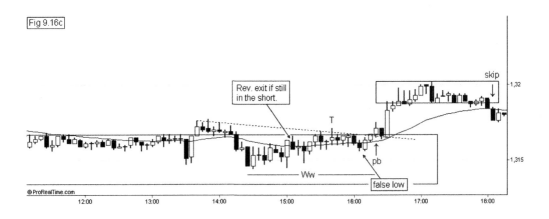

Fig 9.16c

Rev. exit if still in the short.

skip

T

Ww

pb

false low

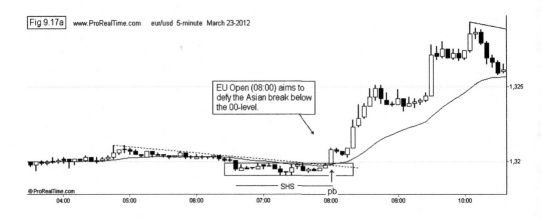

Fig 9.17a   www.ProRealTime.com   eur/usd 5-minute March 23-2012

EU Open (08:00) aims to defy the Asian break below the 00-level.

SHS

pb

Fig 9.17b

evening-star

Res. exit in ceiling test for a bull still in position.

skip

Too aggressive from where we stand.

skip

W

pb

W-pattern middle-part in 50 percent retracement of the opening bull rally.

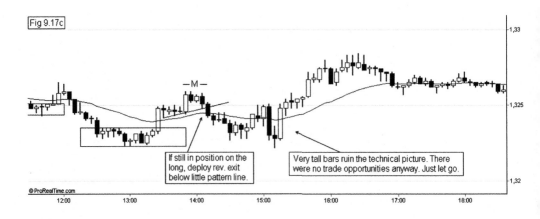

Fig 9.17c

— M —

If still in position on the long, deploy rev. exit below little pattern line.

Very tall bars ruin the technical picture. There were no trade opportunities anyway. Just let go.

266

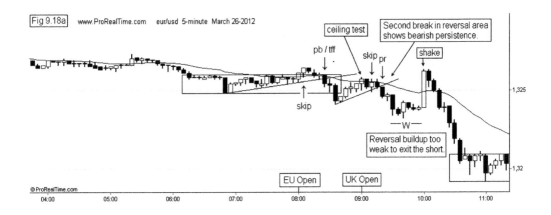

Fig 9.18a   www.ProRealTime.com   eur/usd 5-minute March 26-2012

ceiling test

Second break in reversal area
shows bearish persistence.

pb / tff

skip pr

shake

skip

1,325

W

Reversal buildup too
weak to exit the short.

EU Open   UK Open

1,32

© ProRealTime.com

04:00   05:00   06:00   07:00   08:00   09:00   10:00   11:00

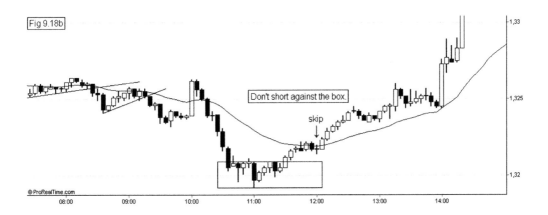

Fig 9.18b

1,33

Don't short against the box.

1,325

skip

1,32

© ProRealTime.com

08:00   09:00   10:00   11:00   12:00   13:00   14:00

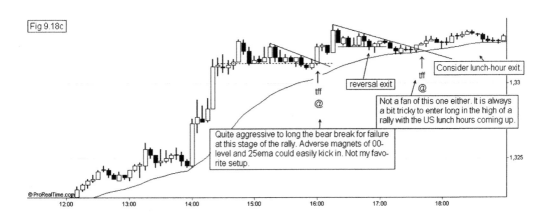

Fig 9.18c

Consider lunch-hour exit.

reversal exit

tff
@

1,33

tff
@

Not a fan of this one either. It is always
a bit tricky to enter long in the high of a
rally with the US lunch hours coming up.

Quite aggressive to long the bear break for failure
at this stage of the rally. Adverse magnets of 00-
level and 25ema could easily kick in. Not my favorite setup.

1,325

© ProRealTime.com

12:00   13:00   14:00   15:00   16:00   17:00   18:00

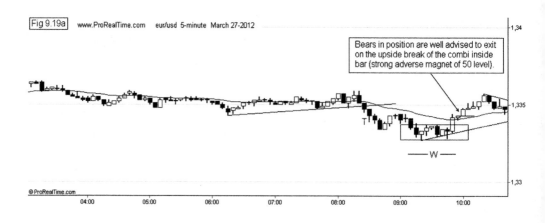

Fig 9.19a — www.ProRealTime.com — eur/usd 5-minute March 27-2012

Bears in position are well advised to exit on the upside break of the combi inside bar (strong adverse magnet of 50 level).

— W —

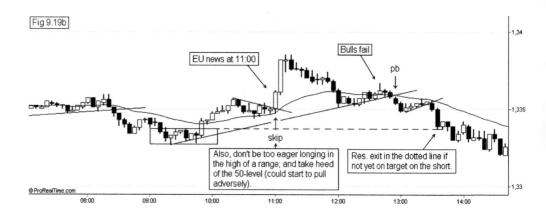

Fig 9.19b

EU news at 11:00

Bulls fail

pb

skip

Also, don't be too eager longing in the high of a range; and take heed of the 50-level (could start to pull adversely).

Res. exit in the dotted line if not yet on target on the short.

Fig 9.19c

Ugly chop. Just stay out.

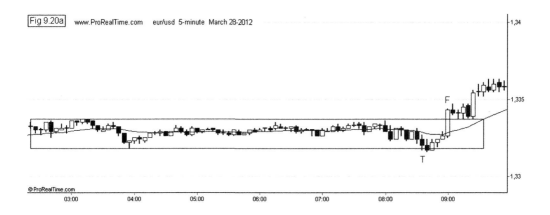

Fig 9.20a   www.ProRealTime.com   eur/usd 5-minute March 28-2012

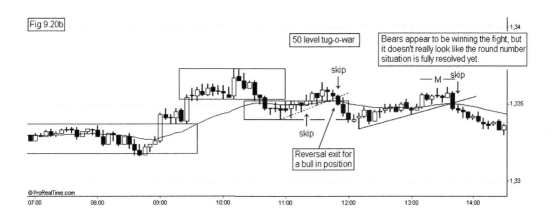

Fig 9.20b

50 level tug-o-war

Bears appear to be winning the fight, but it doesn't really look like the round number situation is fully resolved yet.

skip

M — skip

skip

skip

Reversal exit for a bull in position

Fig 9.20c

pr

skip shorts

magnet

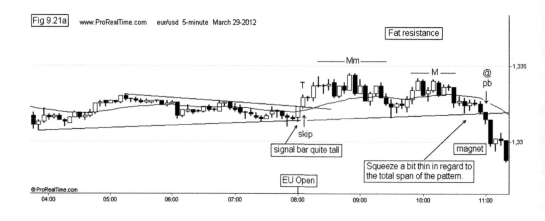

Fig 9.21a   www.ProRealTime.com   eur/usd 5-minute March 29-2012

Fat resistance

Mm

M

@ pb

skip

signal bar quite tall

magnet

EU Open

Squeeze a bit thin in regard to the total span of the pattern.

© ProRealTime.com

Fig 9.21b

false high

pr / pbc

© ProRealTime.com

Fig 9.21c

Depending on how this played out, it is possible to have been shaken out by the entry bar itself.

Pullback too strong

SHS   pb   Rev. exit   skip

magnet

© ProRealTime.com

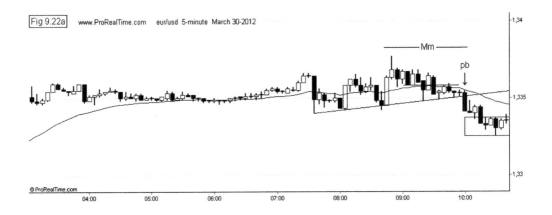

Fig 9.22a   www.ProRealTime.com   eur/usd 5-minute March 30-2012

Mm

pb

© ProRealTime.com

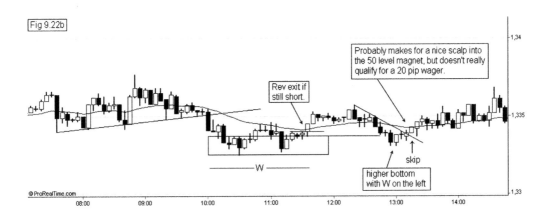

Fig 9.22b

Probably makes for a nice scalp into
the 50 level magnet, but doesn't really
qualify for a 20 pip wager.

Rev exit if
still short.

W

skip

higher bottom
with W on the left

© ProRealTime.com

Fig 9.22c

Signal bar too tall

skip

© ProRealTime.com

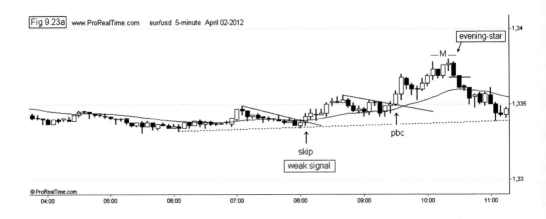

Fig 9.23a   www.ProRealTime.com   eur/usd 5-minute April 02-2012

Fig 9.23b

Fig 9.23c

Fig 9.24a   www.ProRealTime.com   eur/usd 5-minute April 03-2012

T

W — pbc @

Rev. exit if not
yet on target.

© ProRealTime.com

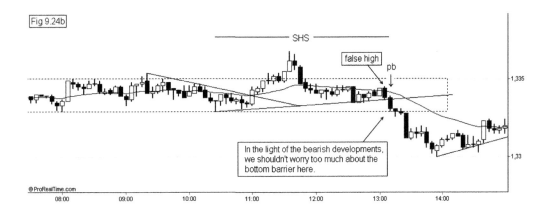

Fig 9.24b

SHS

false high

pb

In the light of the bearish developments,
we shouldn't worry too much about the
bottom barrier here.

© ProRealTime.com

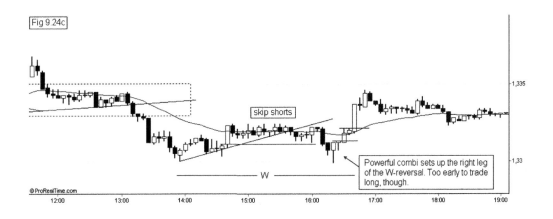

Fig 9.24c

skip shorts

W

Powerful combi sets up the right leg
of the W-reversal. Too early to trade
long, though.

© ProRealTime.com

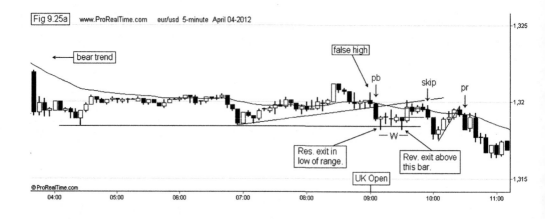

Fig 9.25a www.ProRealTime.com eur/usd 5-minute April 04-2012

bear trend

false high

pb

skip

pr

Res. exit in
low of range.

— W —

Rev. exit above
this bar.

UK Open

Fig 9.25b

skip

skip

Fig 9.25c

ECB interest rate decision due at
13:45. Watch out also for speech
response at 14:30.

skip

— M —

skip shorts

— W —

274

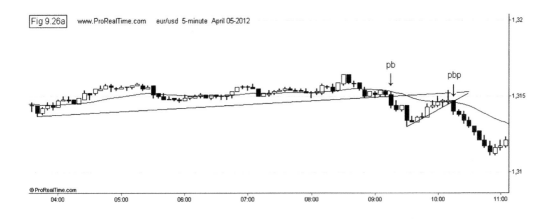

Fig 9.26a   www.ProRealTime.com   eur/usd 5-minute April 05-2012

Fig 9.26b

pb / pr / tff

50 level magnet

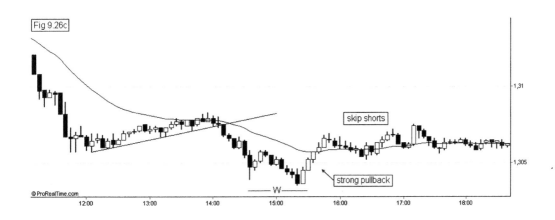

Fig 9.26c

skip shorts

strong pullback

W

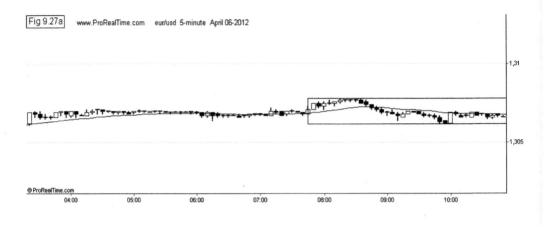

Fig 9.27a   www.ProRealTime.com   eur/usd 5-minute April 06-2012

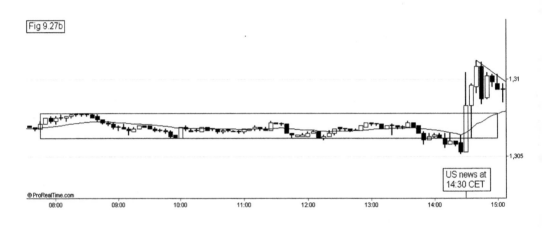

Fig 9.27b

US news at
14:30 CET

Fig 9.27c

News spikes can really mess up the chart. In most instances,
it is best not to engage, particularly when the news flipped
the chart from bearish to bullish (or vice versa). Not too many
traders will play for continuation, which lowers the odds for
follow-through.

skip

276

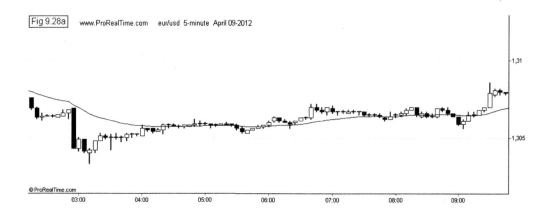

Fig 9.28a   www.ProRealTime.com   eur/usd 5-minute April 09-2012

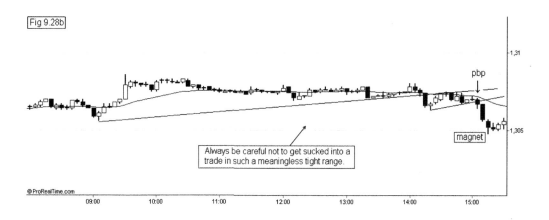

Fig 9.28b

pbp

magnet

Always be careful not to get sucked into a
trade in such a meaningless tight range.

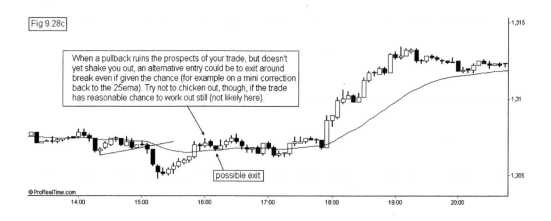

Fig 9.28c

When a pullback ruins the prospects of your trade, but doesn't
yet shake you out, an alternative entry could be to exit around
break even if given the chance (for example on a mini correction
back to the 25ema). Try not to chicken out, though, if the trade
has reasonable chance to work out still (not likely here).

possible exit

Fig 9.29a   www.ProRealTime.com   eur-usd 5/minute April 10-2012

pullback line not yet broken

@ pr

ceiling test

pbp

magnet

EU Open

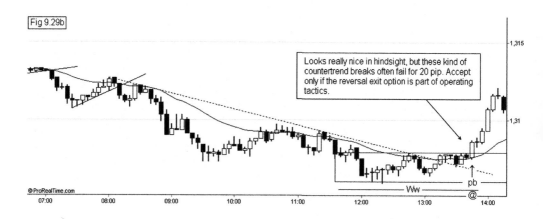

Fig 9.29b

Looks really nice in hindsight, but these kind of countertrend breaks often fail for 20 pip. Accept only if the reversal exit option is part of operating tactics.

pb

Ww

@

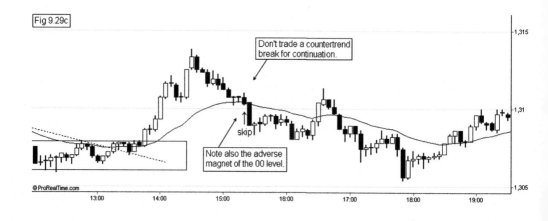

Fig 9.29c

Don't trade a countertrend break for continuation.

skip

Note also the adverse magnet of the 00 level.

Fig 9.30a   www.ProRealTime.com   eur/usd 5-minute April 11-2012

pbp
@

Still a bit tricky, having to trade
away from the 00 level magnet.

Fig 9.30b

skip

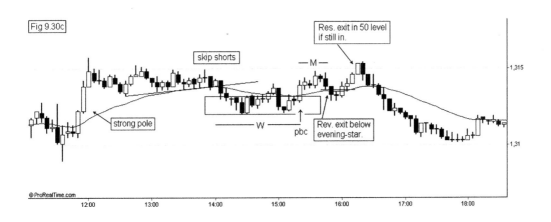

Fig 9.30c

Res. exit in 50 level
if still in.

skip shorts

— M —

strong pole

— W —

pbc

Rev. exit below
evening-star.

Fig 9.31a   www.ProRealTime.com   eur/usd 5-minute April 12-2012

technical test of pattern line

pb

pbp

nice double-bar break

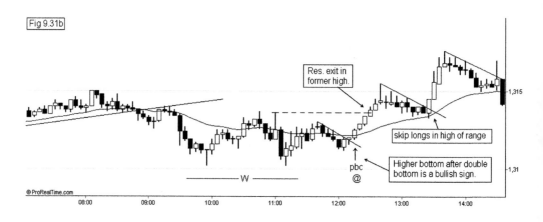

Fig 9.31b

Res. exit in former high.

skip longs in high of range

Higher bottom after double bottom is a bullish sign.

pbc
@

——— W ———

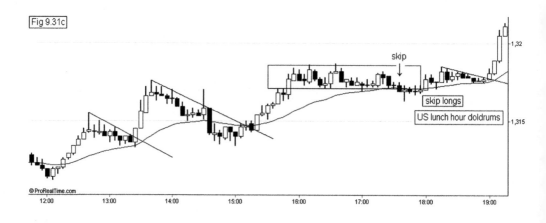

Fig 9.31c

skip

skip longs

US lunch hour doldrums

Fig 9.32a   www.ProRealTime.com   eur/usd 5-minute April 13-2012

ceiling test after tease break

pb   shake

magnet

UK Open

Fig 9.32b

too much overhead resistance

skip

Vww

Fig 9.32c

just let go

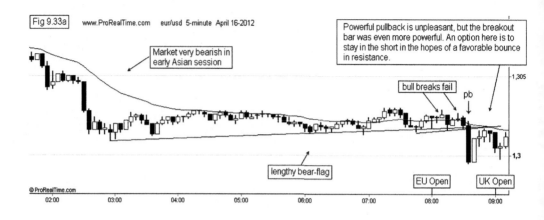

Fig 9.33a   www.ProRealTime.com   eur/usd 5-minute April 16-2012

Market very bearish in early Asian session

Powerful pullback is unpleasant, but the breakout bar was even more powerful. An option here is to stay in the short in the hopes of a favorable bounce in resistance.

bull breaks fail

pb

lengthy bear-flag

EU Open

UK Open

Fig 9.33b

Rev. exit

skip

skip

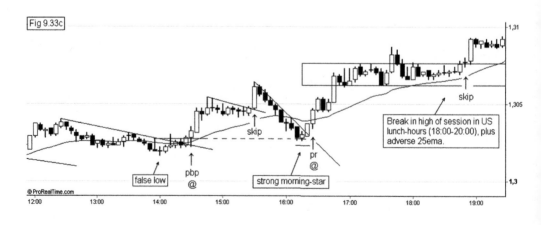

Fig 9.33c

false low

pbp
@

skip

strong morning-star

pr
@

skip

Break in high of session in US lunch-hours (18:00-20:00), plus adverse 25ema.

Fig 9.34a www.ProRealime.com eur/usd 5-minute April 17-2012

Always a bit tricky to trade away from a
round number right before the UK Open.
Be quick to deploy a rev. exit if necessary.

@
pb   Rev. exit

UK Open

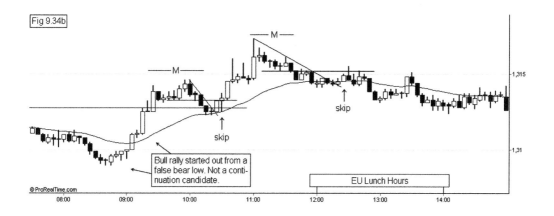

Fig 9.34b

— M —

— M —

skip

skip

Bull rally started out from a
false bear low. Not a continuation candidate.

EU Lunch Hours

Fig 9.34c

ugly chop

just let go

283

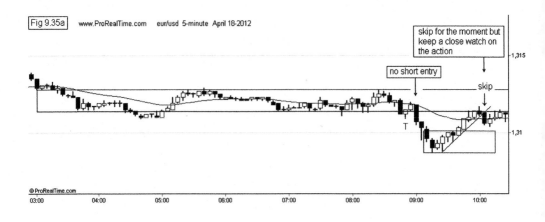

Fig 9.35a — www.ProRealTime.com — eur/usd 5-minute April 18-2012

skip for the moment but keep a close watch on the action

no short entry

skip

Fig 9.35b

No real entry provided to play the pullback reversal in second instance.

Rev. exit below this bar if you went long anyway.

skip

Fig 9.35c

skip

Too early to trade for continuation.

W

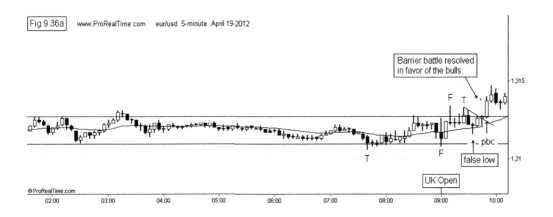

Fig 9.36a   www.ProRealTime.com   eur/usd 5-minute April 19-2012

Barrier battle resolved in favor of the bulls.

pbc

false low

UK Open

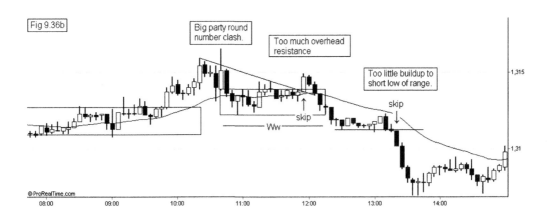

Fig 9.36b

Big party round number clash.

Too much overhead resistance

Too little buildup to short low of range.

skip

skip

Ww

Fig 9.36c

skip

Prices are back in the high of the range. Do not trade for continuation of the bull move anyway.

skip longs

W

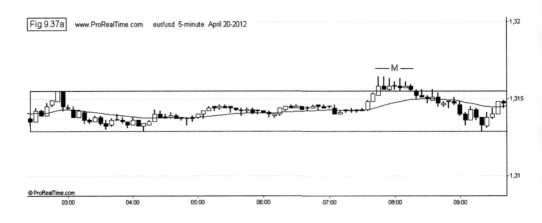

Fig 9.37a   www.ProRealTime.com   eur/usd 5-minute April 20-2012

— M —

Fig 9.37b

Contrarians love to short
these M-patterns, if only to
exploit the 50 level magnet.

— M —

— M —

tff

skip

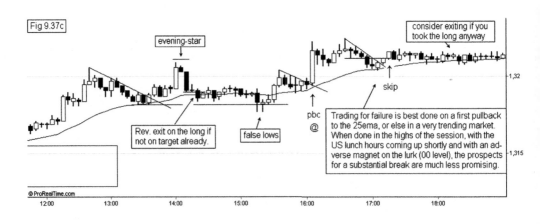

Fig 9.37c

consider exiting if you
took the long anyway

evening-star

skip

Rev. exit on the long if
not on target already.

false lows

pbc
@

Trading for failure is best done on a first pullback
to the 25ema, or else in a very trending market.
When done in the highs of the session, with the
US lunch hours coming up shortly and with an adverse magnet on the lurk (00 level), the prospects
for a substantial break are much less promising.

Fig 9.38a www.ProRealTime.com eur/usd 5-minute April 23-2012

squeeze a bit thin

pbp

Asian range breaks in EU Open

T

EU Open

magnet

Fig 9.38b

false highs demoralizing bulls

pb

T

double-bar break

Fig 9.38c

Rev. exit on the short

tff

skip shorts

W

W

morning-star variant

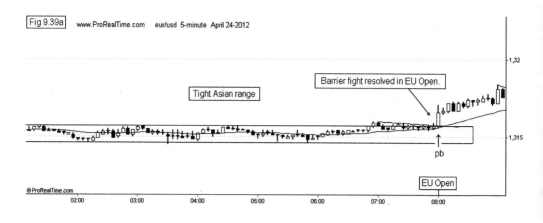

Fig 9.39a www.ProRealTime.com eur/usd 5-minute April 24-2012

Tight Asian range

Barrier fight resolved in EU Open.

pb

EU Open

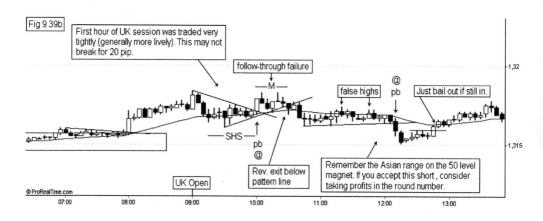

Fig 9.39b

First hour of UK session was traded very tightly (generally more lively). This may not break for 20 pip.

follow-through failure

— M —

false highs

@ pb

Just bail out if still in.

— SHS —

pb @

Rev. exit below pattern line

Remember the Asian range on the 50 level magnet. If you accept this short, consider taking profits in the round number.

UK Open

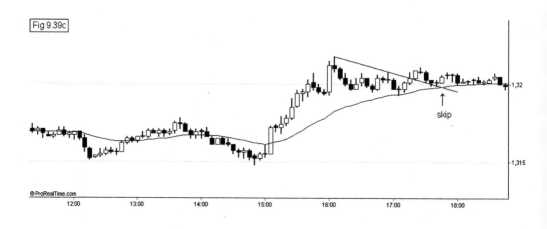

Fig 9.39c

skip

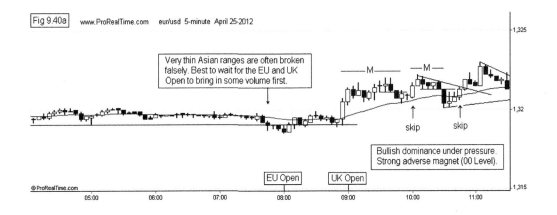

Fig 9.40a   www.ProRealTime.com   eur/usd 5-minute April 25-2012

Very thin Asian ranges are often broken falsely. Best to wait for the EU and UK Open to bring in some volume first.

skip   skip

Bullish dominance under pressure. Strong adverse magnet (00 Level).

EU Open   UK Open

Fig 9.40b

Repeated failure of the bulls to reach the 50 level above.

false high in squeeze

SHS

pb

T
skip

Res. exit level

Stalling prices in 00 level. Res. exit is an option.

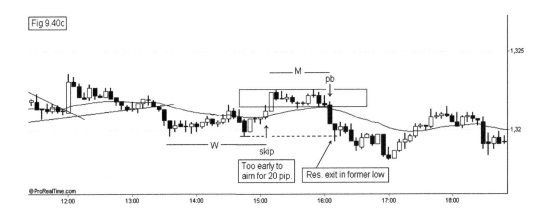

Fig 9.40c

M
pb

W
skip

Too early to aim for 20 pip.

Res. exit in former low

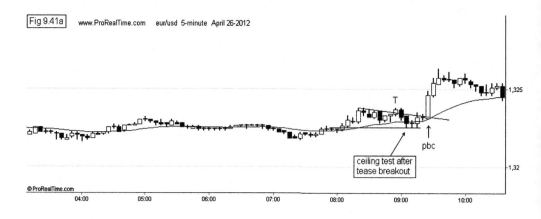

Fig 9.41a www.ProRealTime.com eur/usd 5-minute April 26-2012

T

pbc

ceiling test after
tease breakout

1,325

1,32

04:00 05:00 06:00 07:00 08:00 09:00 10:00

© ProRealTime.com

Fig 9.41b

Evening-star, but signal bar uncomfortably
tall to trade the upside break for failure.

Martket too bearish
to aim for a 20 pip pop.

skip

skip

1,325

1,32

W

08:00 09:00 10:00 11:00 12:00 13:00 14:00

© ProRealTime.com

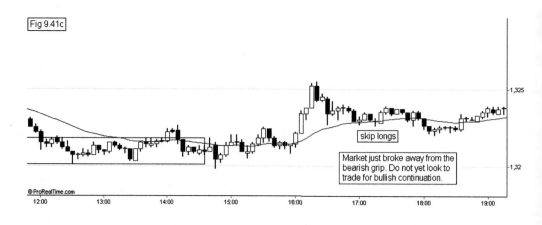

Fig 9.41c

skip longs

Market just broke away from the
bearish grip. Do not yet look to
trade for bullish continuation.

1,325

1,32

12:00 13:00 14:00 15:00 16:00 17:00 18:00 19:00

© ProRealTime.com

Fig 9.42a www.ProRealTime.com eur/usd 5-minute April 27-2012

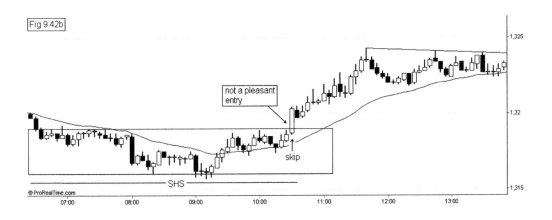

Fig 9.42b

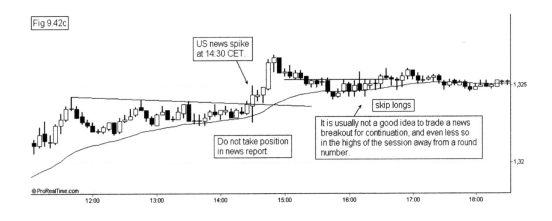

Fig 9.42c

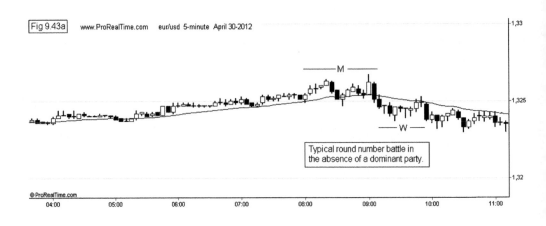

Fig 9.43a   www.ProRealTime.com   eur/usd 5-minute April 30-2012

Typical round number battle in the absence of a dominant party.

Fig 9.43b

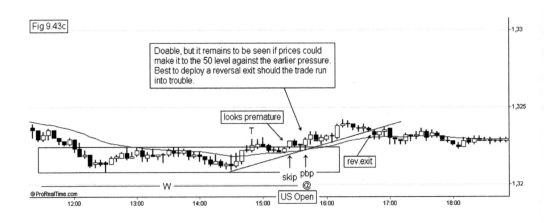

Fig 9.43c

Doable, but it remains to be seen if prices could make it to the 50 level against the earlier pressure. Best to deploy a reversal exit should the trade run into trouble.

looks premature

rev.exit

skip pbp
@
US Open

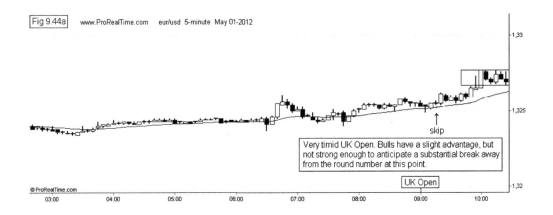

Fig 9.44a   www.ProRealTime.com   eur/usd 5-minute May 01-2012

skip

Very timid UK Open. Bulls have a slight advantage, but
not strong enough to anticipate a substantial break away
from the round number at this point.

UK Open

© ProRealTime.com

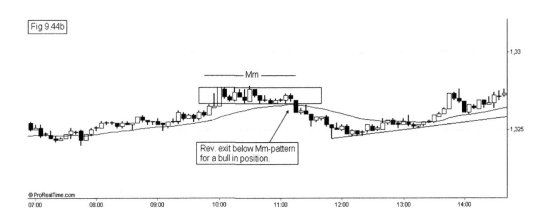

Fig 9.44b

Mm

Rev. exit below Mm-pattern
for a bull in position.

© ProRealTime.com

Fig 9.44c

US news at
16:00 CET

© ProRealTime.com

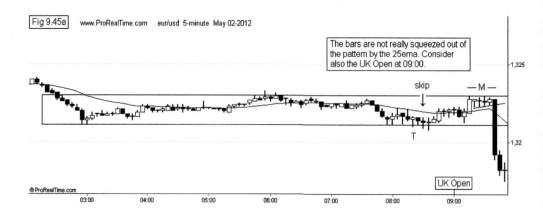

Fig 9.45a   www.ProRealTime.com   eur/usd 5-minute May 02-2012

The bars are not really squeezed out of the pattern by the 25ema. Consider also the UK Open at 09:00.

skip

— M —

T

UK Open

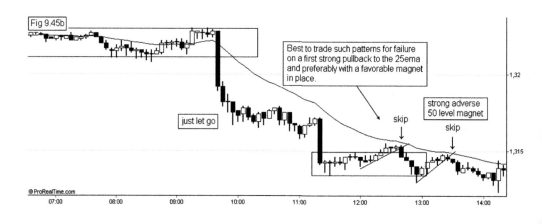

Fig 9.45b

Best to trade such patterns for failure on a first strong pullback to the 25ema and preferably with a favorable magnet in place.

strong adverse 50 level magnet

just let go

skip

skip

Fig 9.45c

Bear trend peters out below 50 level, this will have some scalpers on the lookout for a round number test. Not a great environment to aim for a serious bullish break, though.

skip longs

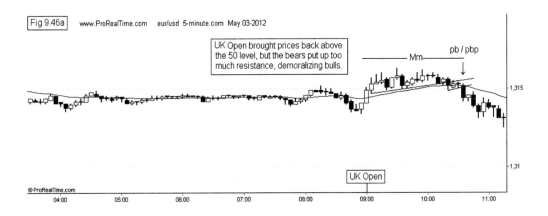

Fig 9.46a   www.ProRealTime.com   eur/usd 5-minute.com May 03-2012

UK Open brought prices back above the 50 level, but the bears put up too much resistance, demoralizing bulls.

Mm

pb / pbp

UK Open

Fig 9.46b

Both are technically valid trades, but with the ECB interest rate decision coming up at 13:45, it is best to stay out. Note also the hefty reaction to the follow-up ECB speech at 14:30.

pb

pbp

Fig 9.46c

Let go

Do not trade a news move for continuation. Do not look to short it either.

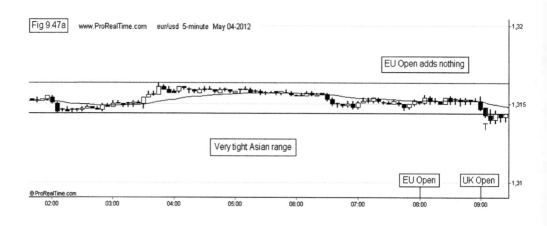

Fig 9.47a   www.ProRealTime.com   eur/usd 5-minute May 04-2012

EU Open adds nothing

Very tight Asian range

EU Open   UK Open

© ProRealTime.com

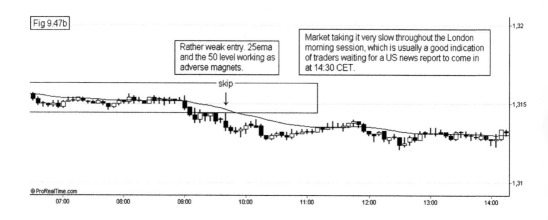

Fig 9.47b

Rather weak entry. 25ema and the 50 level working as adverse magnets.

Market taking it very slow throughout the London morning session, which is usually a good indication of traders waiting for a US news report to come in at 14:30 CET.

skip

© ProRealTime.com

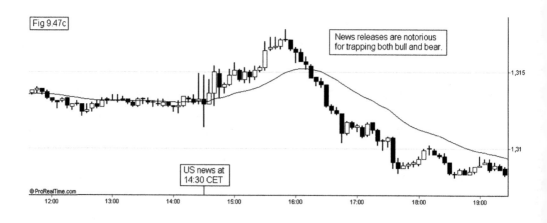

Fig 9.47c

News releases are notorious for trapping both bull and bear.

US news at 14:30 CET

© ProRealTime.com

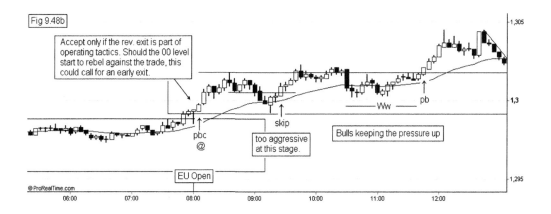

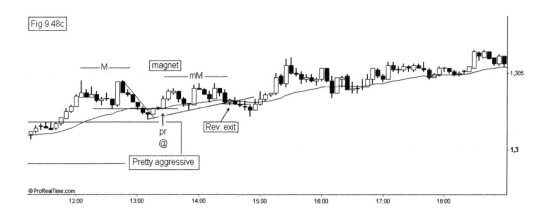

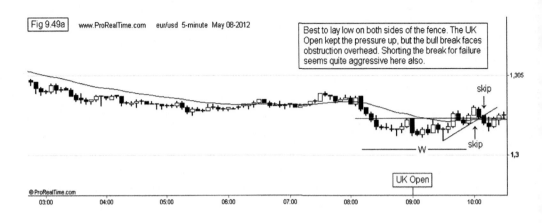

Fig 9.49a   www.ProRealTime.com   eur/usd 5-minute May 08-2012

Best to lay low on both sides of the fence. The UK Open kept the pressure up, but the bull break faces obstruction overhead. Shorting the break for failure seems quite aggressive here also.

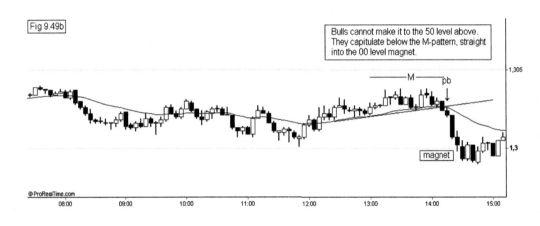

Fig 9.49b

Bulls cannot make it to the 50 level above. They capitulate below the M-pattern, straight into the 00 level magnet.

Fig 9.49c

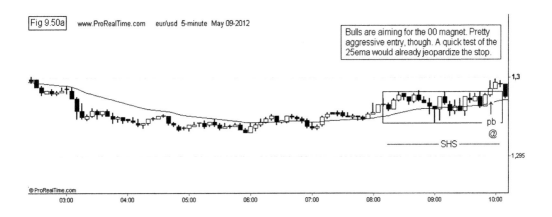

Fig 9.50a   www.ProRealTime.com   eur/usd 5-minute May 09-2012

Bulls are aiming for the 00 magnet. Pretty aggressive entry, though. A quick test of the 25ema would already jeopardize the stop.

pb
@
SHS

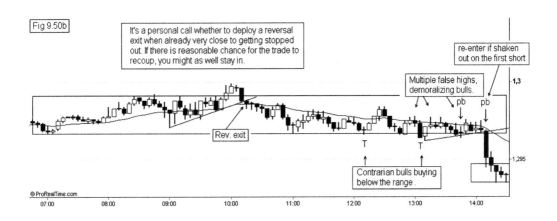

Fig 9.50b

It's a personal call whether to deploy a reversal exit when already very close to getting stopped out. If there is reasonable chance for the trade to recoup, you might as well stay in.

re-enter if shaken out on the first short

Multiple false highs, demoralizing bulls.
pb   pb

Rev. exit

T   T

Contrarian bulls buying below the range .

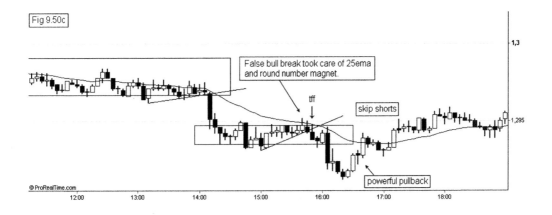

Fig 9.50c

False bull break took care of 25ema and round number magnet.

tff

skip shorts

powerful pullback

299

Fig 9.51a   www.ProRealTime.com   eur/usd 5-minute May 10-2012

Weak setup in UK Open, plus 50 level magnet.

@ pb

M

skip

Res. exit in former low.

UK Open

Fig 9.51b

This is not a trending market and the adverse 50 level magnet is quite strong.

skip

— W —

Fig 9.51c

— M — skip shorts

Bulls still strong (higher lows).

Fig 9.52a | www.ProRealTime.com   eur/usd 5-minute May 11-2012

both long entries are valid

magnet

pbc
pb

Vvw-variant

Fig 9.52b

skip shorts

M

Fig 9.52c

no trades

W

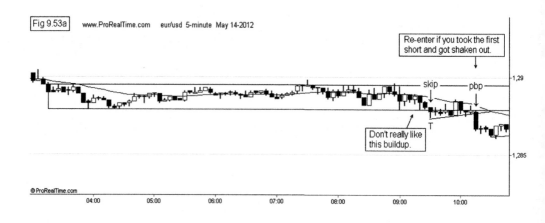

Fig 9.53a   www.ProRealTime.com   eur/usd 5-minute May 14-2012

Re-enter if you took the first
short and got shaken out.

skip ——— pbp

Don't really like
this buildup.

T

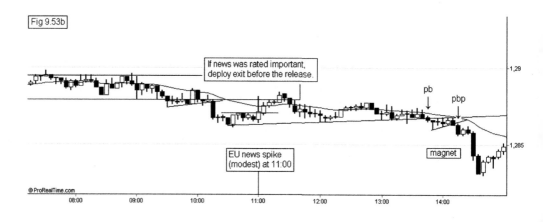

Fig 9.53b

If news was rated important,
deploy exit before the release.

pb

pbp

magnet

EU news spike
(modest) at 11:00

Fig 9.53c

skip longs

bear pressure petering out

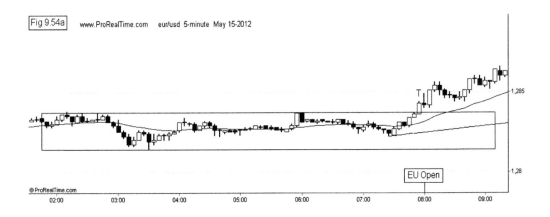

Fig 9.54a   www.ProRealTime.com   eur/usd 5-minute May 15-2012

EU Open

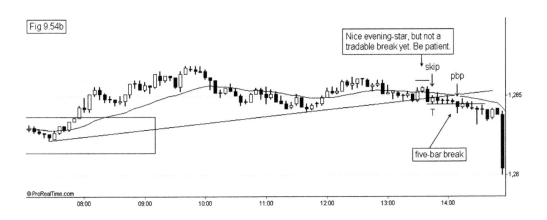

Fig 9.54b

Nice evening-star, but not a tradable break yet. Be patient.

skip   pbp

T

five-bar break

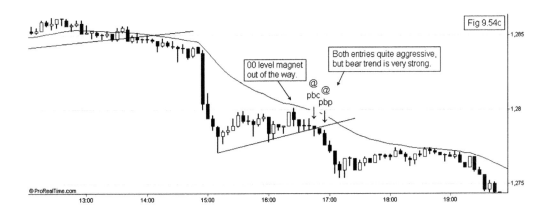

Fig 9.54c

00 level magnet out of the way.

Both entries quite aggressive, but bear trend is very strong.

@   @
pbc   pbp

Fig 9.55a   www.ProRealTime.com   eur/usd 5-minute May 16-2012

Fig 9.55b

Fig 9.55c

Fig 9.56a   www.ProRealTime.com   eur/usd 5-minute May 17-2012

adverse magnets of ceiling
test (dotted line) and 25ema

——— M ———

skip

very shallow pullback

Fig 9.56b

The later you deploy a rev.exit in a pullback,
the bigger the chance of getting trapped out
of a good trade at the worst possible moment.

false high — pbp / pr

pbc

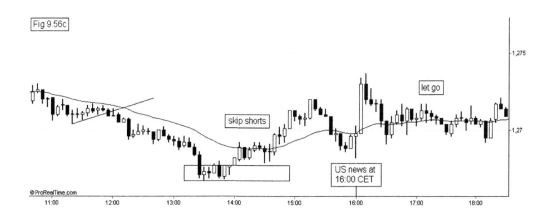

Fig 9.56c

let go

skip shorts

US news at
16:00 CET

Fig 9.57a | www.ProRealTime.com | eur/usd 5-minute May 18-2012

It's too early to defy the bearish pressure.

skip

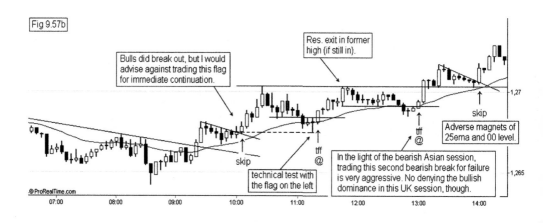

Fig 9.57b

Bulls did break out, but I would advise against trading this flag for immediate continuation.

Res. exit in former high (if still in).

skip

Adverse magnets of 25ema and 00 level.

tff @

tff @

skip

technical test with the flag on the left

In the light of the bearish Asian session, trading this second bearish break for failure is very aggressive. No denying the bullish dominance in this UK session, though.

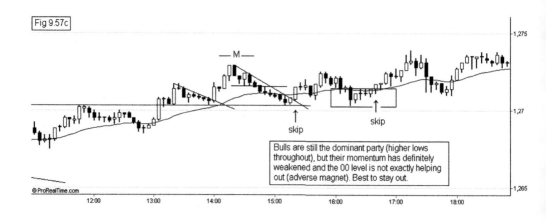

Fig 9.57c

— M —

skip

skip

Bulls are still the dominant party (higher lows throughout), but their momentum has definitely weakened and the 00 level is not exactly helping out (adverse magnet). Best to stay out.

Fig 9.58a   www.ProRealTime.com   eur/usd 5-minute May 21-2012

Bulls fail to break bearish resistance, which could result in a 50 level visit. The action is quite jumpy, though, and the bars are relatively tall. So be patient and await the proper moment.

Fig 9.58b

An option could be to exit the short in this stalling phase, and then put the position back on at a later stage if warranted.

Bulls throw in the towel.

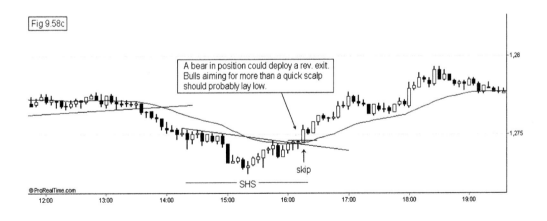

Fig 9.58c

A bear in position could deploy a rev. exit. Bulls aiming for more than a quick scalp should probably lay low.

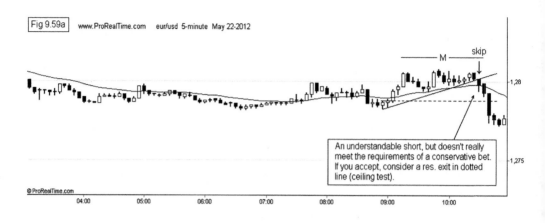

Fig 9.59a   www.ProRealTime.com   eur/usd 5-minute May 22-2012

An understandable short, but doesn't really meet the requirements of a conservative bet. If you accept, consider a res. exit in dotted line (ceiling test).

Fig 9.59b

Evening-stars. The second has more merit from a short side perspective, but nothing to pursue from where we stand.

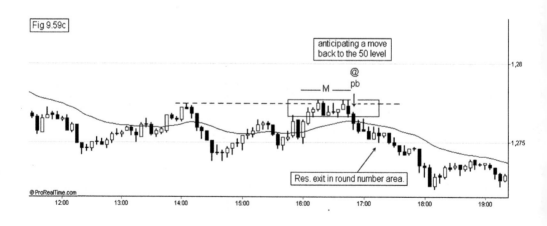

Fig 9.59c

anticipating a move back to the 50 level

Res. exit in round number area.

Fig 9.60a   www.ProRealTime.com   eur/usd 5-minute May 23-2012

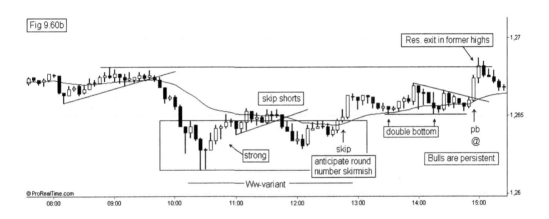

Fig 9.60b

Fig 9.60c

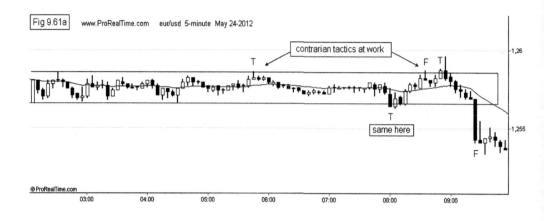

Fig 9.61a   www.ProRealTime.com   eur/usd 5-minute May 24-2012

contrarian tactics at work

same here

Fig 9.61b

Mm-variant

skip shorts

skip

strong pullback

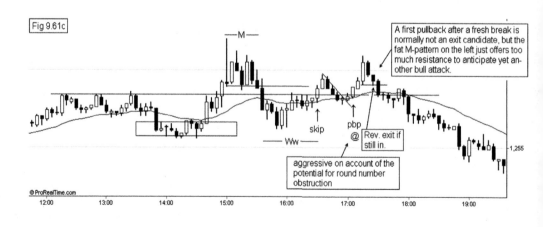

Fig 9.61c

A first pullback after a fresh break is
normally not an exit candidate, but the
fat M-pattern on the left just offers too
much resistance to anticipate yet another bull attack.

M

skip

pbp
@   Rev. exit if
     still in.

Vvw

aggressive on account of the
potential for round number
obstruction

Fig 9.62a   www.ProRealTime.com   eur/usd 5-minute May 25-2012

shake

T

pbc

@

Ww-variant

EU Open   morning-star

Fig 9.62b

ceiling test   @

pb

F

A poorly set bearish break in a
bullish market is a contrarian
favorite.

These second attempts stand a
better chance to follow-through.
Still a pretty aggressive trade.

Fig 9.62c

skip shorts

skip shorts

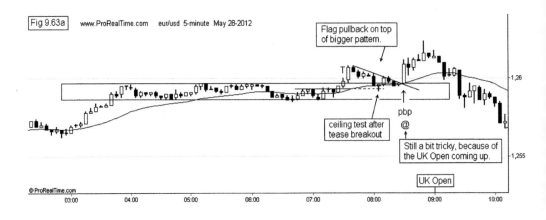

Fig 9.63a · www.ProRealTime.com · eur/usd 5-minute May 28-2012

Flag pullback on top of bigger pattern.

ceiling test after tease breakout

pbp @

Still a bit tricky, because of the UK Open coming up.

UK Open

Fig 9.63b

Squeeze tug-o-war didn't line up with pattern line.

skip

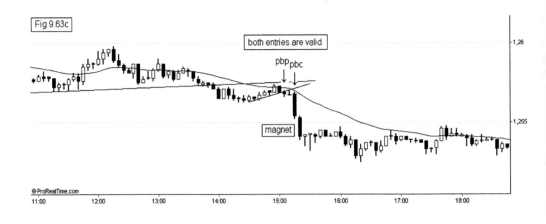

Fig 9.63c

both entries are valid

pbp pbc

magnet

Fig 9.64a   www.ProRealTime.com   eur/usd 5-minute May 29-2012

magnet

false low

tff @

EU Open

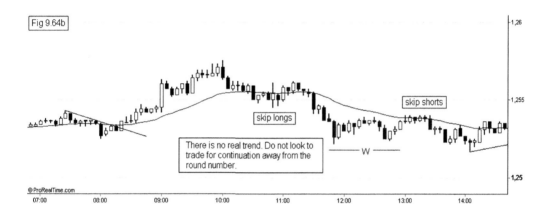

Fig 9.64b

skip shorts

skip longs

There is no real trend. Do not look to
trade for continuation away from the
round number.

W

Fig 9.64c

SHS

M — pb

Entry slightly aggressive, but stop
resides beyond ceiling test level.

a very shortable pattern

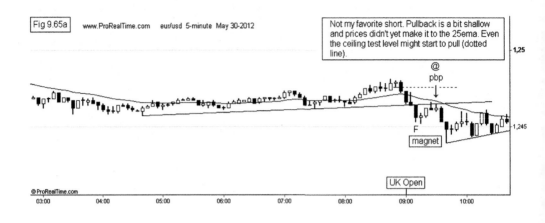

Fig 9.65a   www.ProRealTime.com   eur/usd 5-minute May 30-2012

Not my favorite short. Pullback is a bit shallow and prices didn't yet make it to the 25ema. Even the ceiling test level might start to pull (dotted line).

@
pbp

F

magnet

UK Open

Fig 9.65b

bears counter the news rally

——— M ———

skip

round number skirmish

EU news at
13:00 CET

Fig 9.65c

skip

round number skirmish   skip

——— W ———

Fig 9.66a www.ProRealTime.com eur/usd 5-minute May 31-2012

evening-star

skip

morning-star

Bulls are keeping the pressure up,
but the action is too feverish (bars
too tall) to particpate.

Fig 9.66b

M

skip longs

F

contrarians step in

Fig 9.66c

@
pb

M

T

skip longs

skip longs

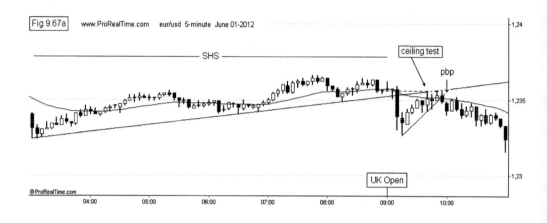

Fig 9.67a   www.ProRealTime.com   eur/usd 5-minute June 01-2012

SHS

ceiling test

pbp

UK Open

Fig 9.67b

tff

Res. exit in low of range

Fig 9.67c

magnet

US news at 14:30 CET

skip

Deploy news report exit before 14:30 if still short.

Personally, I am not a big fan of trading news releases for continuation. This trade set up quite well, though (deep pullback and interesting setup)

Fig 9.68a   www.ProRealTime.com   eur/usd   5-minute   June 04-2012

second breakout attempt premature as well

T   T

pbc

Tease break pullback put in a ceiling test and a 00 level test

W

higer lows throughout

Fig 9.68b

trade has a hard time taking off

rev. exit options

The first barrier test after a break-out is often a bounce candidate.

Fig 9.68c

Let go

false low

pbc

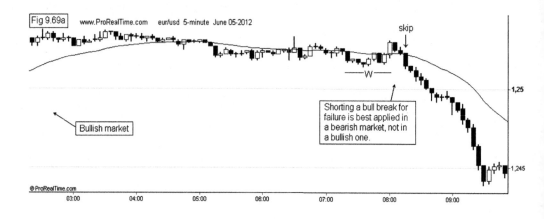

Fig 9.69a   www.ProRealTime.com   eur/usd 5-minute June 05-2012

skip

Bullish market

Shorting a bull break for
failure is best applied in
a bearish market, not in
a bullish one.

@ ProRealTime.com

Fig 9.69b

Typical stalling after huge rally
in UK morning session.

skip shorts

Just let go

@ ProRealTime.com

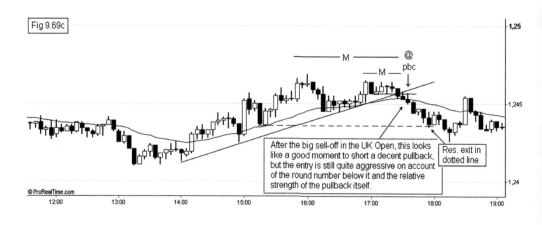

Fig 9.69c

M   @
        pbc
    M

After the big sell-off in the UK Open, this looks
like a good moment to short a decent pullback,
but the entry is still quite aggressive on account
of the round number below it and the relative
strength of the pullback itself.

Res. exit in
dotted line

@ ProRealTime.com

Fig 9.70a   www.ProRealTime.com   eur/usd 5-minute June 06-2012

An extra bar to fatten up the buildup (think combi) would have been nice, but the prospects are good.

EU and UK Open keep the pressure up in a 50 percent retracement of the Asian bull rally. A bullish sign, favoring continuation.

EU Open   UK Open

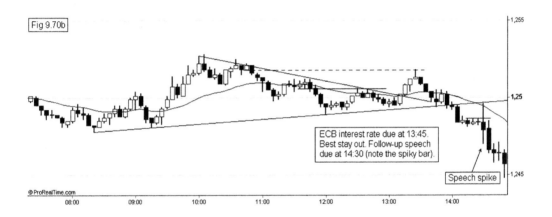

Fig 9.70b

ECB interest rate due at 13:45. Best stay out. Follow-up speech due at 14:30 (note the spiky bar).

Speech spike

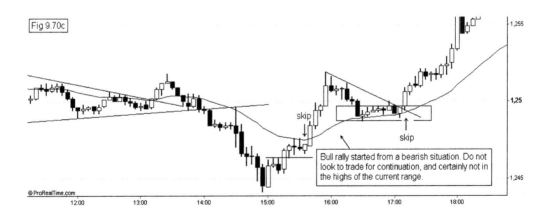

Fig 9.70c

skip

skip

Bull rally started from a bearish situation. Do not look to trade for continuation, and certainly not in the highs of the current range.

Fig 9.71a   www.ProRealTime.com   eur/usd 5-minute June 07-2012

SHS with W

pb

false low, higher low,
ceiling test, 50 level test

© ProRealTime.com

Fig 9.71b

Let go

© ProRealTime.com

Fig 9.71c

US news at
16:00 CET

© ProRealTime.com

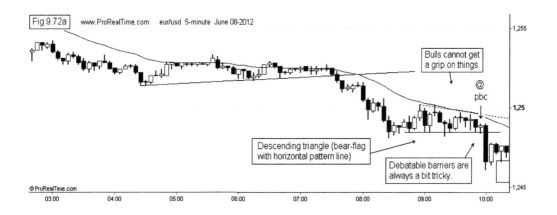

Fig 9.72a   www.ProRealTime.com   eur/usd 5-minute June 08-2012

Bulls cannot get
a grip on things.

@
pbc

Descending triangle (bear-flag
with horizontal pattern line)

Debatable barriers are
always a bit tricky.

© ProRealTime.com

Fig 9.72b

skip longs

W

skip longs

© ProRealTime.com

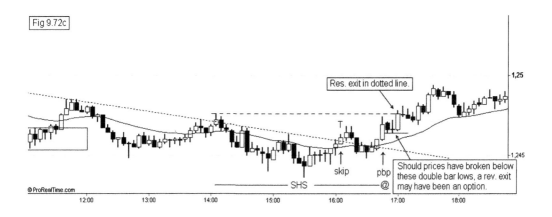

Fig 9.72c

Res. exit in dotted line.

T

skip

pbp

@

SHS

Should prices have broken below
these double bar lows, a rev. exit
may have been an option.

© ProRealTime.com

Fig 9.73a   www.ProRealTime.com   eur/usd 5-minute June 11-2012

Would have been nice to have seen another bar next to the tall signal bar so as to fatten up the squeeze and turn the setup into a combi. The UK Open is known to speed things up a little.

@ pb

magnet

UK Open

Fig 9.73b

pr

Pullback didn't quite make it to the pattern line extension, but did correct 50% of the bear swing when setting up the reversal in the 25ema. Good enough to go.

Fig 9.73c

skip shorts

Let go

US news at 16:00 CET

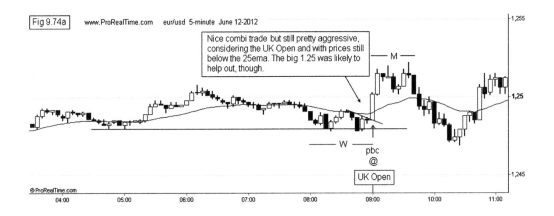

Fig 9.74a   www.ProRealTime.com   eur/usd 5-minute June 12-2012

Nice combi trade but still pretty aggressive,
considering the UK Open and with prices still
below the 25ema. The big 1.25 was likely to
help out, though.

M

W

pbc
@

UK Open

Fig 9.74b

SHS

@
pb

Anticipate 00-level
opposition.

Res. exit

skip

false low is also
a ceiling test

Fig 9.74c

skip shorts

Fig 9.75a   www.ProRealTime.com   eur/usd 5-minute June 13-2012

Would want to see more buildup before trading away from the 00 level magnet.

M

weak setup

magnet fended off?

tff @

skip

skip

EU Open

UK Open

© ProRealTime.com

Fig 9.75b

M

skip

© ProRealTime.com

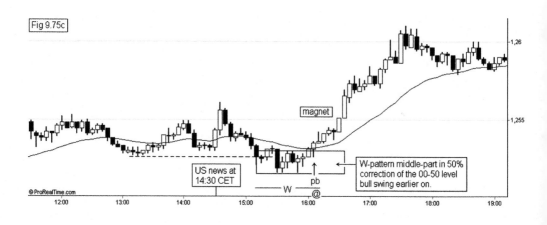

Fig 9.75c

magnet

US news at 14:30 CET

W-pattern middle-part in 50% correction of the 00-50 level bull swing earlier on.

W

pb @

© ProRealTime.com

Fig 9.76a   www.ProRealTime.com   eur/usd 5-minute June 14-2012

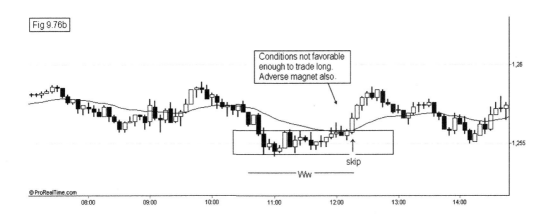

Fig 9.76b

Fig 9.76c

Fig 9.77a www.ProRealTime.com eur/usd 5-minute June 15-2012

very thin price action

F

classic false break trap

UK Open

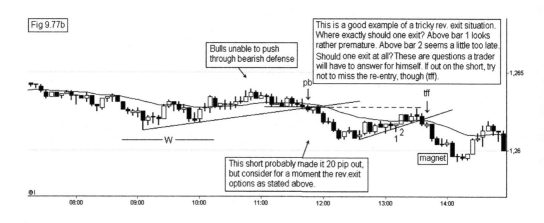

Fig 9.77b

This is a good example of a tricky rev. exit situation. Where exactly should one exit? Above bar 1 looks rather premature. Above bar 2 seems a little too late. Should one exit at all? These are questions a trader will have to answer for himself. If out on the short, try not to miss the re-entry, though (tff).

Bulls unable to push through bearish defense

pb

tff

W

1 2

This short probably made it 20 pip out, but consider for a moment the rev.exit options as stated above.

magnet

Fig 9.77c

Bears in position could consider a rev. exit.

ceiling test

skip

strong pullback

Fig 9.78a   www.ProRealTime.com   eur/usd 5-minute June 18-2012

buildup too thin

skip @ pbp

skip shorts

Res. exit

UK Open

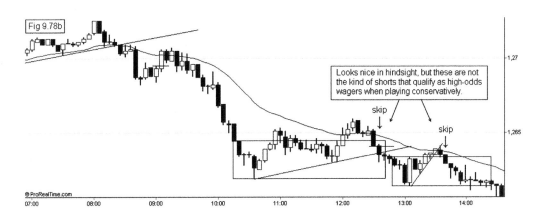

Fig 9.78b

Looks nice in hindsight, but these are not the kind of shorts that qualify as high-odds wagers when playing conservatively.

skip

skip

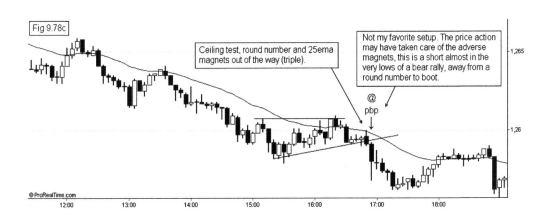

Fig 9.78c

Ceiling test, round number and 25ema magnets out of the way (triple).

Not my favorite setup. The price action may have taken care of the adverse magnets, this is a short almost in the very lows of a bear rally, away from a round number to boot.

@ pbp

327

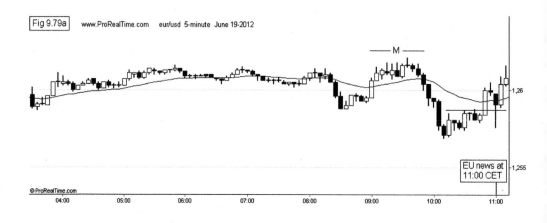

Fig 9.79a www.ProRealTime.com eur/usd 5-minute June 19-2012

——— M ———

EU news at 11:00 CET

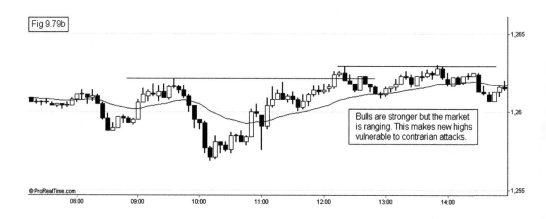

Fig 9.79b

Bulls are stronger but the market is ranging. This makes new highs vulnerable to contrarian attacks.

Fig 9.79c

US traders on a buying spree. Just let go

US Open

Fig 9.80a   www.ProRealTime.com   eur/usd 5-minute June 20-2012

The failure of the short turned into a bull-side opportunity.

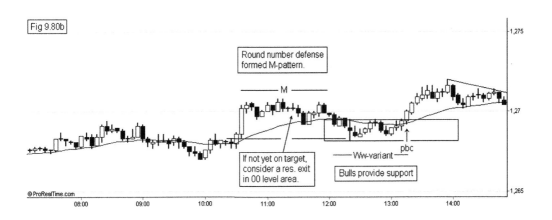

Fig 9.80b

Round number defense formed M-pattern.

If not yet on target, consider a res. exit in 00 level area.

Bulls provide support

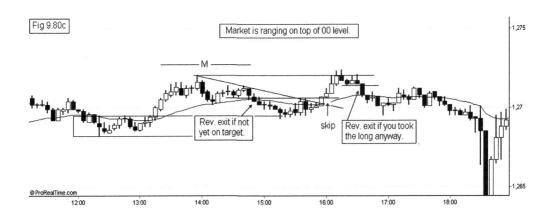

Fig 9.80c

Market is ranging on top of 00 level.

Rev. exit if not yet on target.

skip

Rev. exit if you took the long anyway.

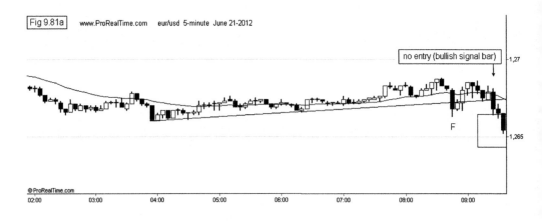

Fig 9.81a   www.ProRealTime.com   eur/usd 5-minute June 21-2012

no entry (bullish signal bar)

F

Fig 9.81b

Conditions not favorable
enough to play long.

M

T

skip

skip

Vvw

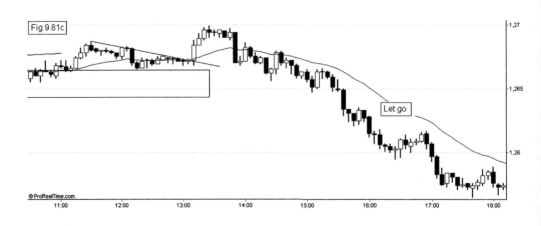

Fig 9.81c

Let go

330

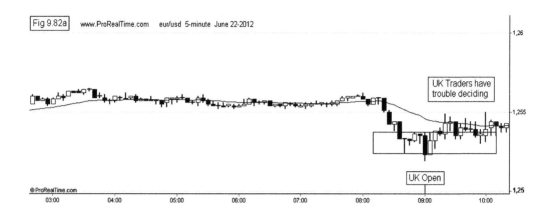

Fig 9.82a   www.ProRealTime.com   eur/usd 5-minute June 22-2012

UK Traders have trouble deciding

UK Open

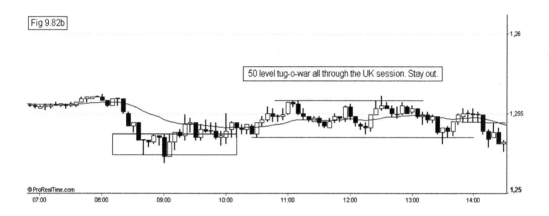

Fig 9.82b

50 level tug-o-war all through the UK session. Stay out.

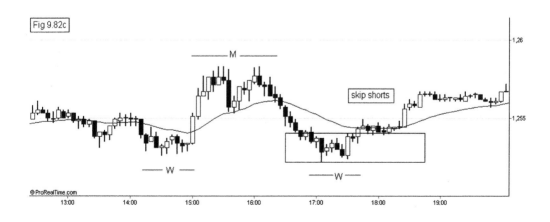

Fig 9.82c

M

skip shorts

W

W

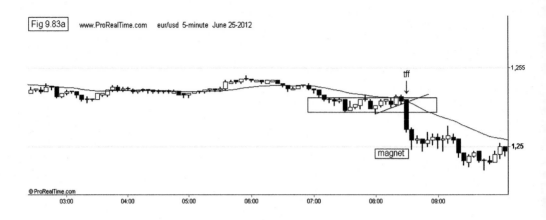

Fig 9.83a   www.ProRealTime.com   eur/usd 5-minute June 25-2012

tff

magnet

Fig 9.83b

anticipate 00 level skirmish

skip

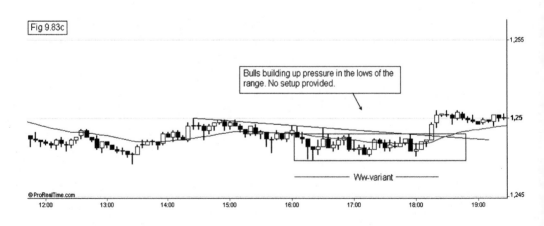

Fig 9.83c

Bulls building up pressure in the lows of the range. No setup provided.

Ww-variant

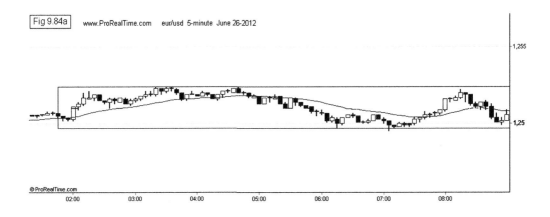

Fig 9.84a   www.ProRealTime.com   eur/usd 5-minute June 26-2012

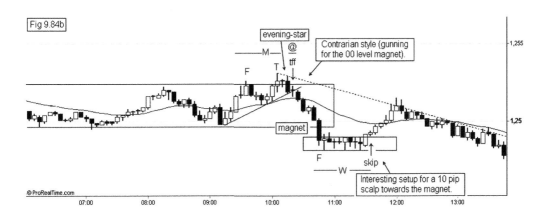

Fig 9.84b

evening-star

Contrarian style (gunning for the 00 level magnet).

magnet

skip

Interesting setup for a 10 pip scalp towards the magnet.

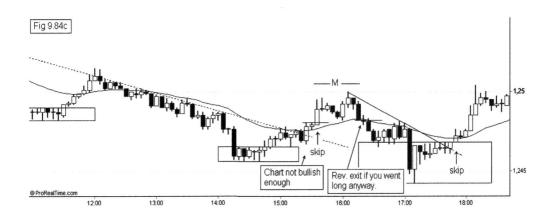

Fig 9.84c

skip

Chart not bullish enough

Rev. exit if you went long anyway.

skip

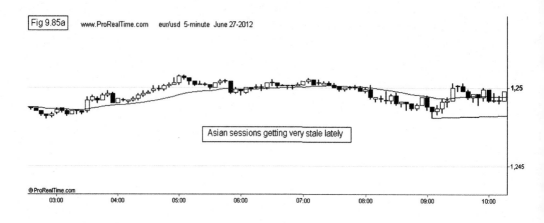

Fig 9.85a www.ProRealTime.com eur/usd 5-minute June 27-2012

Asian sessions getting very stale lately

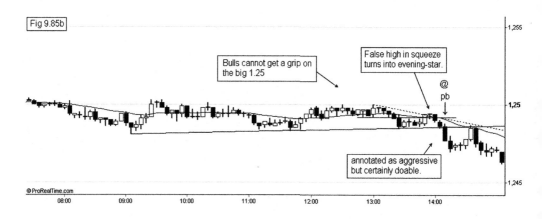

Fig 9.85b

Bulls cannot get a grip on
the big 1.25

False high in squeeze
turns into evening-star.

@
pb

annotated as aggressive
but certainly doable.

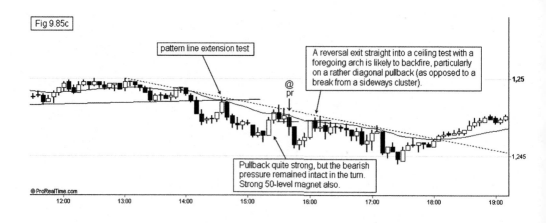

Fig 9.85c

pattern line extension test

A reversal exit straight into a ceiling test with a
foregoing arch is likely to backfire, particularly
on a rather diagonal pullback (as opposed to a
break from a sideways cluster).

@
pr

Pullback quite strong, but the bearish
pressure remained intact in the turn.
Strong 50-level magnet also.

Fig 9.86a www.ProRealTime.com eur/usd 5-minute June 28-2012

bullish re-break failed

— M —

no short entry

ceiling test support

Fig 9.86b

This is not the kind of 25ema pullback you should be looking to short. Market is still digesting the big sell-off in the UK Open.

skip

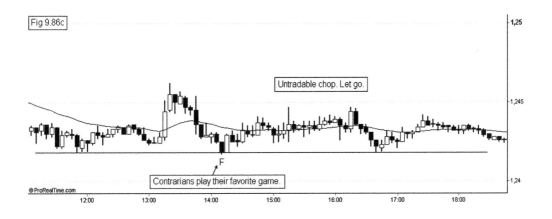

Fig 9.86c

Untradable chop. Let go.

F

Contrarians play their favorite game.

335

Fig 9.87a — www.ProRealTime.com   eur/usd 5-minute June 29-2012

Mm

skip

Quite rare to see the eur/usd spike in the Asian session.

EU and UK Open wondering what to do with the Asian bull spike.

EU Open   UK Open

Fig 9.87b

Market is ranging aimlessly through the UK afternoon.

Fig 9.87c

skip

skip

Try not to short this mega bull rally

Longing for failure is not a good idea, either (big block to dig through). Just stay out.

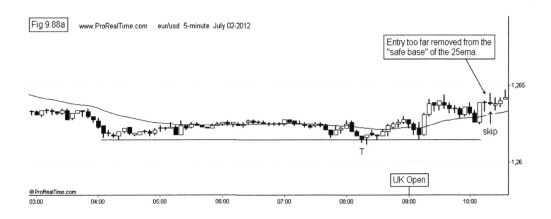

Fig 9.88a   www.ProRealTime.com   eur/usd 5-minute July 02-2012

Entry too far removed from the "safe base" of the 25ema.

Fig 9.88b

Failure of W-pattern reversal

tff

magnet

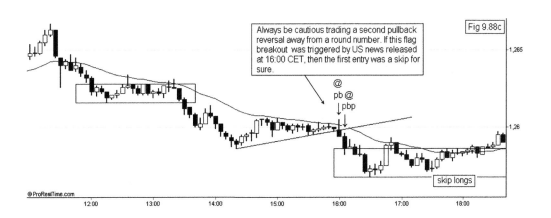

Always be cautious trading a second pullback reversal away from a round number. If this flag breakout was triggered by US news released at 16:00 CET, then the first entry was a skip for sure.

@
pb @
↓ pbp

skip longs

Fig 9.88c

Fig 9.89a   www.ProRealTime.com   eur/usd 5-minute July 03-2012

Best skipped because of the tall signal bar and the risk of an adverse triple (00, 25ema and pattern line test). Should the entry bar have put in the magnet tests prior to taking out the signal bar, the short entry is of better quality (not very likely because of the entry bar's opening price).

skip

UK Open

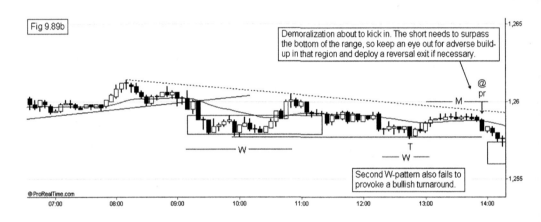

Fig 9.89b

Demoralization about to kick in. The short needs to surpass the bottom of the range, so keep an eye out for adverse build-up in that region and deploy a reversal exit if necessary.

Second W-pattern also fails to provoke a bullish turnaround.

Fig 9.89c

Too early to think long

skip

unfavorable setup

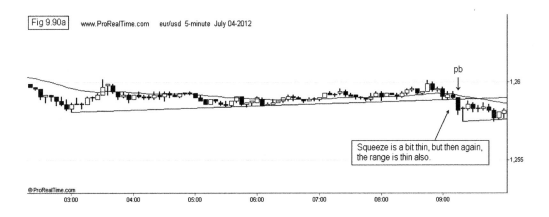

Fig 9.90a   www.ProRealTime.com   eur/usd 5-minute July 04-2012

pb

Squeeze is a bit thin, but then again, the range is thin also.

Fig 9.90b

Reversal exits in a pattern line extension can backfire painfully. If shaken out, always monitor the follow-up action closely and re-enter if the situation calls for it.

Still a reasonable short into the magnet

pb

@ pb

W

magnet

Fig 9.90c

If the trend is agonizingly slow and finally reaches its round number target, a resistance exit is always an option.

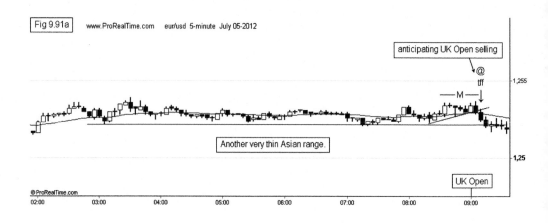

Fig 9.91a   www.ProRealTime.com   eur/usd 5-minute July 05-2012

anticipating UK Open selling
@
tff
— M —
Another very thin Asian range.
© ProRealTime.com
UK Open

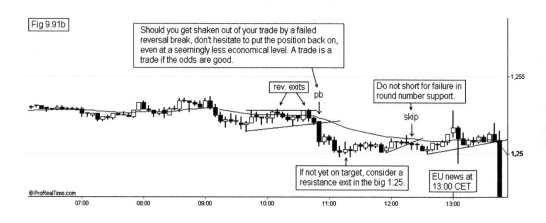

Fig 9.91b

Should you get shaken out of your trade by a failed reversal break, don't hesitate to put the position back on, even at a seemingly less economical level. A trade is a trade if the odds are good.

rev. exits
pb

Do not short for failure in round number support.
skip

If not yet on target, consider a resistance exit in the big 1.25.

EU news at 13:00 CET

© ProRealTime.com

Fig 9.91c

ECB interest rate decisions come out once a month at 13.45 CET. If the rate itself does not bring surprises about, the speech starting at 14:30 may still have a strong impact on the market.

Just let go

skip shorts

© ProRealTime.com

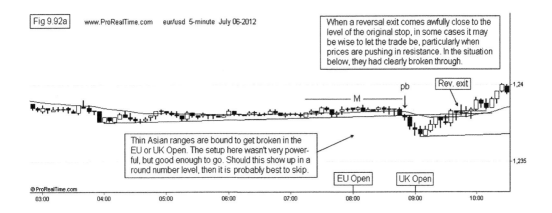

Fig 9.92a   www.ProRealTime.com   eur/usd 5-minute July 06-2012

When a reversal exit comes awfully close to the level of the original stop, in some cases it may be wise to let the trade be, particularly when prices are pushing in resistance. In the situation below, they had clearly broken through.

Thin Asian ranges are bound to get broken in the EU or UK Open. The setup here wasn't very powerful, but good enough to go. Should this show up in a round number level, then it is probably best to skip.

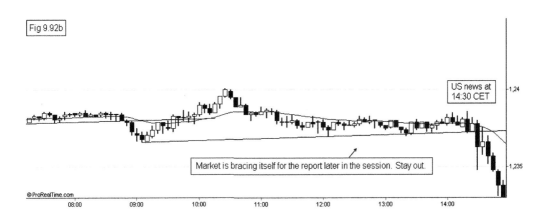

Fig 9.92b

US news at 14:30 CET

Market is bracing itself for the report later in the session. Stay out.

Fig 9.92c

Let go.

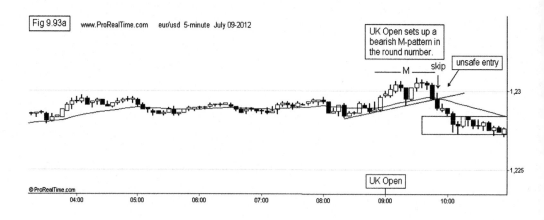

Fig 9.93a   www.ProRealTime.com   eur/usd 5-minute July 09-2012

UK Open sets up a bearish M-pattern in the round number.

M   skip

unsafe entry

UK Open

Fig 9.93b

Best not trade for failure in a ranging market. Consider also the EU lunch hours (12:00-14:00)

skip

Vvw ———— skip

skip longs

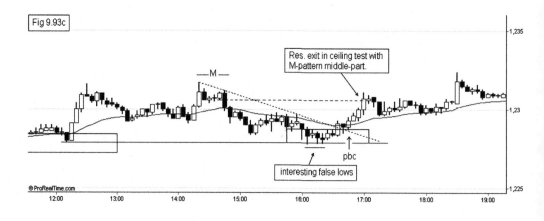

Fig 9.93c

Res. exit in ceiling test with M-pattern middle-part.

— M —

interesting false lows

pbc

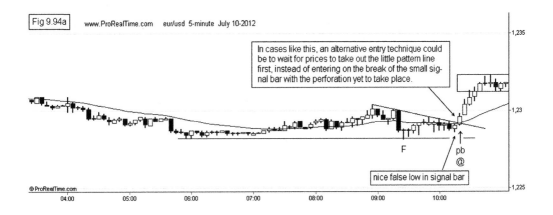

Fig 9.94a   www.ProRealTime.com   eur/usd 5-minute July 10-2012

In cases like this, an alternative entry technique could
be to wait for prices to take out the little pattern line
first, instead of entering on the break of the small signal bar with the perforation yet to take place.

F

pb
@

nice false low in signal bar

Fig 9.94b

False high in squeeze confirms failure to
undo the bear break, demoralizing bulls.

skip   — pbp —

skip

Too early to trade for continuation

Res. exit in ceiling test

Evening-star variant in 60%
retracement of foregoing swing.

— M — pr

Fig 9.94c

skip shorts

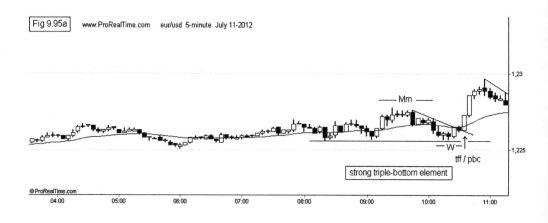

Fig 9.95a   www.ProRealTime.com   eur/usd 5-minute July 11-2012

— Mm —

— W —
tff / pbc

strong triple-bottom element

© ProRealTime.com

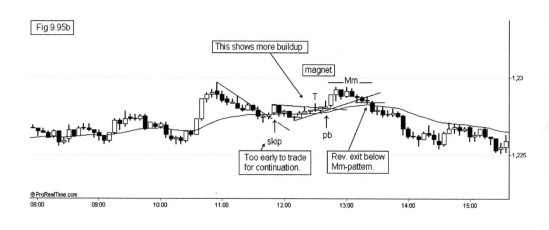

Fig 9.95b

This shows more buildup

magnet

— Mm —

T

skip

pb

Too early to trade
for continuation.

Rev. exit below
Mm-pattern.

© ProRealTime.com

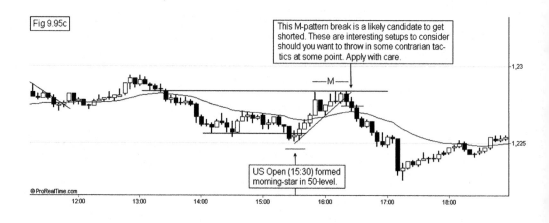

Fig 9.95c

This M-pattern break is a likely candidate to get
shorted. These are interesting setups to consider
should you want to throw in some contrarian tactics at some point. Apply with care.

— M —

US Open (15:30) formed
morning-star in 50-level.

© ProRealTime.com

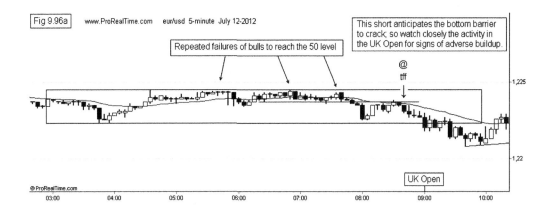

Fig 9.96a   www.ProRealTime.com   eur/usd 5-minute July 12-2012

Repeated failures of bulls to reach the 50 level

This short anticipates the bottom barrier to crack, so watch closely the activity in the UK Open for signs of adverse buildup.

@
tff

UK Open

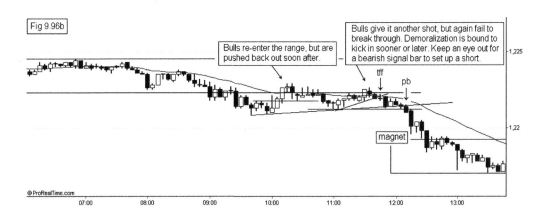

Fig 9.96b

Bulls re-enter the range, but are pushed back out soon after.

Bulls give it another shot, but again fail to break through. Demoralization is bound to kick in sooner or later. Keep an eye out for a bearish signal bar to set up a short.

tff
pb

magnet

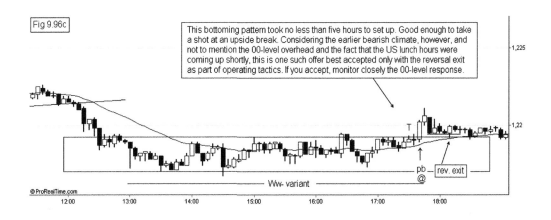

Fig 9.96c

This bottoming pattern took no less than five hours to set up. Good enough to take a shot at an upside break. Considering the earlier bearish climate, however, and not to mention the 00-level overhead and the fact that the US lunch hours were coming up shortly, this is one such offer best accepted only with the reversal exit as part of operating tactics. If you accept, monitor closely the 00-level response.

T

Ww- variant

pb
@

rev. exit

Fig 9.97a www.ProRealTime.com eur/usd 5-minute July 13-2012

skip

These weak squeezes are known to trap traders into a premature break. Not pleasant also was the timing (UK Open) plus the fact that both the 25ema and the 00 level stood to work as adverse magnets.

UK Open

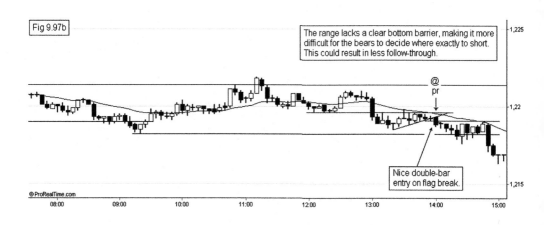

Fig 9.97b

The range lacks a clear bottom barrier, making it more difficult for the bears to decide where exactly to short. This could result in less follow-through.

@ pr

Nice double-bar entry on flag break.

Fig 9.97c

M

skip

Do not trade this rally for continuation.

US Open

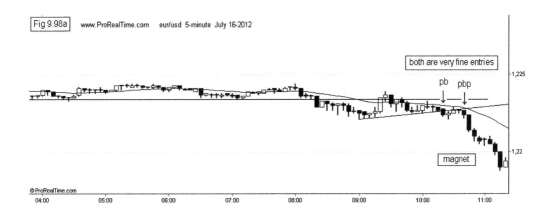

Fig 9.98a   www.ProRealTime.com   eur/usd 5-minute July 16-2012

both are very fine entries

pb   pbp

magnet

Fig 9.98b

An understandable short at first glance, but this was the second pullback to the 25ema (generally not the best trade-for-failure candidate) and the entry suffered risk of the 00-level adverse magnet. Plus there was a US news release coming up at 14:30 CET.

magnet test   skip

EU lunch hours

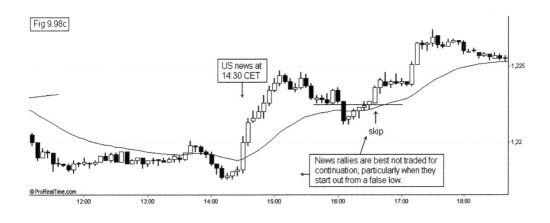

Fig 9.98c

US news at 14:30 CET

skip

News rallies are best not traded for continuation, particularly when they start out from a false low.

Fig 9.99a   www.ProRealTime.com   eur/usd 5-minute July 17-2012

Looks like the bulls are about to gun for the 00 level, but the long does not really set up well. Shady situations in the UK Open can lead to powerful contrarian attacks. Best stay out, and await a better setup.

skip

UK Open

© ProRealTime.com

Fig 9.99b

Let others fight it out in the 00 level

This is a much stronger setup.

skip

tff

Thin buildup in round number. Best be careful.

W

© ProRealTime.com

Fig 9.99c

skip

skip shorts

Market looks to be stalling in anticipation of the news report at 16:00. Exit the short before the news comes out.

US news at 16:00 CET

© ProRealTime.com

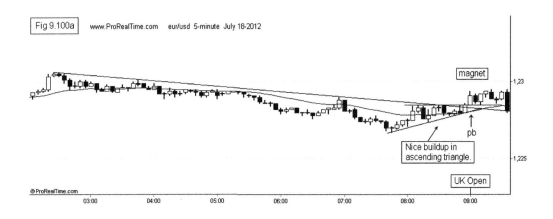

Fig 9.100a   www.ProRealTime.com   eur/usd 5-minute July 18-2012

magnet

Nice buildup in ascending triangle.

pb

UK Open

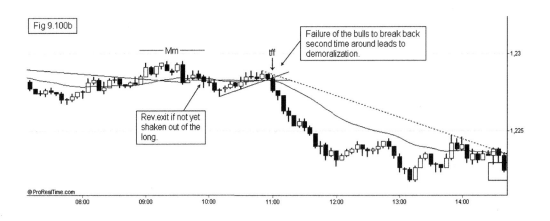

Fig 9.100b

— Mm —

tff

Failure of the bulls to break back second time around leads to demoralization.

Rev.exit if not yet shaken out of the long.

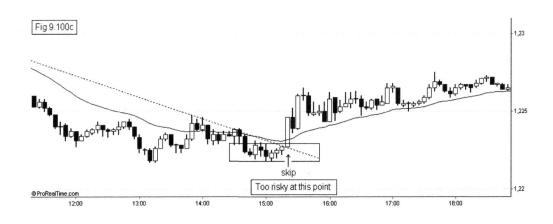

Fig 9.100c

skip

Too risky at this point

349

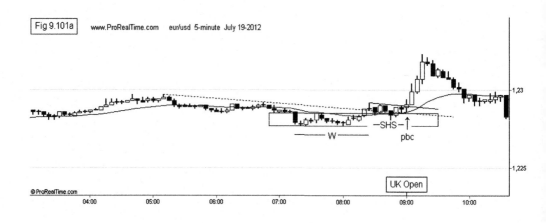

Fig 9.101a   www.ProRealTime.com   eur/usd 5-minute July 19-2012

Fig 9.101b

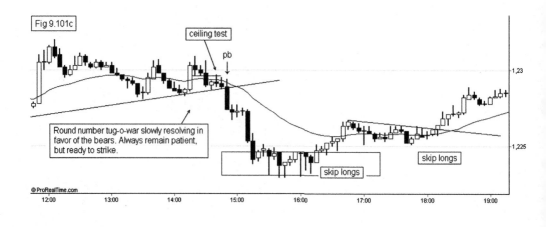

Fig 9.101c

ceiling test

pb

Round number tug-o-war slowly resolving in
favor of the bears. Always remain patient,
but ready to strike.

skip longs

skip longs

Fig 9.102a   www.ProRealTime.com   eur/usd 5-minute July 20-2012

Contrarians gun for the magnet.

skip longs

Ww-variant

Not a great chart to play from the long side. Should prices start to stall in the highs, the 50 level magnet is likely to pull them right back.

@ProRealTime.com

Fig 9.102b

tff

First pullback to the trending 25ema since the 50 level collapse.

@ProRealTime.com

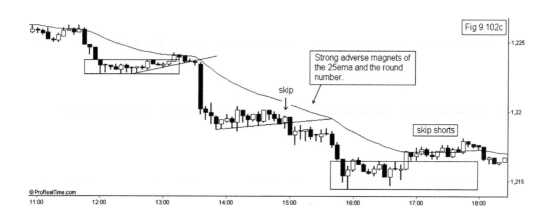

Fig 9.102c

Strong adverse magnets of the 25ema and the round number.

skip

skip shorts

@ProRealTime.com

351

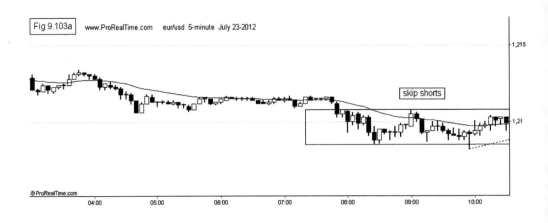

Fig 9.103a www.ProRealTime.com eur/usd 5-minute July 23-2012

skip shorts

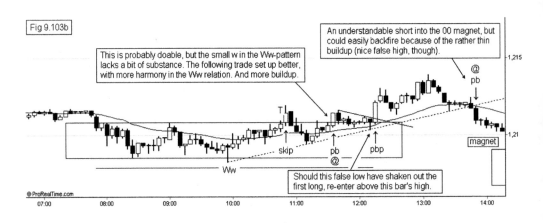

Fig 9.103b

An understandable short into the 00 magnet, but could easily backfire because of the rather thin buildup (nice false high, though).

This is probably doable, but the small w in the Ww-pattern lacks a bit of substance. The following trade set up better, with more harmony in the Ww relation. And more buildup.

@ pb

magnet

skip

pb @

pbp

Ww

Should this false low have shaken out the first long, re-enter above this bar's high.

Fig 9.103c

skip shorts

skip longs

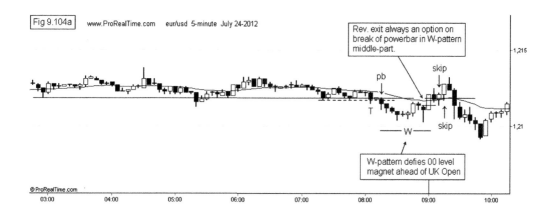

Fig 9.104a   www.ProRealTime.com   eur/usd 5-minute July 24-2012

Rev. exit always an option on
break of powerbar in W-pattern
middle-part.

skip

pb

T

skip

— W —

W-pattern defies 00 level
magnet ahead of UK Open

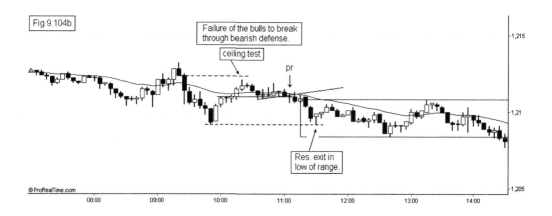

Fig 9.104b

Failure of the bulls to break
through bearish defense.

ceiling test

pr

Res. exit in
low of range.

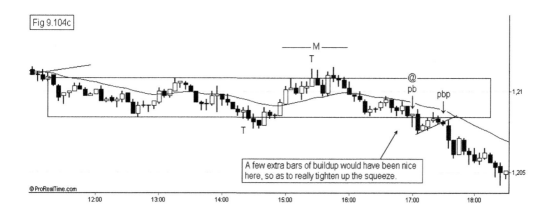

Fig 9.104c

— M —

T

@
pb

pbp

T

A few extra bars of buildup would have been nice
here, so as to really tighten up the squeeze.

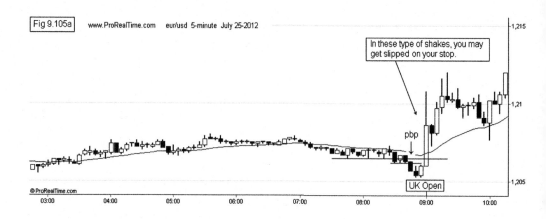

Fig 9.105a — www.ProRealTime.com eur/usd 5-minute July 25-2012

In these type of shakes, you may get slipped on your stop.

pbp

UK Open

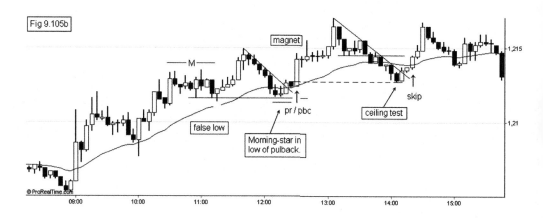

Fig 9.105b

magnet

M

false low

pr / pbc

Morning-star in low of pulback.

ceiling test

skip

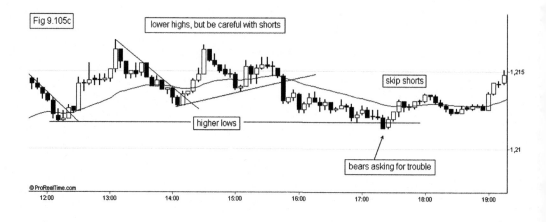

Fig 9.105c

lower highs, but be careful with shorts

skip shorts

higher lows

bears asking for trouble

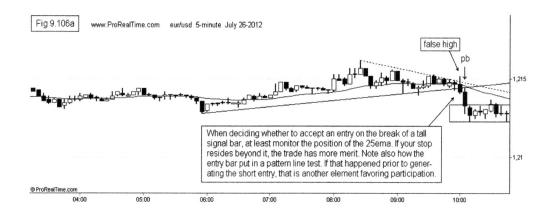

Fig 9.106a   www.ProRealTime.com   eur/usd 5-minute July 26-2012

false high
pb

When deciding whether to accept an entry on the break of a tall signal bar, at least monitor the position of the 25ema. If your stop resides beyond it, the trade has more merit. Note also how the entry bar put in a pattern line test. If that happened prior to generating the short entry, that is another element favoring participation.

© ProRealTime.com

Fig 9.106b

If this rally was induced by scheduled news then entry was best skipped.

Bears still in position should exit above this bar (rev. exit).

magnet

© ProRealTime.com

SHS   pb

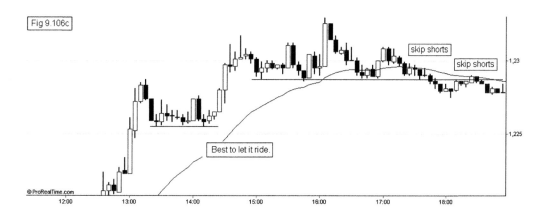

Fig 9.106c

skip shorts
skip shorts

Best to let it ride.

© ProRealTime.com

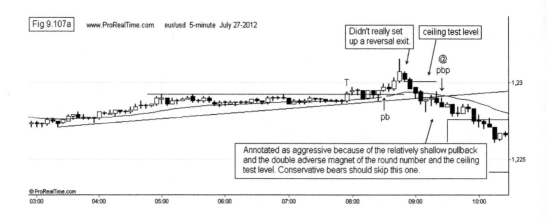

Fig 9.107a   www.ProRealTime.com   eur/usd 5-minute July 27-2012

Didn't really set up a reversal exit.

ceiling test level

@ pbp

pb

Annotated as aggressive because of the relatively shallow pullback and the double adverse magnet of the round number and the ceiling test level. Conservative bears should skip this one.

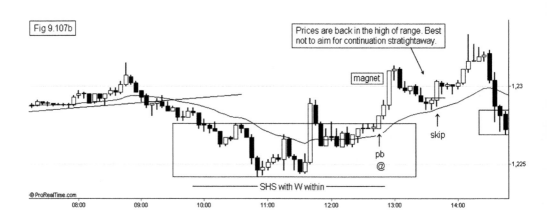

Fig 9.107b

Prices are back in the high of range. Best not to aim for continuation stratightaway.

magnet

skip

pb @

———— SHS with W within ————

Fig 9.107c

— M —

Let go

skip

An understandable long, but very aggressive.

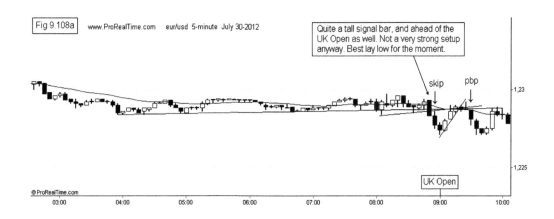

Fig 9.108a   www.ProRealTime.com   eur/usd 5-minute July 30-2012

Quite a tall signal bar, and ahead of the UK Open as well. Not a very strong setup anyway. Best lay low for the moment.

skip

pbp

UK Open

Fig 9.108b

Rev. exits on a diagonal pullback (more or less) will often trap you out of your trade. Not all can be avoided, though.

A classic development : neckline of head-and-shoulders pattern breaks falsely (T) and then a fourth arch is added (squeeze) to set up the short in high-odds fashion.

SHS

false high

pb

W

T

magnet

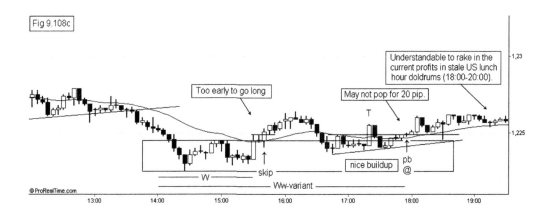

Fig 9.108c

Understandable to rake in the current profits in stale US lunch hour doldrums (18:00-20:00).

Too early to go long

May not pop for 20 pip.

T

W

skip

Ww-variant

nice buildup

pb
@

357

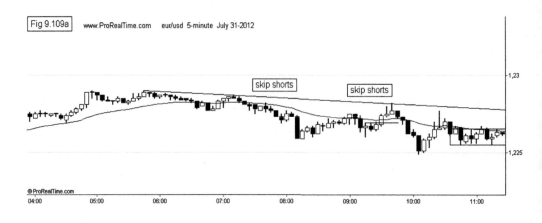

Fig 9.109a   www.ProRealTime.com   eur/usd 5-minute July 31-2012

skip shorts

skip shorts

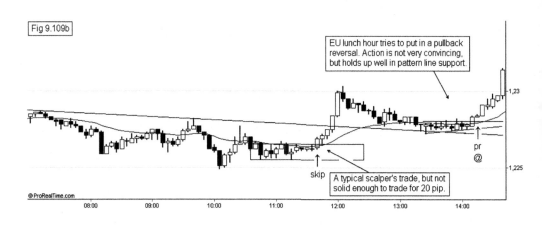

Fig 9.109b

EU lunch hour tries to put in a pullback reversal. Action is not very convincing, but holds up well in pattern line support.

pr @

skip

A typical scalper's trade, but not solid enough to trade for 20 pip.

Fig 9.109c

Bars exceed their average span. Best to lay low.

W

US Open

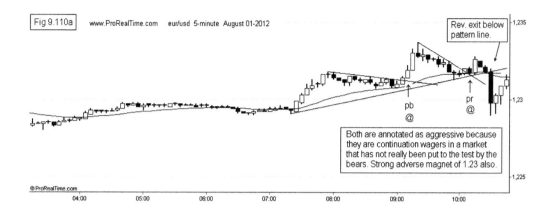

Fig 9.110a   www.ProRealTime.com   eur/usd 5-minute August 01-2012

Rev. exit below pattern line.

Both are annotated as aggressive because they are continuation wagers in a market that has not really been put to the test by the bears. Strong adverse magnet of 1.23 also.

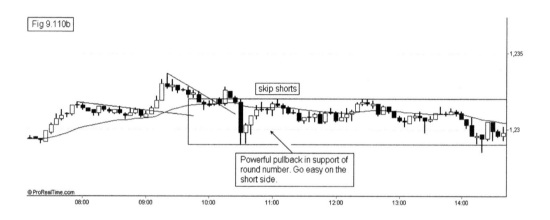

Fig 9.110b

skip shorts

Powerful pullback in support of round number. Go easy on the short side.

Fig 9.110c

An understandable scalp to rake in some pip on the way to the 00 level magnet, but this did not set up well for our purposes.

skip

Fig 9.111a   www.ProRealTime.com   eur/usd 5-minute August 02-2012

Pullback after tease breakout turns into flag on top of range barrier.

false low

skip

Looks a little premature.

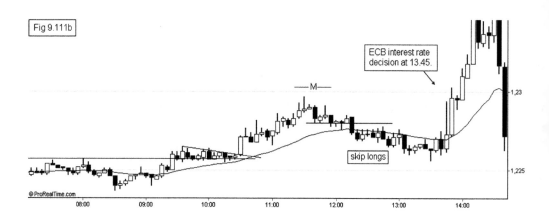

Fig 9.111b

ECB interest rate decision at 13.45.

skip longs

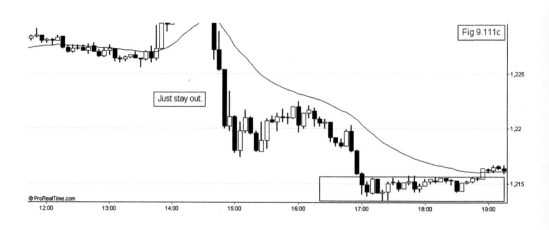

Fig 9.111c

Just stay out.

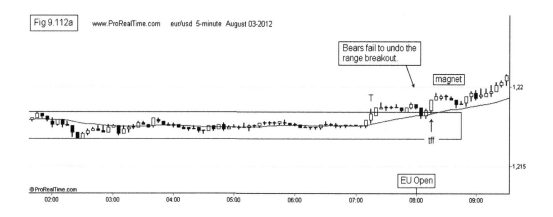

Fig 9.112a   www.ProRealTime.com   eur/usd 5-minute August 03-2012

Bears fail to undo the range breakout.

magnet

tff

EU Open

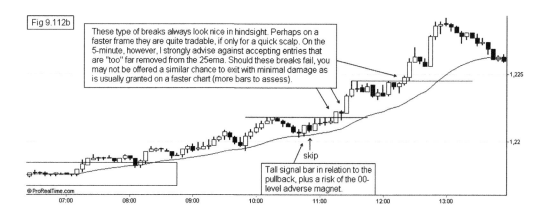

Fig 9.112b

These type of breaks always look nice in hindsight. Perhaps on a faster frame they are quite tradable, if only for a quick scalp. On the 5-minute, however, I strongly advise against accepting entries that are "too" far removed from the 25ema. Should these breaks fail, you may not be offered a similar chance to exit with minimal damage as is usually granted on a faster chart (more bars to assess).

skip

Tall signal bar in relation to the pullback, plus a risk of the 00-level adverse magnet.

Fig 9.112c

US news at 14:30 CET

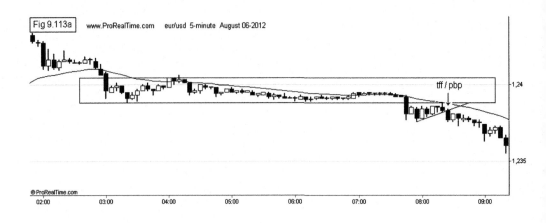

Fig 9.113a — www.ProRealTime.com — eur/usd 5-minute August 06-2012

tff / pbp

Fig 9.113b

skip shorts

powerful pullback

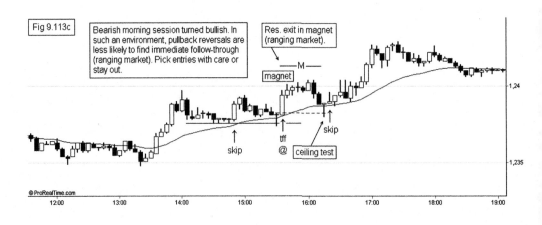

Fig 9.113c

Bearish morning session turned bullish. In
such an environment, pullback reversals are
less likely to find immediate follow-through
(ranging market). Pick entries with care or
stay out.

Res. exit in magnet
(ranging market).

—— M ——

magnet

tff
@

skip

ceiling test

skip

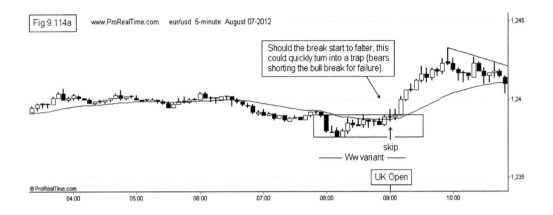

Fig 9.114a   www.ProRealTime.com   eur/usd 5-minute August 07-2012

Should the break start to falter, this
could quickly turn into a trap (bears
shorting the bull break for failure).

skip

——— Ww variant ———

UK Open

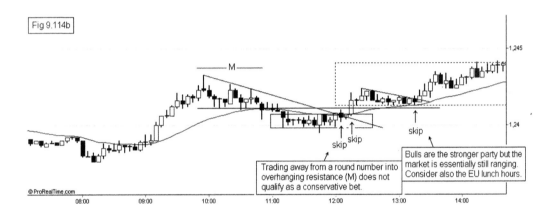

Fig 9.114b

——— M ———

skip skip

skip

Trading away from a round number into
overhanging resistance (M) does not
qualify as a conservative bet.

Bulls are the stronger party but the
market is essentially still ranging.
Consider also the EU lunch hours.

Fig 9.114c

skip shorts

Fig 9.115a   www.ProRealTime.com   eur/usd 5-minute August 08-2012

London Open W-block looks
pretty strong. Do not trade for
failure.

skip

skip

magnet

skip

pb
@

W

Vvv

Market is clearly building up to a reversal.

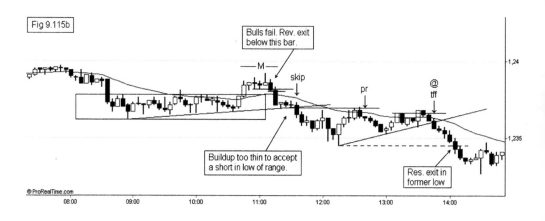

Fig 9.115b

Bulls fail. Rev. exit
below this bar.

— M —

skip

pr

@
tff

Buildup too thin to accept
a short in low of range.

Res. exit in
former low

Fig 9.115c

Overhead resistance a
little above the 00 level.

skip longs

Vvv

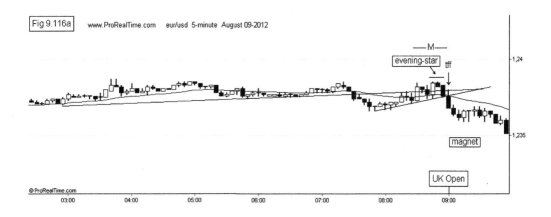

Fig 9.116a   www.ProRealTime.com   eur/usd 5-minute August 09-2012

— M—
evening-star
tff
magnet
UK Open

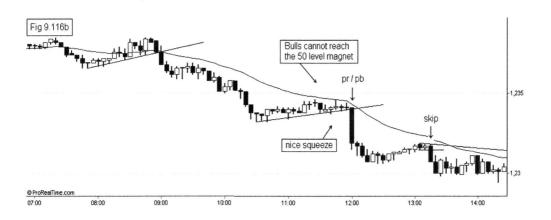

Fig 9.116b

Bulls cannot reach
the 50 level magnet

pr / pb

skip

nice squeeze

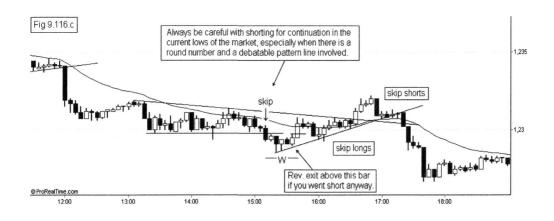

Fig 9.116.c

Always be careful with shorting for continuation in the
current lows of the market, especially when there is a
round number and a debatable pattern line involved.

skip

skip shorts

skip longs

— W —

Rev. exit above this bar
if you went short anyway.

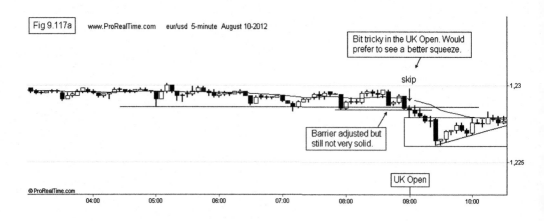

Fig 9.117a   www.ProRealTime.com   eur/usd 5-minute August 10-2012

Bit tricky in the UK Open. Would prefer to see a better squeeze.

skip

Barrier adjusted but still not very solid.

UK Open

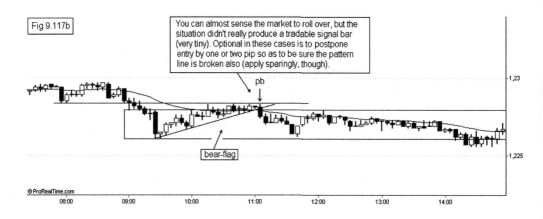

Fig 9.117b

You can almost sense the market to roll over, but the situation didn't really produce a tradable signal bar (very tiny). Optional in these cases is to postpone entry by one or two pip so as to be sure the pattern line is broken also (apply sparingly, though).

pb

bear-flag

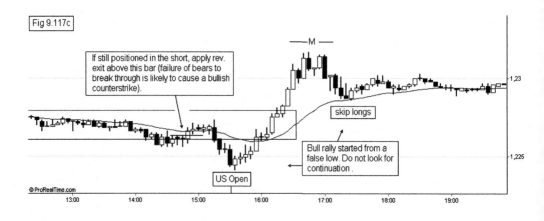

Fig 9.117c

— M —

If still positioned in the short, apply rev. exit above this bar (failure of bears to break through is likely to cause a bullish counterstrike).

skip longs

Bull rally started from a false low. Do not look for continuation .

US Open

Fig 9.118a   www.ProRealTime.com   eur/usd 5-minute August 13-2012

— W —

Bullish breakout in the making

© ProRealTime.com

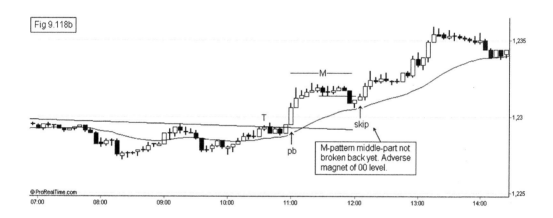

Fig 9.118b

— M —

T

skip

pb

M-pattern middle-part not broken back yet. Adverse magnet of 00 level.

© ProRealTime.com

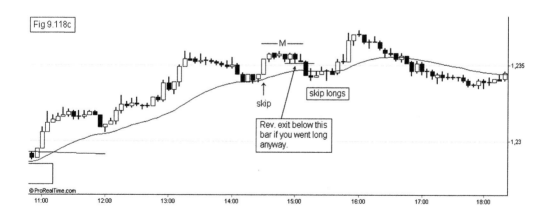

Fig 9.118c

— M —

skip

skip longs

Rev. exit below this bar if you went long anyway.

© ProRealTime.com

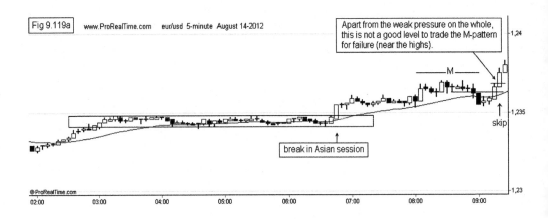

Fig 9.119a   www.ProRealTime.com   eur/usd 5-minute August 14-2012

Apart from the weak pressure on the whole, this is not a good level to trade the M-pattern for failure (near the highs).

M

skip

break in Asian session

Fig 9.119b

M

skip shorts

skip

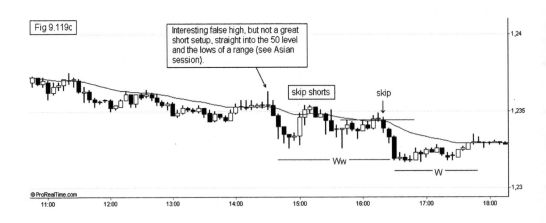

Fig 9.119c

Interesting false high, but not a great short setup, straight into the 50 level and the lows of a range (see Asian session).

skip shorts

skip

Ww

W

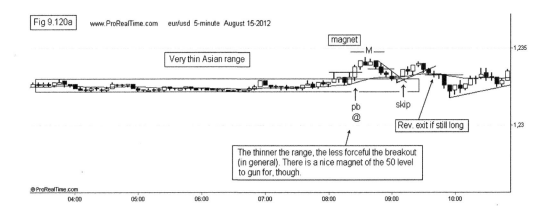

Fig 9.120a   www.ProRealTime.com   eur/usd 5-minute August 15-2012

magnet

M

Very thin Asian range

pb
@

skip

Rev. exit if still long

The thinner the range, the less forceful the breakout
(in general). There is a nice magnet of the 50 level
to gun for, though.

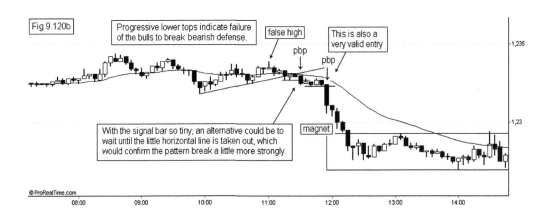

Fig 9.120b

Progressive lower tops indicate failure
of the bulls to break bearish defense.

false high

pbp

This is also a
very valid entry

pbp

With the signal bar so tiny, an alternative could be to
wait until the little horizontal line is taken out, which
would confirm the pattern break a little more strongly.

magnet

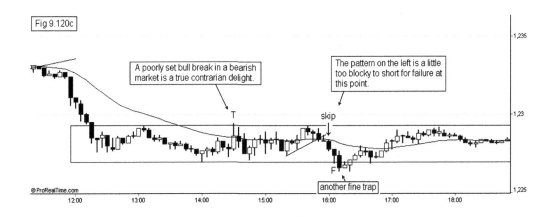

Fig 9.120c

A poorly set bull break in a bearish
market is a true contrarian delight.

The pattern on the left is a little
too blocky to short for failure at
this point.

T

skip

F

another fine trap

Fig 9.121a   www.ProRealTime.com   eur/usd 5-minute August 16-2012

Nice scalp to the top of the range ; pretty aggressive trade if you aim for 20 pip, though.

Res. exit

1,23

Ww

pb

@

1,225

EU Open   UK Open

© ProRealTime.com

04:00   05:00   06:00   07:00   08:00   09:00   10:00

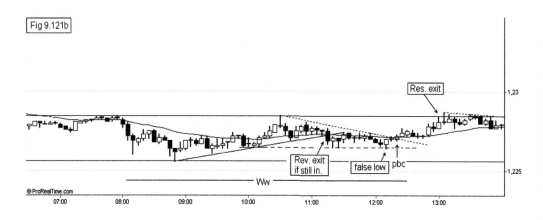

Fig 9.121b

Res. exit

1,23

Rev. exit if still in.

false low   pbc

Ww

1,225

© ProRealTime.com

07:00   08:00   09:00   10:00   11:00   12:00   13:00

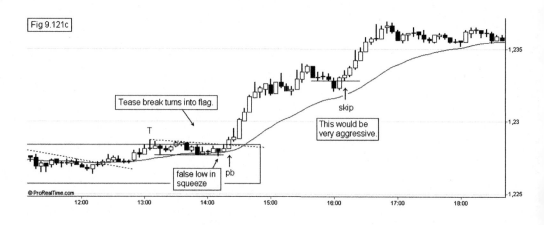

Fig 9.121c

1,235

Tease break turns into flag.

T

skip

This would be very aggressive.

1,23

false low in squeeze   pb

1,225

© ProRealTime.com

12:00   13:00   14:00   15:00   16:00   17:00   18:00

Fig 9.122a   www.ProRealTime.com   eur/usd 5-minute August 17-2012

If you traded long and not yet on target, deploy a reversal exit below this bar to avoid 50-level magnet

Bullish dominance not convincingly established in 50 level.

— M —

skip

EU Open

Fig 9.122b

— M —

skip shorts in lows of range

skip longs

Fig 9.122c

double false highs

@
tff

This short goes up against a pretty strong block (below 50 level), but the bears definitely hammered back the bullish charges above the round number, proving their dominance once more (worth a shot).

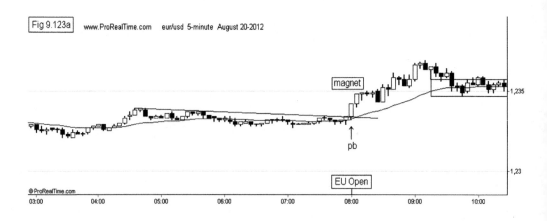

Fig 9.123a   www.ProRealTime.com   eur/usd 5-minute August 20-2012

magnet

pb

EU Open

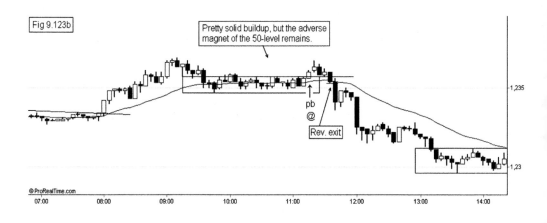

Fig 9.123b

Pretty solid buildup, but the adverse
magnet of the 50-level remains.

pb
@

Rev. exit

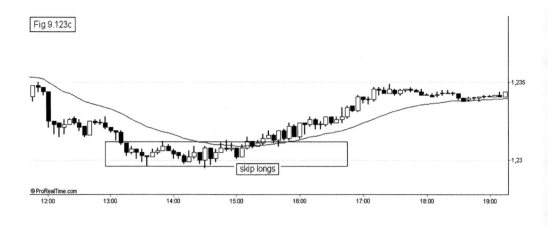

Fig 9.123c

skip longs

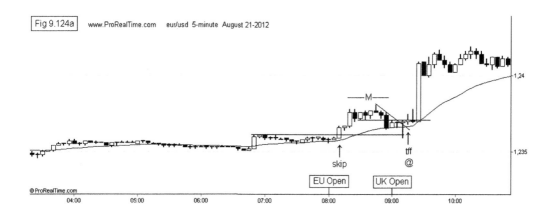

Fig 9.124a   www.ProRealTime.com   eur/usd 5-minute August 21-2012

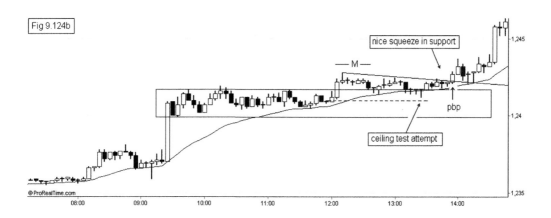

Fig 9.124b

Fig 9.124c

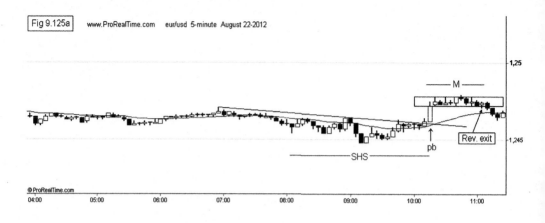

Fig 9.125a   www.ProRealTime.com   eur/usd 5-minute August 22-2012

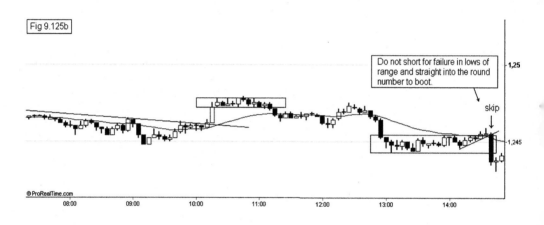

Fig 9.125b

Do not short for failure in lows of range and straight into the round number to boot.

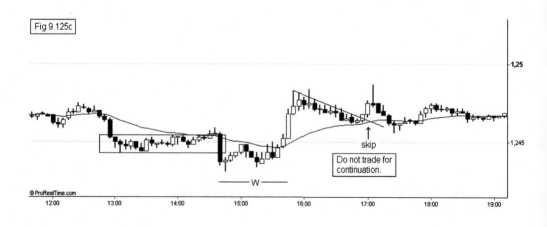

Fig 9.125c

Do not trade for continuation.

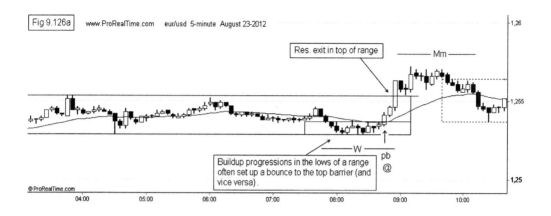

Fig 9.126a   www.ProRealTime.com   eur/usd 5-minute August 23-2012

Res. exit in top of range

Mm

Buildup progressions in the lows of a range
often set up a bounce to the top barrier (and
vice versa).

W

pb
@

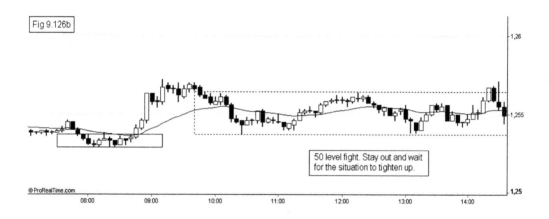

Fig 9.126b

50 level fight. Stay out and wait
for the situation to tighten up.

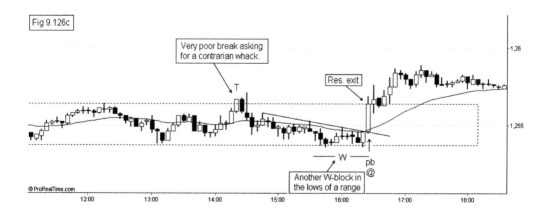

Fig 9.126c

Very poor break asking
for a contrarian whack.

T

Res. exit

W

pb
@

Another W-block in
the lows of a range

375

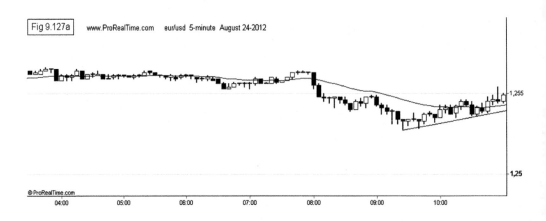

Fig 9.127a   www.ProRealTime.com   eur/usd 5-minute August 24-2012

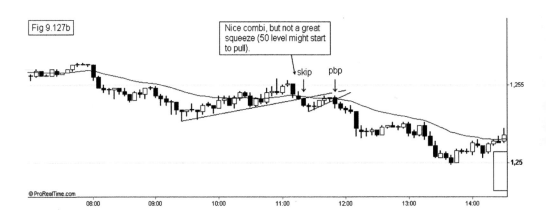

Fig 9.127b

Nice combi, but not a great squeeze (50 level might start to pull).

skip

pbp

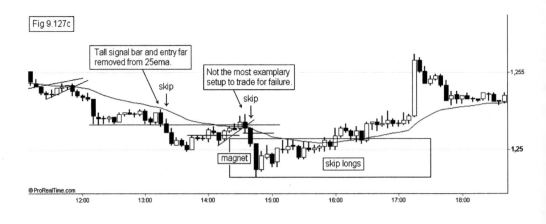

Fig 9.127c

Tall signal bar and entry far removed from 25ema.

skip

Not the most examplary setup to trade for failure.

skip

magnet

skip longs

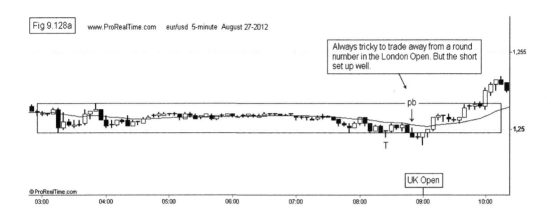

Fig 9.128a   www.ProRealTime.com   eur/usd 5-minute August 27-2012

Always tricky to trade away from a round
number in the London Open. But the short
set up well.

pb

T

UK Open

Fig 9.128b

Very thin price action. Let go.

Fig 9.128c

Summer months can be awfully stale. When confronted with these lackluster
sessions, a very common mistake is to overtrade. It's better to lay low instead.

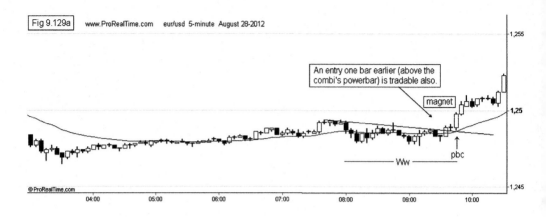

Fig 9.129a www.ProRealTime.com eur/usd 5-minute August 28-2012

An entry one bar earlier (above the combi's powerbar) is tradable also.

magnet

pbc

Vvw

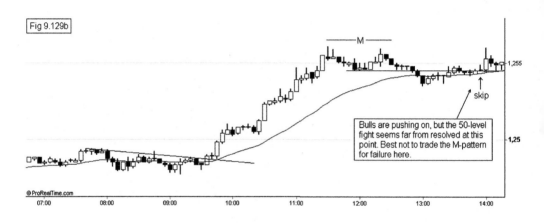

Fig 9.129b

M

skip

Bulls are pushing on, but the 50-level fight seems far from resolved at this point. Best not to trade the M-pattern for failure here.

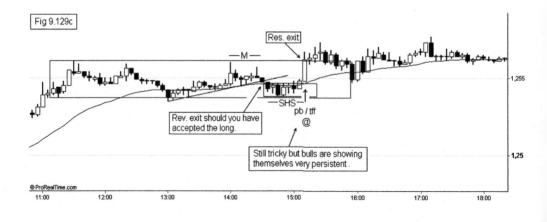

Fig 9.129c

Res. exit

M

SHS

pb / tff
@

Rev. exit should you have accepted the long.

Still tricky but bulls are showing themselves very persistent .

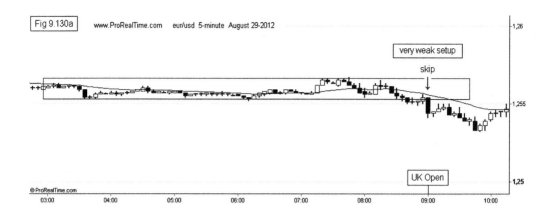

Fig 9.130a   www.ProRealTime.com   eur/usd 5-minute August 29-2012

very weak setup

skip

UK Open

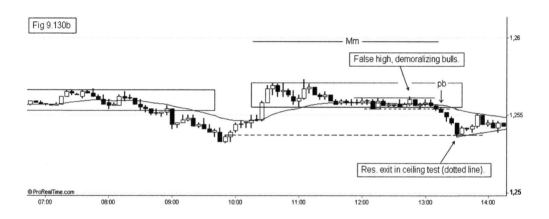

Fig 9.130b

Mm

False high, demoralizing bulls.

pb

Res. exit in ceiling test (dotted line).

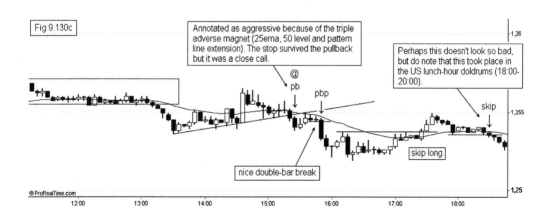

Fig 9.130c

Annotated as aggressive because of the triple
adverse magnet (25ema, 50 level and pattern
line extension). The stop survived the pullback
but it was a close call.

Perhaps this doesn't look so bad,
but do note that this took place in
the US lunch-hour doldrums (18:00-
20:00).

@
pb

pbp

skip

skip long

nice double-bar break

Fig 9.131a   www. ProRealTime.com   eur/usd 5-minute August 30-2012

50 level range

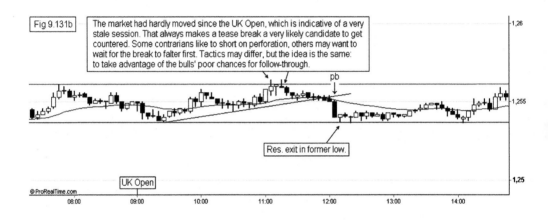

Fig 9.131b   The market had hardly moved since the UK Open, which is indicative of a very stale session. That always makes a tease break a very likely candidate to get countered. Some contrarians like to short on perforation, others may want to wait for the break to falter first. Tactics may differ, but the idea is the same: to take advantage of the bulls' poor chances for follow-through.

pb

Res. exit in former low.

UK Open

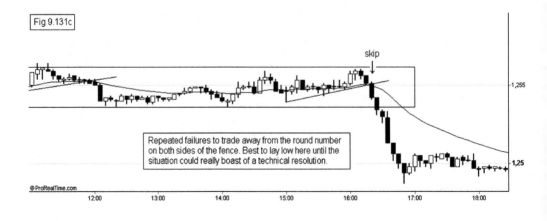

Fig 9.131c

skip

Repeated failures to trade away from the round number on both sides of the fence. Best to lay low here until the situation could really boast of a technical resolution.

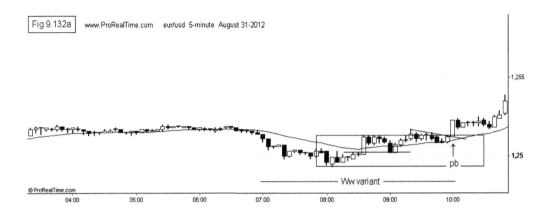

Fig 9.132a   www.ProRealTime.com   eur/usd 5-minute August 31-2012

Ww variant

pb

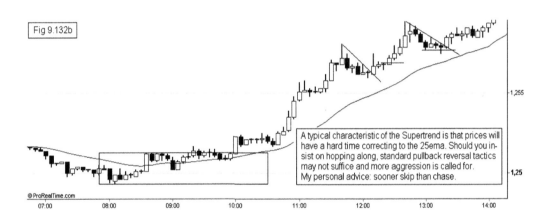

Fig 9.132b

A typical characteristic of the Supertrend is that prices will
have a hard time correcting to the 25ema. Should you insist on hopping along, standard pullback reversal tactics
may not suffice and more aggression is called for.
My personal advice: sooner skip than chase.

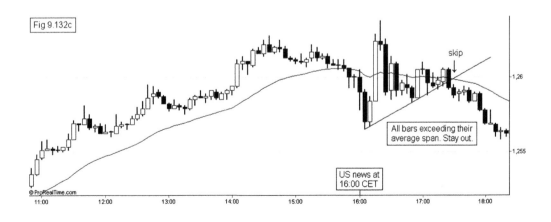

Fig 9.132c

skip

All bars exceeding their
average span. Stay out.

US news at
16:00 CET

Chapter 10

Trade Size—Compounding

With so much of the attention directed towards the technical side of trading, it is easy to overlook the importance of accounting, and that of trade size in particular. For all who take their trading seriously—in essence, as a business—devoting a few moments to read up on this most essential topic will be time well spent.

What will be offered in this chapter is not a set of hard-and-fast rules on how to apply volume per trade "correctly"; the variables regarding capital, skill and appetite for risk are just too widespread for accounting to be molded into a one-fits-all format. What we can do, however, is look at it from the perspective of the average, relatively underfunded trader and find out how a better understanding of trade volume can have a major impact on the bottom line over time. All this is completely separated from the technical side of trading. It really is an accounting matter.

The essence of trade sizing is very simple at heart. The basic idea is to always apply a certain amount of units per trade in relation to the available funds in the account. As the account grows, so should the number of units played. If this is done in strict accordance with a certain percentage of capital, it is referred to as *compounding*. For example, if an account grows from $5,000 to $5,500 and the risk is set to 1 percent per trade, a compounding trader will have increased his number of units by 10 percent but his risk per trade still stands at 1 percent. Likewise, when the account shrinks in value, so should the amount of units per trade, yet the risk per wager will remain the same in terms of percentage.

When exactly to adjust one's volume is a personal call. Scalpers, trading a single instrument, may want to do so every new session; but the principle of compounding works equally well when done from a weekly perspective, or even on a monthly basis. Variations on the compounding theme are practically infinite, and all will show different results, but more important than the exact application is to grasp the advantage of steadily increasing units in accordance with a growing account. For ease of use, we will explore the compounding factor based on *weekly* adjustments.

Note: The following accounting suggestions are specifically geared towards traders who have been showing positive results for, say, at least a few months. Those still struggling to come out ahead are best advised to work on their trade selection first and not think too much about account buildup. They should either do their trading on a paper-trade account or, preferably, on a live account on superlight volume. The latter option is a great asset of trading spot Forex: you can participate in the actual market and see your orders *filled*, but without the psychological disadvantage of having too much capital at stake in the learning stages. (Many retail brokers allow you to trade as low as nickels and dimes.)

A widely accepted and generally sound idea is to risk between 1 and 2 percent of capital per trade. While there is of course room on the low side, it is strongly advised not to risk more than 2 percent on a single wager; sooner or later, such hastiness is bound to backfire—and there isn't much call for it either. Compounding units on a more conservative risk model may have the account growing at a calmer pace, but the inevitable drawbacks will have less of an impact also, and in the end, this may benefit account growth much more than slow it down.

To fully understand the virtues of compounding let us compare the trading results of two traders who scored the exact same points per week for 48 weeks on end. Trader A kept trading the same units per trade, despite his growing account, yet Trader B incorporated the compounding factor on a weekly basis. Let us further assume that both traders started out on a $5,000 account, risking 2 percent per trade ($100) and that they consistently scored 2.5 points per week. (A single stop represents 1 point, so this would be 25 pip per week when working with a 10 pip stop on a trade.)

For Trader B, the compounded outcome as shown below can be computed with a so-called *compound interest calculator*, we will get to that in a moment. The results are as follows:

Trader A consistently took out $250 per week, which means his assembled profit for the year is $12,000 (250 x 48), bringing his account up to a total of $17,000. Quite a respectable feat.

Trader B started out with the same $250 profit in his first week, but then immediately incorporated these gains into his trading volume for the next week. And he kept applying the compounding factor every new week. After 48 weeks, this trader's bottom line will amount to a whopping $52,000.

Do realize that both traders scored the *exact* same points per week for 48 weeks straight; they may even have taken the very same trades and managed them the exactly same. In other words, the huge difference in bottom line is solely a consequence of accounting.

Of course, somewhere down the line, Trader A, in the face of his steadily growing account, will surely have increased his volume per trade. But then again, it is certainly not uncommon for a profitable trader to remain stuck on the same volume for many months on end, for example when trading the futures markets (it's quite a step to go from 1 to 2 contracts), or when habitually pulling out monthly earnings to cover living expenses.

Necessities and preferences aside, it is plain to see that the ideal situation is to run a trading account purely for trading purposes, without taking anything out for as long as possible. This way, even a "small" account can prosper pleasantly over time.

It is interesting to note also that if both traders had managed to take out not 2.5 but 5 points per week, the yearly profits of Trader A would have doubled to $24.000 (bringing his account to $29.000), but not so with Trader B. In fact, after 48 weeks of compounding 5 points per week on a 2-percent model, his account would have shown an incredible figure of $485,000. Such can be the power of compounding.

Please understand that all of the above just serves to point out the virtues of running a trading business effectively. It is not about projecting hypothetical riches into the future. These figures, however, do illustrate the amazing differences in bottom line between two traders doing the exact same thing, but who take a different approach to accounting. It is therefore highly recommended to start implementing the compounding factor into the trading volume as soon as possible when profitable across the board.

Quite intriguing also is that compounding not only proves its merits on the positive side of the equation. It works equally well in protecting an account from full depletion. In fact, it is virtually impossible to blow up an account when strictly abiding by the rules of compounding. After all, on a shrinking account, each new week will be traded with less volume (but with the same percentage of capital risk per trade). For example, if we once again picture a trader with a $5,000 account, risking 2 percent per trade, and we now let this trader *lose* 2.5 points per week for 48 weeks straight, then his account would still show a *positive* figure of about $426.

In other words, for a non-profitable Forex trader to add funds to a shrinking account is a folly, for he can theoretically trade as long as he wants without ever depleting his initial stake. Adding funds to fatten up an account should only be done when profitable across the board and never in a desperate attempt to swing things around by trading bigger. Granted, this holds up mainly for the Forex market and may not apply to futures or stocks, where you may not be able to place a trade without a certain minimum balance in the account. But do check with your Forex broker on this matter also, because some may have put up a minimum barrier as well.

The great benefit of trading spot Forex, and particularly functional when compounding, is that we can increase our trade volume in the smallest of increments. Instead of having to add a full contract, as in the case of the futures market, we can add just a handful of units on the next trade if we so desire (100,000 units being a full contract).

To check the amazing benefits of compounding for yourself, you could run your numbers through a rather complicated mathematical formula, but a much quicker way is to look up a *compound interest calculator* on the web. There are many of them freely available. (Find a simple one that only compounds interest annually, not quarterly.) Since these calculators are originally designed for annual interest computations, you have to discard the years-to-grow box and read it as if it says weeks-to-grow. You only have to type in three entries: Current principle (your account balance), weeks-to-grow (the number of weeks you want to project) and the interest rate (see below). If there is a box for annual addition, just set it to zero. Some calculators may not allow you to type in more than 40 weeks (years basically); just find one that has no limit. Always cross check your results with another calculator, just to make sure you can trust the figures presented.

What to put in the interest rate box is dependent on the number of points per week you wish to project, and on the chosen percentage of risk per trade. Regardless of what bracket settings are used, a full stop-out always equals 1 point (in our bracket a full winner equals 2 points). On a 1-percent risk model, 1 point equals 1 percent. So, in the interest rate box, type 3 when you want to see the results of 3 points of profit per week compounded. When using a 2-percent model, type 6 for these same 3 points per week, and so on.

To check if your calculator works properly, a random example should look like this: Current principle ($10,000); weeks-to-grow (48); interest rate (3); The future value should read: $41,322.52.

As you can check as well, scoring the same points per week consistently on a more aggressive 2-percent model will not just double the results. In the example above, after 48 weeks the balance will stand at no less than $163,938.72 (in the interest rate box, enter 6 instead of 3).

Does this imply that a profitable trader is depriving himself when applying a risk model of less than 2 percent? In all fairness, no one can answer this for another. Being more comfortable with a lesser amount of capital at stake may very well outmatch the benefits of playing an aggressive 2-percent model. When just starting to emerge on the profitable side, a trader may still lack the confidence and emotional stability that comes with experience over time. In this promising yet often brittle phase, perhaps an idea could be to start out with, say, a 0.5 percent risk per trade and then gradually work up to a 1-percent model in the coming weeks; and from there on to a full 2-percent model. It's all up to the trader.

Note: It should be stressed that the calculations derived from the compound interest calculator are based on a consistency of points per week that is virtually untenable in practice. Even when two traders take out the same points per month, their weekly results will probably differ and so will the way they compound. For example, one trader may have taken out 5 points per week for 4 weeks straight (very consistent), and in his case the computations of the calculator will match up. But another trader may hypothetically have scored 0 points in the first three weeks and then 20 points in the last. His result for the month will amount to a lesser total in comparison with his more consistent fellow trader, simply because he had no profits to compound in the first three weeks of the month.

As we can see, the possible variations on the compounding theme are practically infinite and all will show different results. (Think also of losing weeks and having to *lower* volume on the next week.) In other words, playing around with the calculator can be fun, but it is highly recommended not to indulge in silly fantasies on future riches. Moreover, once the practical advantages of compounding are established, my advice would be to fully discard this tool. Not only is it unrealistic to project hypothetical gains into the future, should the weekly objectives not be met, this may add an unwelcome element of stress and frustration. Much more useful is to concentrate on improving consistency first; the rest will follow by itself.

As to deriving the right amount of *units* per trade, there are calculators freely available on the web, but perhaps it is wise to briefly examine how these computations can be done by hand. If you have no direct need for this, just skip the following paragraphs. Anyway, here goes:

To compute the amount of units to be assigned on the next Monday's trades, we need to know (a) the account balance, (b) the risk model, and (c) the "stop factor" on the instrument in question.

To understand the latter, let us examine the specifications of the eur/usd contract first. The pair is made up of a base currency (eur) and a quote currency (usd). A full contract represents 100,000 units, but the value of the contract in US dollars is dependent on the currency rate. If the pair stands at, say, 1.3000, the value of a full contract is 100,000 x 1.30 = $130,000. If the rate goes up 100 pip, it will stand at 1.3100 and the contract now represents a value of $131,000. From this we can derive that on a *full* eur/usd contract, 1 pip equals $10, regardless of the current rate.

The "stop factor" is key in the computation of units. It is derived as follows. A theoretical 1 pip stop requires a factor 100. If we use a 10 pip stop in our bracket, we need to divide 100 by 10, and so our stop factor is 10. Should we want to use, say, a 12,5 pip stop, then we should divide 100 by 12,5 and our stop factor will be 8, and so on. For ease of use, let's stick to the 10 pip stop, representing a stop factor of 10.

Thus, on a $5000 account and a 2-percent risk model, a trader can compute his units as follows: 5000 x 2 x 10 = 100,000 units (a full contract). Should the account go up with, say, $250 for the week (25 pip profit), the new balance will stand at $5,250 and the computation of volume for the next Monday session is as follows: 5250 x 2 x 10 = 105,000 units.

When using a 1-percent model, it is just a matter of adjusting the risk model in the computation: 5000 x 1 x 10 = 50,000 units. After the same 25 pip of profit for the week, the balance will stand at $5,125. The next week can now be traded with 5125 x 1 x 10 = 51,250 units.

The computations above apply to an account held in US dollars. If you hold an account in, say, euro, you need to incorporate a "conversion factor" as well. For this you need to look at the current rate of the eur/usd instrument. The easiest way to do this is to first compute the number of units as if holding an account in US dollars (as shown above) and then multiply by the rate. Let's say the eur/usd is quoted at 1.3000. To compute the units on a euro account of €5,000, the computation for a stop factor of 10 on a 2-percent model is: 5000 x 2 x 10 x 1.3 = 130,000 units.

Of course, the rate can fluctuate substantially during the course of the week, which, strictly seen, would demand adjustment along the way. However, much more important than being absolutely meticulous about compounding is to understand the importance of steadily increasing unit size.

The easiest way to do all your trade sizing is to find a *Forex Position Size Calculator* on the web, freely available. With this tool you can compute in just a few seconds the right amount of units for *any* currency pair in relation to your risk model, account balance and account currency. When doing your calculations by hand, take specific note of pairs that are quoted with different decimals, such as the Japanese yen. Always make sure, though, to check your volume in actual risk per trade. Chances are, your platform will already warn you when a preset unit size is way off the mark (margin error notification).

Note: For "ease of use", some brokers do not specify a full contract in the standard 100,000 units, instead they name a full contract as 10 units. For example, should you want to trade 135,000 units, you may now have to type in 13.5 in the order ticket. And your next possible step up would be 13.6. Although this will affect the *exact* application of unit size in terms of capital percentage, the incremental steps are still small enough to allow a steady increase of trade volume, which is what compounding is all about. For what it is worth, one silly trade that could have been avoided will have a much bigger impact on your weekly earnings than a unit size that was slightly below or above the desired percentage.

To summarize on the above, let it suffice to say that responsibly increasing your volume along the way, regardless of how exactly it is done, is a most vital aspect of running your business effectively. The advantages of compounding simply cannot be ignored.

Chapter 11

Adapting to Low Volatility

It could be personal preference, but I would say the Forex markets are the best place for traders to start out their trading careers. One of the main benefits, as explained in the previous chapter, is to be allowed to play almost any volume of choice (on the low side) and to be able to increase trade size in the smallest of incremental steps. Furthermore, although not equally active in every time zone, the markets are open 24/5 and there is always an interesting Open to play, with usually enough action going on in the first few hours of the session to make some decent profits for the day.

But there is a drawback also. Although this can hit other markets in equal fashion, Forex markets, from time to time, can go very, very stale; this could be due to a news release later in the session, but it is certainly not uncommon for currency pairs to travel in a tight, meandering range for days, weeks, and sometimes even months on end. At the time of writing these pages, July 2014, we are currently experiencing record-low volatility (at least on an intraday basis), which is perhaps not so strange if we take into account the unprecedented near-zero interest rates across the board and the fact that most central banks have openly declared not to intervene on the upside anytime soon.

Regardless of its actual cause, a persistent environment of low volatility seldom makes for pleasant trading (savvy contrarians might think differently). It surely isn't much fun to see prices meander aimlessly in a tight range for hours on end, and painstakingly slow at that. In such a climate, with little follow-through on balance, the breakout trader in particular is at risk of becoming at least a little frustrated. But not all is lost. Depending on when you read these pages, the markets may be swinging generously to and fro again, but in case low volatility persists, or perhaps reappears, let's have a look at how we can deal with these matters in terms of adaptation.

First of all, it should be noted that the price action principles are never affected, for they stand above the nature of the session; as long as there are traders around, action will cause reaction and this will have the principles of supply and demand do their thing as in any active session. Consequently, there isn't much need for revising the game plan on a *technical* basis; the changes will mostly regard strategic procedure.

Typical adjustments that spring to mind are to tighten the standard bracket to a smaller span (if only on the target side) and to lay very low on quick continuation trades that stem from little buildup, particularly when the highs or lows of the session are in play. Another popular adjustment is to switch over to a faster time frame, in the hopes of finding more opportunities in the smaller motions of the market.

Experienced traders, having seen every possible climate a hundred times over, may not find it too hard to adjust their game to a slower pace; for a novice trader, lacking technical reference and overall experience, this may not be so easily done and it could take a serious number of losing or otherwise aborted trades to even come to terms with the change in climate. Of course, a novice, too, will quickly come to realize that the conditions are out of the ordinary and that follow-through on breakouts is often treacherously brittle; but it is no easy chore to come up with an adequate answer on how to adapt to this kind of setting.

This chapter is meant to offer some insights on the matter, but before we proceed, allow me to suggest a very worthy alternative first, which is *not* to adjust, but to simply set up more markets to trade. Needless to say, this doesn't release a trader from practicing patience still, but at least it is fair to assume that trading more markets simultaneously should increase the amount of opportunities offered. By trading, say, four markets, as opposed to a single instrument, it requires a mere fourth of the average points per market to come out ahead with similar results as before. In addition to adding markets, a trader could also split up his working day into two shifts, so as to focus on the hours of most activity, which are usually the first few hours following an Open. For example, Asian traders can trade the Asian and the EU morning (00:00-04:00 and 08:00-12:00 CET). European traders can trade the EU and US morning (08:00-12:00 and 14:00-18:00); American traders can trade the early US morning, and then perhaps give it another go in the Asian Open later on (14:00-18:00 and 00:00-04:00).

But even with these countermeasures in place, days may still go by without a single trade running to target, or even being offered in conservative fashion—such can be the nature of a stale environment. Yet if you can see past the foolish notion of needing to score profit on a *daily* basis and instead look upon your business from, say, a *monthly* perspective (or yearly, for that matter), the prospects for decent returns are seldom very bleak, even in poor conditions.

So why adjust at all? It's hard to speak for another, but whenever a persistently harsh environment starts to weigh heavy on a trader's psyche, affecting also the way the opportunities that *do* occur are perceived, it might indeed pay to explore some tried-and-tested alternatives.

The reader will recall that the 5-minute chart merely served a vehicle role for price action illustrations and strategy design. If we so desire, we should have little difficulty transposing our earlier findings to a faster chart with hardly any need for technical adjustment.

Before we go this route, it is important to understand that slow conditions do affect the faster frames as well. So patience and trade selection are still key. On the good side, if we set up a few of these charts rather than just one, this is likely to offer enough action to at least keep us sharp and in good spirits.

This then leaves us to decide on a frame of choice. Obviously, the options are plentiful. Next to popular time frames, like the 1 or 2-minute, there are tick, range and volume charts in any customizable setting, and some platforms even offer traders the possibility to code their own frames by parameters of choice.

In order not to deviate too much from the visual characteristics of the 5-minute chart, allow me to suggest a frame that looks pleasantly familiar but is much faster on the whole: the 200-tick. (A single tick is a transaction between buyers and sellers, regardless of the volume traded.) Depending on the current pace of the market a 200-tick setting could resemble a 2 or 3-minute frame on a Forex chart, but this is never a matter of absolutes. A specific advantage of the tick frame setting is that when there is little trading done, the chart does not have to print an obligatory bar as in the case of a time frame setting; instead it will accumulate whatever is traded and then only print a bar when the preset tick number is matched. Thus, where a stale phase might print, say, thirty non-descriptive bars in a row on the 2-minute frame (an hour of nothingness), on a 200-tick chart this may only show, say, six such bars. But as soon as the action picks up pace, the 200-tick and the 2-minute frame may start to resemble one another more closely again.

The above implies that by trading the 200-tick frame, we can benefit from the advantages of a faster time frame, like the 2-minute, but without the disadvantage of seeing the chart stretched out into nothingness when there is little trading done.

In all fairness, tick charts are not unanimously appreciated and there is indeed a disadvantage when compared to time frame charts: due to the endless variety of possible settings, and not to mention the fact that different providers produce different tick data (we'll get to that in a minute), few tick chart traders will look at the *exact* same action, bar-wise, on their screens. It can therefore be argued that the break of a tick bar may not trigger the kind of spicy response that is often seen on the break of a time bar. On a faster chart, however, this is seldom an issue of concern. Since we aim to trade away from buildup, the break of a signal bar on the 200-tick is not likely to be a standalone event, not even on a swift pullback reversal. There are always more bars involved and together they will set up our buildup boundaries in very visible fashion, just like we have come to appreciate on the 5-minute frame in our earlier studies. In fact, they may even line up more neatly.

But why not let the reader judge for himself. Following below is a series of examples on the eur/usd, aud/usd and usd/jpy, all seen from the perspective of the 200-tick. Once these studies are completed, we will wrap up this chapter with a brief exploration of some popular non-Forex markets: the S&P 500, the Nasdaq 100 and the Dow mini. If nothing else, all this will demonstrate that price action concepts do not discriminate from market to market, nor from frame to frame, be it tick or time.

Note: The tick settings in the charts below reflect the data feed of Prorealtime, a standalone charting provider. Since currencies are not traded on a centralized exchange, transaction data is bundled in bits and pieces from all over the globe and the way this is done is likely to differ from one provider to the next. Should you work with another provider, you may have to alter your tick setting to a different number to resemble the charts shown, but close is always good enough. (And perhaps your preference goes out to another chart pace anyway, slower or faster.) In any case, there exists no such thing as a superior time or tick frame. More important is to use a setting that sits well with your personal idea of pleasant charting and trading.

When experimenting with a new setting, of whatever kind, it is essential to allow yourself sufficient time to obtain a good feel for the new market pace. When you have limited access to historical data, it is much advised to take screenshots of relevant market situations and to file them for future reference. This will not only build up a solid database of study material, it will surely help to speed up the testing period in which to train your eyes to the specific characteristics of the new setting.

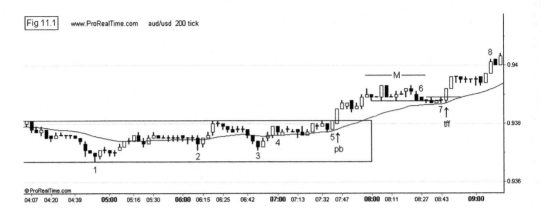

Figure 11.1 Since our operating tactics will be based on the same principles previously discussed, our focus in this new series is best directed
towards the strategic differences in trading the 5-minute and the 200-
tick. For starters, it is recommended to replace the thinly plotted 00
and 50-levels with the so-called 20-levels in the chart (00, 20, 40, 60
and 80). This is not to imply that the 50-level has lost relevance, most
certainly not, but in a low-volatility environment, prices do show a re-
lentless tendency to back and fill between two 20-levels, for hours on
end, rather than marching more voluptuously between 00 and 50. (But
always pay extra attention in the area between 40 and 60.) Surely this
meandering habit is detectable also on the 5-minute frame, but a faster
chart might offer a better chance for exploitation. With this tighter perspective in mind, however, it is recommended not to shoot for 20 pip on
a single breakout, but to look more in the range of 8 to 10 pip targets.
On the stop side, protection can usually be set within an 8 pip range, as
will be shown. It is of course essential to keep the spread as close to 1
pip as possible. On popular pairs like the eur/usd, aud/usd and usd/
jpy, this should not be a problem with most brokers. Attached to your
entry, you can set up a bracket with, say, a 12 pip target and 10 pip
stop, but your exits are best executed on a discretionary basis within
this range, especially on the stop side. You can enter also with an open
target, but always put in a stop to minimize the harm in the event of a
platform crash or connection failure.

So let's have a look at a practical example. First off, on the faster
frames a proper understanding of box technique is paramount. Engag-

ing in quick continuation scalps after a corrective motion to the 25ema is not necessarily discouraged, but your best shot, on balance, is to play your breaks from a lengthy box progression (but still from the base of the 25ema, and always from a buildup phase). Although this aud/usd chart may seem suspiciously cherry-picked for its beauty and double-pressure follow-through, this type of price action, and the box breakout in particular, is a very common sight, as any modest backtest will confirm.

As to the technicals, the top barrier of the box was easily found. The 2-3 element on the other side was a higher double bottom with the low at 1; the 4-5 progression was a classic squeeze between the 25ema and the top of the box. Note also how the 80-level played a crucial role in the bearish defense. You can enter on the break of the box and set your stop below the last low in the squeeze prior to entry. (A buildup element of 4 pip in span will demand a 7 pip stop, which includes a break on either end and a 1 pip spread.) You can place your stop also below the absolute low of the squeeze, but there is little point in setting it wider still (hope-and-pray tactics). For a target, you could of course aim for the 00-level above, but in a slow market that can be quite a distance to cover without running the risk of having to exit the trade on a reversal break first. The suggested alternative here is to pocket the profits on the first bout of follow-through somewhere halfway the two levels, for about 8 or 9 pip, and then perhaps see if the market is kind enough to set up a continuation entry in the direction of the higher magnet.

Note: Even though the 200-tick setting may print most of the bars within a 2 to 4 pip range, this doesn't necessarily mitigate their individual significance. Therefore, it is once again preferable to enter long above a bullish bar and short below a bearish one. Naturally, there is no escaping the many neutral dojis on this frame. They can serve as signal bars as well.

Despite most bars being smaller in span, the price action mechanics on a faster frame aren't much different from what we have seen on the 5-minute. Was it any harder to detect the features of the M-pattern halfway the 80 and 00-level? And what about the way this bear block broke out at the bottom, below combi 6, straight into a trending 25ema;

didn't that spell trade-for-failure the same way it would have done on a 5-minute frame?

Above bar 7, we can now shoot for the 00-level (8), with a tight stop below the four bars prior to entry. Do keep in mind that continuation scalps like these tend to be more failure-prone than a solidly built up break from a box progression, especially in the lunch-hour doldrums where volume is often ultra thin; in the early morning activity, however, they are generally worth a shot.

Note: The mere suggestion of using a 5 or 6 pip stop in the currency markets may strike some readers as highly aggressive, if not plain suicidal. Allow me to stress that this is based on a low-volatility environment and very much seen from a scalper's perspective; other than that, it is still a matter of risk versus profit in regard to the most probable outcome. But before venturing out on the scalper's path, a rock-hard understanding of pressure, conditions and buildup is of the utmost importance. Never underestimate the potential for opposition, and always be very, very patient, even on these "faster" frames. Make it a habit also to review all your wagers well, your losers in particular, to see if further improvements can be made on the part of trade selection.

Tip: To keep track of the "ticks-left-to-go" within the current bar in progress, set up a *tick-counter* in the corner of your chart. This is the tick equivalent of the popular *time-counter* which keeps track of the minutes or seconds-left-to-go in the time bar of the moment. While not an indispensable asset in trade execution, a counter is a handy little tool that can only facilitate the timing of a break; a decent charting package will offer both the tick and time-counter as a standard feature.

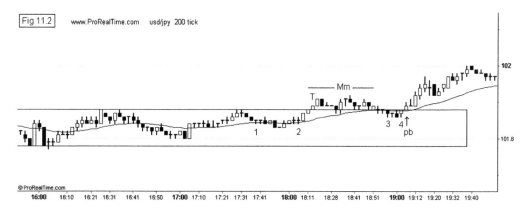

Figure 11.2 Here is another common box situation, taken from the usd/jpy 200-tick. This time prices had found support in the 80-level, with typical resistance in the 90-level area (top of the box). A lengthy fight halfway two "20-levels" is always worthy of attention, for a break may benefit from a favorable magnet about 10 pip out. By the same token, however, a *failed* breakout may soon have the opposite round number kick in, to the detriment of those positioned in the break. But as we know, not every first failed attempt is a harbinger of complete failure. Quite the contrary.

The first bull break through the bearish defense was set up by the 1-2 progression, which had formed a higher low in the box; but there was too little buildup directly below the barrier to look upon this break as a high-odds play, at least from where we stand. Hence the tease annotation (T). As prices struggled in the breakout area, this formed a bearish Mm-variant on top of the barrier, so not particularly promising for the bulls. But take specific note of the response to the break below it: instead of bulls jumping out, new bulls stepped in on a ceiling test with the 1-2 element on the left (3-4).

As we have already witnessed many times over, a failure of the defending party to undo a box breakout *convincingly* is always an interesting tell, for this could set up a re-break soon after, and possibly with better odds attached. So whenever the attacking parties show signs of persistence, be prepared for a second break attempt; but before hopping along, do make sure that the technical situation is favorable still, and always trade from buildup.

Entry here can be taken on the break of bar 4 with a tight stop below the 3-4 element. This is also a trade-for-failure setup in regard to the failed Mm-reversal in the 25ema. Target is the 00-level.

Figure 11.3 The high of this aud/usd range found resistance in the 20-level, with lower highs along the way. Slowly but surely the market was moving towards an encounter with the 00-level magnet. There was an early bear attempt to break away from the box, but not built up very tightly yet (T). Note also the very poor bull break at F earlier on, a classic false break trap.

Soon after the bullish T-1 riposte fell short of breath, prices slid down to the bottom barrier again (2). After a quick bounce up and a false high at 3, the barrier was breached second time around, but once again a bit prematurely. Best to lay low. Should the market immediately take off, so be it. As is often seen, though, bulls did their best to fend off the break, and this set up the trade in a much better fashion (2-4 squeeze). With three identical lows 1 pip below the box barrier, we can now draw an alternative box boundary at this level. As to the exact entry, my advice would be not to short below bar 4 straightaway, but to wait for the little horizontal line to be broken.

In this instance, the distance to the 00-level magnet was only about 6 or 7 pip from entry, meaning that prices needed to break this level by a few pip to render the trade profitable in the 8 to 10 pip range. In such cases, whether to pocket profits immediately on impact with the 20-level (00 here) or to aim for a modest perforation is always a personal call. What may help to decide on this matter is of course the nature of the session's overall pressure, but consider also the width of your box; provided the climate is indeed favorable, very often the breakout swing will try to mimic this vertical span. The width of the box here was about 10 pip. Check Figure 11.2 for similar mechanics.

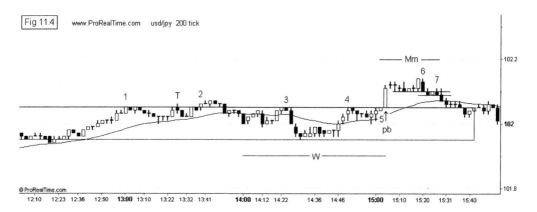

Figure 11.4 This chart serves well to point out the caution necessary when there is a round number running straight through the center of a box pattern. As we know from plenty of examples on the 5-minute frame, these situations tend to make the number work as an adverse magnet, especially on the first few attempts to trade away from it. This usually means that more buildup is required to make the breakout worth our while. In this session, bulls had successfully worked their way through the 00-level on the far left, and then proceeded with two quick breaks at T and 2. Both attempts can be considered premature. Particularly in a slow environment, I strongly advise against pursuing these hasty continuation trades away from a newly conquered round number. Best to give the market a chance to establish a firm footing in the level first. Should prices have broken out above the level of 1 at 3, that would have made for an uncomfortable entry as well. Despite the better buildup, the false perforations of T and 2 on the left had rendered the barrier of the box debatable at that point. Just give it some more time.

In terms of buildup, the W-pattern between 14:00 and 15:00 is of much better quality. Interesting to note here is that despite the earlier perforations, the original high at 1 had remained the level of most attention. Hence the box drawn as depicted. At the bottom side, the low of the W had bounced bullishly away from the cluster on the far left.

The 4-5 buildup represents a squeeze between the box barrier and the 25ema, with the 00-level offering support (note the false low in it). Entry can be taken above bar 5.

Although the trade was good to go, this doesn't immediately rule out the adverse magnet issue (the 00-level below was still nearer than the 20-level above). On wagers like these, an idea could be to trail your trade a little more aggressively than usual. A reversal exit may have been deployed below bar 6 (at the risk of getting trapped out of the trade), but most certainly below bar 7, which was now the break of an Mm-variant and very likely to invite a corrective motion back to the 00-level magnet.

For future purposes, it may be useful to compare the conditions on this box breakout with those in Figure 11.1. Technically seen, the prospects for a successful wager were better in the earlier chart than in the session here above. The reason is found within the issue of the adverse magnet. Since the box break in Figure 11.1 more or less took place from the base of the 80-level, the top barrier and the round number coincided, providing double support should a pullback have come to test the breakout (no immediate risk for our stop yet). In the situation above, the round number magnet resided well *below* the top barrier, and uncomfortably close to where we put our stop. While the mere eventuality of a hurtful pullback is not necessarily a reason to skip an otherwise decent break, it remains an element of concern with the trade up and running. In other words, whenever a stop resides in the conspicuous pull of an adverse magnet, it may pay to deploy a reversal exit on a W or M-pattern break more quickly (as opposed to hanging in, in the hopes of a failed reversal).

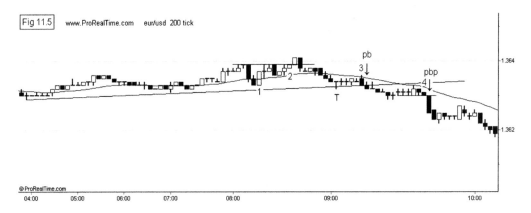

Figure 11.5 This eur/usd 200-tick example nicely illustrates the danger in going up against the resistance of a "new" round number, as well as the benefits of trading in its favorable pull.

As first sight, trading the break above bar 2 does not seem such a bad proposition. There was decent buildup within the 1-2 element and perhaps the trade may have benefitted from the always prominent 50-level magnet about 10 pip higher up. But there was still the 40-level to crack. Note also that there were no earlier bull attempts to perforate this level, which already tends to compromise the prospects of an *immediate* break. Especially in these slow markets it is crucial not to be too eager to participate on any first break; sooner anticipate a new 20-level (40 here) to initiate resistance than to be broken substantially with little ado.

Another thing to have taken into account is that the break took place prior to the UK Open at 09:00; in a more lively setting this may not be a major element of concern, but in a tight market this could keep the bulk of breakout traders on the sidelines still, particularly when there is room for reservation as to the offer itself.

The bear break at T, set in the UK Open, can be regarded as a tease and thus an easy skip. More interesting was the follow-up action, the T-3 squeeze. Although its features were quite modest, this buildup definitely gained attraction when the bar on the right showed a false breakout on the bull side prior to closing bearishly on the pattern line (3). This set up an acceptable short in the potential pull of the 20-level below. Whether to shoot for the magnet itself, about 12 pip out, or to be satisfied with 8 or 10 pip profit is a personal call, but the activity on the way to target can have a say in this decision. For example, when the post-breakout action failed to break back the broken pattern line and then was broken on the bear side in turn (nice six-bar break below 4), this made the 20-level a very likely level to be targeted. Furthermore, if in position from below bar 3, a bear could now trail his stop above the new squeeze, risking only a few pip in a worst-case scenario. Bears in position from below bar 4 would probably do well to cash in on the round number also.

It is not hard to grasp the staleness of the environment here. There was virtually no trading done in the Asian hours prior to the EU Open at 08:00 and even the UK Open at 09:00 could hardly boast of trader excitement. But as we can see also, there were still ways to anticipate some early morning follow-through.

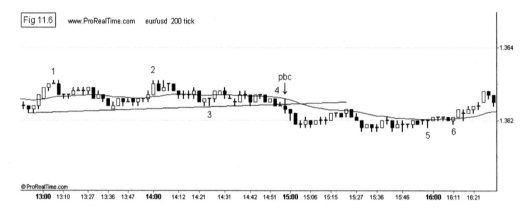

Figure 11.6 Here's another fine example of round number resilience. The break below combi 4 was preceded by the 3-4 squeeze, which was essentially a flat lower-top arch following the double top on the left (1-2). So no problem with this short in pressure terms. The entry, however, was somewhat uncomfortably located on account of the 20-level directly underfoot. If you accept a trade like this, it is essential to do so with always a good eye on the round number response. A pleasant thing about these type of entries, though, is that the level may initially work as a favorable magnet, which will have the trade already a few pip in the plus on impact. If so, this generally means that there is a somewhat better

chance of getting out with minimal damage, or even unscathed, should the trade fall apart and need to be scratched. But do be mindful not to use this prospect as an excuse for accepting entries of *dubious* quality.

Even the US Open at 15:30 failed to bring life to this market, such can be the extent of trader absence in a noncompliant environment; if not already out before, eventually this short had to be exited, either above bar 5 on a re-break of the 20-level (after buildup and a false low in bar 5), or else above bar 6.

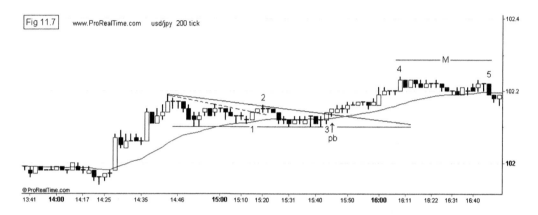

Figure 11.7 When the market is a little more lively, a flag pattern can make for a nice setup, too, but very essential is to consider the extent of buildup prior to the break, as well as the distance from entry to the nearest 20-level opposition. Technically seen, when bar 1 was broken topside, the flag at that point looked fairly decent in relation to its pole, but a troubling factor here was the short distance to the 20-level over-head (102.20). When prices shoot up rather "abruptly" from one round number to the next (US news at 14:30?), it is generally wise to an-ticipate bearish opposition in the latter, if only for the likelihood of bull parties taking profits there. Consequently, I would recommend not to trade the break above bar 1.

But when the 2-3 element was added and then broken topside, the situation had definitely gained merit. After all, this action let on that bears had proved unsuccessful in fully countering the bull break above bar 1, and then suffered a second bull break in turn (note also the triple-bottom boundary of the flag). The extra buildup, and not to mention the moral victory over the bears, had now improved the odds for a 20-level breach most considerably (enter long above bar 3).

If still in position when prices "corrected" from the high of bar 4, there was ample time to exit this trade in the 4-5 progression. Just because we are aiming for profits in the 8 to 10 pip range does not mean we cannot bail out beforehand *without* a specific reversal exit notification. Whenever prices start to seriously stall, particularly in an area of resistance, always an option is to pocket whatever gains are in place and be done. Do recall that we are exploring these 200-tick charts from the perspective of a *low-volatility* environment; this generally calls for more caution on entries and less optimism on the target side. In any case, to have stayed in the trade below bar 5 would have been in defiance of standard reversal exit policy (M-pattern break).

Figure 11.8 Next to box progressions and flag patterns, multiple-arch formations on top of a pattern line are a very common sight on the 200-tick as well. The pattern on the aud/usd here was a head-and-shoulders variant with an M-pattern top in the middle (1-2). Some bears may have deemed the M-pattern already telling enough to take their chances on the sell side below bar 2, but that can be considered pretty aggressive from where we stand. But for a bull to have entered long in bar 3, in an attempt to the trade the M-pattern break for failure, would have been a flat-out mistake. There was simply no bullish dominance visibly present to justify this trade-for-failure option.

The reader may recall from our earlier discussions that a repeated failure of one party to reach its round number very often sets the stage for a successful run on the number at the other side. As bulls conspicuously failed in reaching the 20-level above, this will have turned plenty of eyes in the direction of the 00-level, particularly with such a fine pattern line in place. Depending on one's appetite for aggression, an option may have been to short the break of the pattern line in bar 4 straightaway, so as not to run the risk of missing the ride to the magnet. But definitely shortable was the break below bar 5, a classic pattern break pullback entry.

Quite commonplace in a slow market is a first-touch bounce on a round number (at 6). If not yet on target, such development could quickly eat back all the current profits on the trade; but rather than being upset or fearful, it is crucial to keep assessing the odds from a probability perspective. Below the pattern line, bears still had the best of the action, meaning that prices were more likely (technically speaking) to bend down to the 00-level again than to shake out the trade beyond the last arch on top of the pattern line. Should prices indeed turn favorably again, it is up to the trader whether to stay in for a 20-level breach or grab profits in the level second time around and be done. The overall pressure of the session could have a say in this decision.

If out on the trade, definitely not a good idea would have been to reposition the short in bar 7 or thereabouts. Apart from this being done in the tricky area of the prominent 00-level, just consider the distance to the 25ema. On *any* time or tick frame, continuation breaks are best deployed from the "safe base" of this average, and most preferably with a favorable magnet in sight.

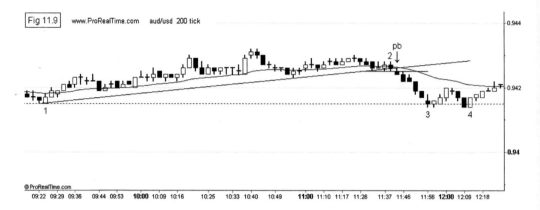

Figure 11.9 After several hours of trying to work their way through the 30-level, bulls finally succumbed to the bearish opposition, which left the market highly vulnerable to the 20-level test. Hence the short below bar 2 (triple-bar break). In cases like this, you can shoot for a round number breach—otherwise skip—but perhaps with the intention to deploy a resistance exit in the former low of 1 at 3 (dotted line). Especially in very tight markets, always anticipate at least some form of opposition in the new round number *area*, even after an initial perforation. If still in on the short, a reversal exit above bar 4 will have been a valid call (W-pattern middle-part break).

Figure 11.10 This picture shows the follow-up action to the previous chart, Figure 11.9. Considering the extent of buildup within the 2-3 progression, entering short below bar 3 appears justified, but as we know, even solid buildup does not rule out the false break potential. A

favorable element here was the prominent 00-level already in view, but the adverse 20-level was still very close. A thing that may have favored the short also was the pole-flag-swing potential, meaning a break below bar 3 could have resulted in a follow-through swing that would mimic the length of the 1-2 pole from which the 2-3 "flag" (descending triangle) was hanging. But even with fine prospects in play, always keep good track of the trade once open. A first diagonal pullback may not pose an immediate threat, but whenever a sideways cluster shows up, and then gets broken against the trade, there is a serious risk of breakout failure.

A clear indication of trouble was the 4-5 element, which harbored the unmistakable features of a W-pattern middle-part, complete with false lows and a bullish "powerbar" on the right. A reversal exit above bar 5 is a defensible call, but do accept that there is always a risk of getting trapped out of the trade on a false adverse break.

Despite the opposition in the extension of the pattern line, bulls remained persistent and eventually forced a break above bar 6. This certainly didn't improve the odds for a 00-level visit anytime soon. If still short, best to bail out above bar 6 with minimal damage.

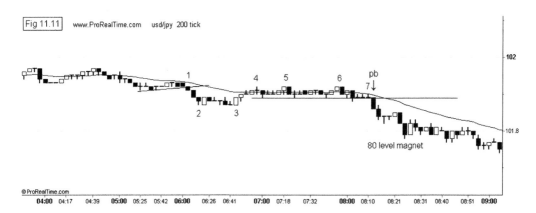

Figure 11.11 The importance of exploiting a favorable magnet *in combination with sufficient buildup* cannot be stressed enough. In strict technical terms, the flag-break short in bar 1 appears a reasonable proposition, but do note that the action at that point was incredibly thin. With only about 12 bars printed per hour, the 200-tick resembled the 5-minute chart, with most bars standing just 1 pip tall (not uncommon in the

latter half of an already stale Asian session). This was definitely not the kind of environment that called for a quick continuation scalp, favorable magnet or not. Things may have been equally stale when bar 7 was broken, but at least the buildup to this break was about four times as extensive. We could say that the 4-7 progression was a lengthy tug-o-war that ultimately proved the counterbreak above the 2-3 middle-part a failure. Note also the bearish triple-top within (4-5-6). Taking into account as well that the break below 7 took place shortly after the EU Open at 08:00, some extra volume was likely to come in on the sell side, if only for early-bird bears to take their chances on an 80-level touch. It is a personal call whether to take profit on impact with the number or to allow for a little breach so as to pocket a few more pip on the trade. Definitely not advisable here was to greedily stay in for even more profit when the action went sideways in the 80-level, particularly with the often rebellious UK Open next on the agenda (09:00).

Figure 11.12 This chart shows a flag breakout on the aud/usd that took place in the first half of the Asian session (generally more active than the latter half). From the start of the session at 00:00, prices had remained in bearish mode, which basically meant that all conservative trades on the bull side were off. Of course, this does not release a trader from practicing caution on the sell side as well. Trading breaks for continuation always requires a certain form of buildup, and most preferably on a correction of sorts to the 25ema. Advisable also is to take position with a

favorable magnet in play. These are simple things to assess at any level in your trading career.

From about 02:00 to 03:00 bulls had tried hard to break away from the bearish pressure but each time they came to reclaim possession of the 25ema, they failed to break through, giving rise to the impression that the 80-level magnet below was more likely to get targeted than the 00-level above. But even with the dominant pressure well established and a favorable magnet in sight, patience still remains a most crucial virtue within all of our operating tactics. We should always give the market a fair chance to set up our trades *properly*.

From a conservative point of view, an opportunity came presented shortly *after* the flag was broken at 4 (tease) and then followed by a pullback that put in a ceiling test with the last arch prior to the break (high of bar 5 hit upon the low of bar 3). Once this test was completed, it took only a few bars for a short to set up below bar 6 (nice double-bar break). Best to place a stop above bar 5, or at least above the false high of the entry bar.

From the moment of entry, follow-through was pleasantly forthcoming, with not a bullish bar printed before the 80-level was hit. Considering the bearish pressure at hand, we could take our chances on a little breach of the level so as to pocket profits in the 10 pip range. Perhaps we could even say, somewhat optimistically, that the 1-2 maneuver was the pole from which the 2-6 flag was hanging, leaving the bears the task to mimic this stretch on the way down, with potential profits somewhere in the 15 pip range (pole-flag-swing); but my personal advice would be not to push your luck too much beyond a newly broken round number, especially when the markets are awfully tight on the whole.

Fig 11.13   www.ProRealTime.com   Nasdaq 100 e-mini 200 tick

Figure 11.13 Just to show that our techniques can indeed be applied to any market and frame of choice, let's wrap up this chapter with a couple of charts from the popular futures markets. It's beyond the scope of this guide to delve into the finer differences between Forex and Futures trading, but none of it relates to the technical side anyway. Quite the contrary, things are very much the same.

This is a picture of the Nasdaq 100 e-mini. I set up the chart with a 200-tick frame but it merely shows an example. The time axis depicts the hours in EST, meaning a standard session of the underlying market would run from 9:30 (US Open) to 16:00 (US Close); but futures can be traded also in the hours outside this stretch. While activity tends to be minimal in the after-hours, it usually picks up in the pre-hours of the next day, when the EU/UK markets are up and running. Understandably, action is the heaviest around the US Open, or perhaps already one hour before if major US news is released at 8:30 EST (which is 14:30 CET).

Not seldom, the US opening hour will print some very tall and fickle bars on a 5-minute frame, which can be rather cumbersome to trade, especially with a tight stop. To cut the bars to a smaller span you can of course set up a faster time frame, say, the 2-minute, but I would recommend using a tick chart setting on account of the benefits mentioned earlier on. In any case, a faster frame always improves the visual on buildup, and will allow you to trade with a tighter technical stop as well. Helpful also is to strip all clutter from the chart and to set it up with only the 25ema showing, and of course the thinly plotted horizontal lines of relevance. On the Nasdaq chart above, I put in the 5 and 10-levels.

As can be derived from just a quick glance, the price action mechanics are virtually identical to those of the Forex markets—and so is the way the poorer breaks tend to get punished. The break at F was a classic false break trap; the one at T, despite the better buildup, showed all the makings of a tease break venture. Note that this picture displays just an hour of price action, so there is not much info here on the pressures of the overall session. Nonetheless, bulls who took a shot at the range break at F were simply asking for a good whack. Bears who shorted at T are best advised to work on their patience.

Definitely more interesting was the break above bar 4 which came about as a consequence of the 1-4 buildup, which in turn had found technical footing in the cluster on the left. This was an ascending triangle variant hanging from the pole T-1. Consequently, you could play this break with a technical target equaling the T-1 stretch, which would bring prices more or less to the next 5-level at 3.875. A stop could be placed either below bar 4 or bar 3, but there is little point in setting it below bar 2 or lower still; after all, the premise behind trading a break from a *buildup* progression is that prices should either follow through in double-pressure fashion, or the trade is best closed out with a minimal loss without much ado.

Since this break took place in mid-range, it would have been rather optimistic to have aimed for a target that equaled the width of the box when counted from the *top* barrier. A very common theme to have anticipated here was for prices to bounce back from 3.875 to put in a test with the range barrier, or even a deeper ceiling test with the 1-4 cluster. By simply raking in the profits in bar 5 (yielding a favorable risk/reward ratio of close to 1:2), a trader not only keeps it simple, he keeps it profitable as well.

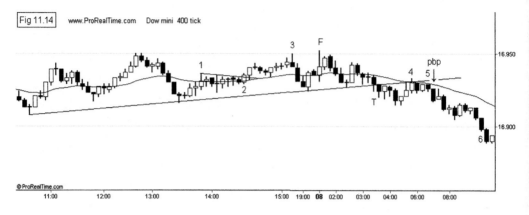

Figure 11.14 On the Dow mini, it makes sense to plot the 00 and 50-levels as the round numbers of most relevance. With prices traveling up to 17.000, this is basically comparable to a currency pair in the 1.70 range. This time I chose the 400-tick to cut the bars to a tradable span. Is this price action any different from what we have seen on countless eur/usd 5-minute chart examples? Hardly. A few things are worthy of attention, though. On the time axis, note the very small stretch between 15:00 and 19:00: only a few bars got printed in four hours time. While the futures market may still be open after the close of the underlying Dow Index (16:00), these after-market hours are traded very thinly and follow-through is not likely to be substantial. Should you have been in position from above the 1-2 buildup, always a defensible call is to grab profits into the regular close at 16:00, or thereabouts; and particularly when this coincides with a touch on a conspicuous round number or technical resistance of sorts.

The tall bars within the 3-F arch may give off an impression of strong after-hours activity, but if we consider the time in which this took place, it is basically an optical illusion brought about by the tick frame setting. It is interesting to see, though, that even in the after-hours, price action mechanics do remain active, as can be derived from the false break at F.

It is very interesting to note also that by plotting tick bars instead of time frame bars, price action on a faster frame still remains pleasantly compressed and visibly "tangible", even when building up a pattern from one session to the next. Some may argue that a pattern boundary on a tick chart possesses less relevance when compared to its time frame counterpart, but I believe this to be a misconception. Just look at the way the arches formed on the pattern line, and take specific note of the typical way the post-breakout action fought it out with the line's extension.

The break at T, set in the UK morning, was a little premature from where we stand and can be rightfully skipped. It then took about three hours for a pullback to test back the pattern line at 4, and then another hour for the pattern break pullback short to set up as depicted (enter below bar 5, with a stop above bar 4 and a target at the 00-magnet).

All this may seem terribly demanding on the part of a trader's patience, but the trick here is not necessarily to *trade* the US futures in the early UK session, but to simply have these charts up and running for when activity picks up, at least a few hours prior to the US stock markets Open at 09:30 EST. (But do take heed of major news releases, which are often scheduled at 8:30 EST.)

Figure 11.15 On the S&P 500 e-mini, contracts can change hands very swiftly which is why a we can set up the chart with a much larger tick number (2000 here). On this instrument, round number levels can be plotted in increments of 5 points as depicted (5 and 10-levels).

Once again, the price action here looks awfully familiar. Bulls were clearly in charge in the 1-2 upswing, which may have left plenty of sideline bulls on the lookout for a correction of sorts. Hopefully it needs no explaining that the "morning-star" pattern at 3 offered a very poor base for a trade on the long side (skip entry in bar 4). Trading for continuation near the highs of a bull swing, and in resistance of a round number to boot, seldom makes for great odds. Unfavorable also was the relatively wide stop needed for "technical" protection (below 3). Just skip and await a better opportunity.

About an hour later, this came presented as a result of very fine buildup within the 5-7 element, which was part of a Vw-variant starting at 4. Prior to the breakout there were false lows at 6, always an interesting tell. A very straightforward pattern line was broken at T, and from there on it was just a matter of waiting for the trade set up in high-odds fashion (a pattern break combi long above bar 7).

On a trade like this you can set your stop either very sharply below bar 7, or more conservatively below the lows of the triple-bottom element at 6. A nice target here would be the former high of 2. If not fully there yet, consider an exit into the close of the underlying S&P 500 index at 16:00 EST.

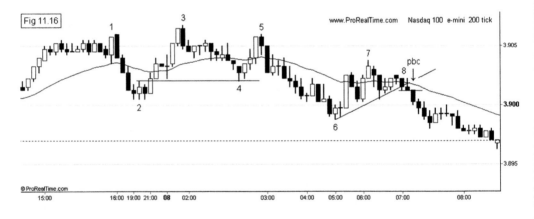

Figure 11.16 There can be strong correlation in directional pressure from market to market, even when traded on different continents. It may not always be so evident who exactly is leading who at any point in time, but that is basically irrelevant also since we best concentrate on what the charts themselves are saying. Perhaps the 5-6 bear swing was a consequence of the EU/UK stock markets opening bearishly for the day (03:00 EST is 09:00 CET), but the 1-3-5 triple top already gave fair warning to the bulls. Before we take up the particulars of the pattern

break combi setup at 8, several hours later, let us run briefly through the earlier action.

For starters, longing the break above bar 1 was a poor choice on the part of the parties involved. Not only was it a low-odds continuation attempt technically, the break was set straight into the close of the previous session at 16:00. Even if presented during regular trading hours, just look at where a technical stop needed to be placed (below bar 1). That's way too far out for our taste.

Next day, early in the EU morning, the 3-4 bear swing had put in a "ceiling" test with the floor of the 1-2-3 arch, which was eagerly bought. Not surprisingly, little of this enthusiasm was left when prices entered the danger zone of the double-top in the round number above (1-3). Eventually this had the market sliding down to the 00-level in the 5-6 bear swing.

With this downswing quite prominently displayed, plenty of bears will surely have started to examine their pullback reversal options within the 6-8 follow-up. This was a rather rough bear-flag formation hanging from the pole 5-6, and had taken a few hours to complete. Notice the false high at 7 (what were these bulls thinking), which was essentially an aborted ceiling test with the low of bar 5. About an hour later, combi 8 set up a double-bar break outside the boundary of the flag, but still pleasantly close to the base of the 25ema (no adverse magnet on entry).

On this short, prices needed to break the 00-level to offer decent profit, but it's fair to say that the action set up thick enough to take a shot on the sell side here. The dotted line depicts a level of a former low from the previous session, which may have served as a resistance exit level as an alternative to the low of bar 6. Some bears may even have set up their short targets at a level that would more or less mimic the length of the 5-6 bear swing, measured from the high of combi 8, but that can be regarded as quite optimistic, particularly if we take into account the bounce potential at the dotted line, if only for prices to test back the prominent 00-level magnet.

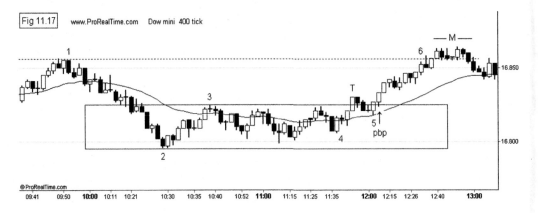

Fig 11.17   www.ProRealTime.com   Dow mini 400 tick

Figure 11.17 Purely from a technical perspective, the break above bar 5 offers an excellent entry on the long side, but in case the market was very bearish earlier on (not visible), there is a slight issue of concern. Although the preceding range was pretty solidly built up, the break was offered in a 50 percent retracement of the 1-2 bear swing, which is always a bit tricky and could induce renewed activity from the contrarian camp. This is not to say that the break was a definite skip in a bearish market (which is after all dependent on one's appetite for aggression), it is just to point out that we should not forget to assess the overall pressure first so as to determine whether the conditions are not too unfavorable to play along for the ride.

Should the earlier action have been very bullish, though, then we can basically regard the 1-2 bear swing as a pullback that tested the 00-level magnet, and from this perspective, the pattern break pullback entry above bar 5 was of indisputable quality, both in setup and conditions.

Note that I plotted the top of the bottom range at 3, the first high in the bounce away from the magnet. This level was only challenged in the break at T, which was a tease breakout in technical terms and thus a skip. Subsequently, the T-5 pullback put in a very familiar ceiling test with the highs of the combi at 4, from which prices bounced up, with the close of bar 5 back outside the range. How many times have we not seen a similar flag-shaped pullback as a response to a tease breakout on our eur/usd charts.

A good bracket on this trade would be the 50-level target (exit in bar

6) with the stop below bar 5. Prices perforated the former high a bit, but then a little M-progression took shape, a fair indication that the pull of the adverse magnet was kicking in.

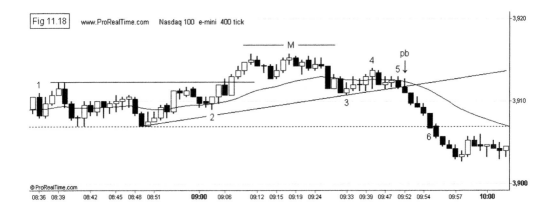

Figure 11.18 Let's conclude our studies with one last example taken from the Nasdaq 100 e-mini. This time I plotted the chart in the 400-tick setting with the round numbers standing at the 10-levels (you can put in the 5-levels also).

Progression 1-2 was a round number fight in the US Open in which the bulls seemed to have a slight advantage over the bears (note the W-characteristics within). Personally I would advise against trading long above bar 2, and to refrain from action above the horizontal barrier as well (tease break candidate). Round number defense can be very re-silient and in these fickle skirmishes it never takes much of a counter push for a tight stop to get shaken out.

Bulls did manage to break away, but their banners of victory never caught a favorable wind. First there appeared an M-pattern in defiance of the break, soon followed by a bear-flag (3-5), which had now turned the adverse pressure into an Mm-variant.

The false high in bar 4 was a brave attempt of the bulls to worm themselves a way out of the squeeze, but straight into resistance of the cluster to the left. As we know, such failure is not likely to boost the bullish morale, but it can do wonders for that of the bears. When bar 5 popped up, closing bearishly on the flag line, we could not have wished for a better setup to take advantage of the situation (enter short on the break of bar 5).

Since this trade set up so well, there was little reason for concern regarding the round number directly underfoot—would *you* buy below bar 5 with an M-pattern and a bear-flag overhead?

This is not to say, though, that the level could no longer pose a problem once in position, even with the short well underway; since this market was far from trending yet, the lows of the range were likely to get bought (dotted line), and that could have turned the broken round number, if not the flag cluster a little above it, into an adverse magnet. Why not avoid all that by simply cashing in when the profits are good and up for the taking (resistance exit in bar 6). And then on to the next trade.

Chapter 12

Final Words

If there has been one leading theme throughout this entire work, it can only reflect the very premise as stated from the outset: the market's ways are highly repetitive and thus exploitable given practice and time. Strategy and tactics may vary from trader to trader, yet all have to abide by a small set of elementary principles that repeat over and over again in any chart.

But please recall that all of the foregoing can only offer a platform for further trader development. By and large, success as a trader will be a direct function of one's willingness to study price action on hundreds, if not thousands of charts, available at the push of a button in any decent charting package. For the evidence is clear: the markets are not particularly forgiving to those who take their education too lightly or deem themselves above it. But the odds are excellent for all parties who embrace a more diligent approach.

Always keep in mind that the losses of one will pay for the profits of another. To emerge on the favorable side of this equation simply requires that you study harder than your opponent in the field. There really is no point in putting capital on the line unless you are absolutely convinced to have obtained an edge in this game. This cannot be stressed enough. So study hard and give yourself that fighting chance. Aim for your goals, but do take pride and enjoyment in the journey as well.

Bob Volman, July 2014

About the Author

Bob Volman (1961) is an independent trader working solely for his own account. He is the author of *Forex Price Action Scalping*, a book widely acclaimed by active scalpers for its ingenuity and practical usefulness, and in continuous demand since its first publication in 2011. *Understanding Price Action* is his second volume on price technical trading, containing all the insights and practicalities any trader could ever hope to find within a single trading guide.

For more information, the author can be reached at:

upabook@gmail.com

Free excerpts of the book can be downloaded from:

www.upabook.wordpress.com

Index

Note: Since many of the following references appear on a continual basis throughout the entire book, the page numbers refer to where they are first introduced, as well as explained with the most attention for practical detail (when applicable).

Printed in Great Britain
by Amazon

19565008R00249